Building Switched Networks

Building Switched Networks

Multilayer Switching, QoS, IP Multicast, Network Policy, and Service Level Agreements

Darryl P. Black

ADDISON–WESLEY

An Imprint of Addison Wesley Longman, Inc.

Reading, Massachusetts • Harlow, England • Menlo Park, California
Berkeley, California • Don Mills, Ontario • Sydney
Bonn • Amsterdam • Tokyo • Mexico City

The publisher offers discounts on this book when ordered in quantity for special sales. For more information, please contact:

AWL Direct Sales
Addison Wesley Longman, Inc.
One Jacob Way
Reading, Massachusetts 01867
(781) 944-3700

Visit AW on the Web: http://www.awl.com/cseng/

Library of Congress Cataloging-in-Publication Data

Black, Darryl P.
    Building switched networks : multilayer switching, QoS, IP multicast, network policy, and service level agreements / Darryl P. Black.
        p.   cm.
    Includes bibliographical references and index.
    ISBN 0-201-37953-8
    1. Computer networks.   2. Packet switching (Data transmission)
3. Multicasting (Computer networks)   I. Title.
TK5105.5.B555   1999
004.6—dc21
                                                                    98–43438
                                                                        CIP

ISBN 0-201-37953-8
Text printed on recycled paper.
1 2 3 4 5 6 7 8 9 10—MA—0302010099
First printing, January 1999

To my entire family,
for their support throughout this project

Contents

Preface

Introduction

It wasn't all that long ago when Local Area Networks (LANs) were composed of Ethernet running on long segments of coaxial cable. In yesterday's LANs, several Personal Computers (PCs) and workstations shared the same cable and took turns using the network. As the segments grew beyond device and cable length constraints, bridges were added, providing an effective way to extend the number of devices and overall span of the LAN. Routers were used to access the Wide Area Network (WAN) and Internet. From the local router, data traveled across the Internet to its destination. The Internet was composed of a mesh of routers providing a communication infrastructure for moving data a few kilometers, many thousands of miles, or completely around the world.

Telnet, File Transfer Protocol (FTP), and other character cell interfaces provided both local area access and wide area access to the network. Graphical interfaces were used locally and often minimally.[1] The network provided only limited communication, complementing the primary sources of information such as the telephone, face-to-face conversations, mailed reports, and nightly batch processing.

It is unclear whether the surge of networking began with the introduction of Microsoft Windows networking, the use of networked Graphical User Interfaces (GUIs), or just the need to distribute more and more data. Today's network growth could be due to the influx of the Web browsers and servers providing the ability to link multimedia (graphics, text, and sounds) with hypertext—after all, this was key to the World Wide Web (WWW) explosion. Or perhaps it was the penetration of client/server applications (sometimes classified as

---

1. One notable exception is MIT's X Window System. This system is an early graphical interface noted for its voracious appetite of network bandwidth. Today the MIT campus uses a switched infrastructure.

bandwidth "hogs"), distributed databases, e-mail environments, and file servers that was responsible for its proliferation. One other reason might be that technology has become much easier to deploy with the introduction of 10BaseT, twisted-pair wiring, and hubs. Most likely though, the popularity of networking came as a result of many, concurrent requirements and events.

Whatever the cause, the strain on the network gradually became very apparent. In the LAN, the standard 10 Mbps-shared Ethernet started to crumble, showing large periodic faults, consistent spikes of activity, and general sluggishness. More and more traffic on the Internet resulted in a bigger and bigger routing mesh. A larger mesh meant more routing change updates and more states of routing flux. In short both the LAN and the WAN were becoming unreliable and unbearably slow.

In the past few years we have seen radical changes in our networks: Bridges have been retired; there is less and less shared Ethernet in the LAN; the Internet is now composed of many Autonomous Systems (ASs) that are managed independently; and traffic is routed between the ASs at only a few external points in each AS. In short, our hunger for networking has resulted in a new generation of networking composed of technologies that scale to meet our needs.

Switching is the core to this new era of networking. Switches help networks scale by addressing performance and robustness and encapsulating network intelligence. In the LAN, switching provides the answer for bandwidth-hungry applications. Switching resolves the problems of shared networks by providing dedicated or minimally shared pipes between devices; and Ethernet switches provide dedicated 10 Mbps, 100 Mbps, and 1000 Mbps pipes, allowing for fat files, graphics, and remote data to flow without congestion. Switches bring together many layer-2 technologies including Fiber Distributed Data Interface (FDDI), Ethernet, Token Ring, and Asynchronous Transfer Mode (ATM), providing a great deal of flexibility for building LANs. It is no wonder that LAN switching became such an important technology so quickly and is so popular today.

Switching is also becoming the common denominator of the WAN. We are seeing more and more ATM switches that provide the needed capacity for moving large amounts of data quickly deployed in the WAN. ATM comes with the promise of Quality of Service (QoS) and a rich base on which to deliver that promise. Frame relay switches, commonly used to build corporate Intranets (private geographically dispersed networks), provide an effective way to connect LANs that are widely separated.

This book is about switched networks and the technologies incorporated within them—switching in the LAN and WAN, switching today, and switching tomorrow. Switches, including workgroup switches, backbone switches, access switches, edge switches, multiservice edge switches, and core switches, are the devices that are satisfying our insatiable appetite for more and more bandwidth. These switches span from the workgroup to the backbone in the LAN and from the edges to the core of the WAN; they are being combined with networking technologies to provide significant networking advances.

In short, switches are being positioned to take us into the next generation of networking. Layer-3 switching, layer-4 switching, multiprotocol label switching (MPLS), Virtual LANs (VLANs), 802.1Q, 802.1p, Class of Service (CoS), Quality of Service (QoS), Resource ReSerVation Protocol (RSVP), Internet Protocol (IP) multicast, Service Level Agreements (SLAs), and policy-based networking are all being actively introduced into switch architectures. These technologies are discussed in this book, as they are becoming part of our overall networking (switching) infrastructure.

Organization of This Book

Figure I.1 provides a conceptual view of the book. We work from the bottom up to establish our networking base and discuss current switching technologies in the LAN and WAN. Then (moving from left to right) we discuss technologies that are expected to shape tomorrow's switched networks greatly. We conclude with a discussion of networking policy and network management—the glue that holds our switched networks together.

This book consists of eight chapters.

- Chapter 1 underscores our demands on networking—today and tomorrow. This chapter introduces the demands and the possible solutions that will be used to satisfy the networks of tomorrow.

- Chapter 2 provides a concise summary of background technologies prerequisite information for the rest of the book. It selectively introduces the key underpinnings of networking and uses a simple WWW example to put the technologies into a useful context.

- Chapter 3 focuses on switching and Virtual Local Area Networks (VLANs). It clearly identifies what switching is and discusses switching in the LAN and WAN. VLANs are presented, and the 802.1Q and 802.1p standards are explained. This chapter provides the switching base that we employ today and begins the launch into new technologies with recent VLAN developments.

- Chapter 4 delves into all of the various types of switching. The chapter discusses in detail switching at various layers and multiprotocol label

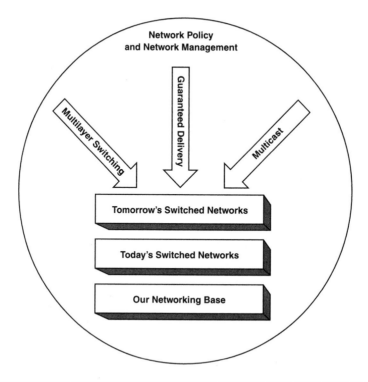

Figure I.1 Conceptual view of this book

switching (MPLS), the emerging standard. In addition, all of the other recent switching developments are presented.

■ Chapter 5 is about quality of service (QoS) and providing delivery guarantees. Providing differentiated services is key to tomorrow's switched networks. This chapter covers the fundamental components of resource management and developments by the ATM Forum and the Internet Engineering Task Force (IETF).

■ Chapter 6 discusses IP multicast in depth. Although this technology has had a very slow penetration into our networks, it is believed to be a fundamental component of tomorrow's switched networks. Clearly having the ability to go beyond point-to-point communication is instrumental in making our networks scale.

- Chapter 7 reinforces the book's focus by discussing Service Level Agreements (SLAs), network policy, and a few rapidly developing network services. Virtual Private Networks (VPNs) and Voice over Internet Protocol (VoIP) are two new emerging services that underscore the needs of switching, quality of service, and IP multicast.

- Chapter 8 concludes the book by discussing the additional network management needs that are required as our networks mature. Clearly as our switched networks become more sophisticated, management tools must become more intelligent to reduce the burden on the network operators. This chapter stresses the desires of tomorrow's networks, the plausible solutions, and the management that will glue everything together.

In summary we start by defining our demands on networking and our network base in Chapters 1 and 2. We then cover switching today in Chapter 3. Chapters 4, 5, and 6 cover multilayer switching, guaranteed delivery, and multicast, respectively. Finally we look at network policy and advanced network management, which tie together tomorrow's switched networks.

Audience

Throughout the book it is assumed that you have some familiarity with networking, although time is taken up front to review some key networking concepts that are important to understanding the material in the book. The book assumes that you are pragmatic and interested in information that you can use to extend your existing set of networking knowledge and that you are after solutions and the motivations behind the technologies, not just a regurgitation of Requests for Comments (RFCs). For the most part, the book tends to stay away from the actual bits and bytes that go across the wire since this depth would require a book for each subject covered. Care has been taken to condense a lot of material into a few hundred pages that deal with the central theme of switched networks.

This book is written for corporate network analysts, network managers, information technology managers, network planners, network designers, technicians, and other technical management personnel who need exposure to these new technologies. It provides the necessary concrete information for planning an upgrade from a shared to a switched environment and a knowledge base of new, emerging technologies that are expected to be core to switching solutions carrying us into the next millenium. This book may also serve the engineering community or be used as a college text for a course in data communications.

If you look carefully at the list of people who will benefit from *Building Switched Networks: Multilayer Switching, QoS, IP Multicast, Network Policy, and Service Level Agreements,* you will extract one very common characteristic—all of these people are extremely busy! Like my last book, *Managing Switched Local Area Networks: A Practical Guide,* this book addresses this need by being concise and to the point, yet it is written in a friendly, easy-to-understand style. Books that can provide focused, pragmatic, integrated text are the most valuable ones for today's busy technical reader. This book attempts to be precisely that by focusing on some very interesting networking technologies, covering a lot of ground, and telling a complete story about switched networks.

Acknowledgments

As you read this book, you will quickly learn just how much information you need to know to understand the essence of networking. Over the past fifteen years I have been exposed to several network experts and many rich development environments. I have also been fortunate to go to many trade shows and external training events that provided a way to learn from experts in the industry. This book is a culmination of my experiences and knowledge, and it would not have been possible without the daily water-cooler talk, periodic brainstorming, critical thinking with colleagues, and exposure to the technical gurus across the industry.

My experiences at Wang Laboratories, Digital Equipment Corporation, 3Com, and, most recently, Nortel Networks are the basis for this effort. Although there are too many people to mention, I am very indebted to the technical community in which I work. I therefore offer a big thanks to all of my colleagues of yesterday and today.

Quality book writing has many critical components, and one vital component is first-class reviewers. I'm not completely knowledgeable of the process used to write books at other companies, but Addison Wesley Longman uses a series of very intense reviews during the writing process. These reviews make their books as technically accurate as possible, yet the books flow well. This book went through some very tough reviews by some strong network experts. I would personally like to thank Dr. Stuart Cheshire of Apple Computer, Dave Crocker, J. Alan Gatlin, Dave Hannum, Peter Haverlock, Glen Herrmannsfeldt, Mukesh

Kacker, Jeffrey Mogul, Bob Natale of ACE°COMM Corporation, Radia Perlman, Linda Richman, Ed Volkstorf, and William Welch of Nortel Networks for their critical reviews and helpful suggestions and comments.

Last, but clearly not least, I would like to commend key members of the Addison Wesley Longman team who provided a tremendous amount of coordination, guidance, and support along the way. Writing a technical book is not a small task, and without a crew like this, you would see many sparse technical bookshelves. Many thanks to Karen Gettman, Mary Hart, and Maureen Willard for helping me pull this effort together into a book.

CHAPTER 1

Our Demands for Networking

1.1 Introduction

Over the past few years networking has become increasingly fundamental to most people's lives. In order to progress from satisfying today's network requirements to tomorrow's, networks will need to grow in sophistication, span, and performance. This chapter captures the motivation for this emerging era of networking by presenting the prerequisites of today and the challenges of tomorrow. The chapter concludes by introducing some of the emerging technical solutions that will help us to realize tomorrow's networking challenges.

1.2 Key Problems Addressed

Simply stated, networks allow us to move information. They provide us with the ability to share data and resources across a room, building, campus, or the world. With today's global economy, information is often not local; access to information anywhere in the world is vital to the success of many businesses. Networks provide the critical infrastructure to move, access, and consolidate information far and near.

Reliability, performance, accessibility, and security are important characteristics of networks; these are the main qualities used to measure a network's viability. A network that is constantly "down" is of little use. Likewise a network in which security is consistently challenged is problematic. Slow networks are tolerated to a point, but they clearly limit network utility.

Today's largest data network, the Internet, is plagued with many problems that are characteristic of data networks:

- **Distance matters a lot:** Generally speaking, the greater the span between two communication end points, the slower and more expensive the communication. The delay is largely due to the number of interconnection devices (that is, switches) through which traffic must be routed as distances increase. Simply stated, interconnection devices provide the glue that binds networks together, enabling communication among many users at the same time. Each interconnection device can be thought of as a traffic intersection through which data must be queued, redirected, and often (unfortunately) delayed. Network service providers often charge more to span longer distances simply because their cost to cable and maintain network spans is often proportional to the distances they must go.

- **Time of the day, week, and month has a big impact on performance:** Network traffic exhibits the characteristics of rush hour traffic and often has daily, weekly, and monthly peaks. Different parts of the globe "wake up" at different times, and devices suddenly appear on the network; in many ways traffic travels with the sun. Holidays also result in aberrations of network use.

- **Congestion can have an impact on networking performance:** Networks that are clogged often drop traffic, only to have traffic regenerate and further exacerbate the problem of congestion. Sometimes when the network is slow and the latency is high, traffic is regenerated, and congestion again increases.

A S I D E . . .

When the Transmission Control Protocol (TCP) over Internet Protocol (IP) (known as TCP/IP) detects congestion, it reduces the number of packets that will be injected into the network; this clearly helps keep the Internet from melting down. In other words, TCP/IP reduces the number of outstanding packets it maintains for which it is waiting for an acknowledgement. This lessens the demand on the network for the TCP/IP communication session, but it may severely limit the viability of TCP for time-sensitive data, such as interactive voice and video.

- **End point positioning in the network determines the overall network performance:** A network connection is as good as its weakest link. If a user connects via a modem or uses wireless technologies, the network may appear sluggish, even if the other end of the connection is a fat pipe. A "thin" connection at the other end can be equally problematic.

- **The type of information transmitted matters:** Interactive voice traffic is least tolerant to delay, then real-time (or interactive) video, and finally ordinary data. Real-time video is very sensitive to the smallest network capacity between the two communication points. A video stream going primarily across an unloaded gigabit connection may be severely handicapped as it makes its final connection across a 28-Kbps dial-up connection. Real-time transmission does not work well across networks with intermittent delays; buffering data at the receiving end points is often used to smooth out video transmission.

- **Redundant data is prevalent in most networks:** Transmitting the same data to many end stations is common in the network. Just imagine how many recipients of the same market-price stock data there are, especially within the same company! Releasing a new, popular, Web-downloadable version of software almost guarantees a subsequent flood of networking activity of the same download across the world. Clearly our Internet is largely consumed with redundant data, reducing the overall capacity of the network.

  Unfortunately redundant data is not typically multicast across our network, reducing the overall impact of the transmission. Multicasting provides a way to send information to many users at the same time without a separate stream of information for each user; rather, packets are "fanned out" to individuals only at the very end of communication transmission.

- **Predictability and reliability matter a lot:** As our lives become more complex with increased demands, elements of predictability become increasingly important. We survive increased demands by building upon a foundation of service expectations. For example, performing A yields B; if e-mail is sent today, it will satisfy a deadline; and so on. The United States phone network is very reliable and is usually available, unless, of course, an earthquake or other natural disaster happens. Networks provide an important alternative service, and they need to be predictable.

1.3 Communication Paradigms

There are only three communication paradigms that networks must satisfy: one-to-one communication, one-to-many communication, and many-to-many communication. Figure 1.1 illustrates these forms of communication.

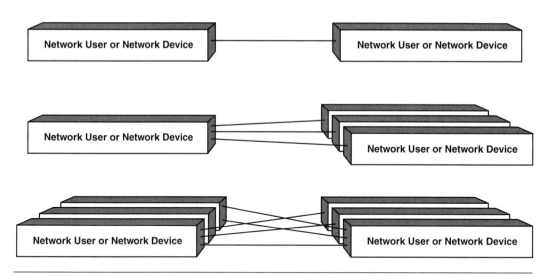

Figure 1.1 Communication paradigms

One-to-one communication, commonly known as *unicast,* is the simplest form of communication. You send an e-mail to colleague x, colleague x returns a reply to you, you send a file to the printer: These are instances of unicast communication.

One-to-many or many-to-many are forms of *multicast* or *broadcast* communication. Multicast refers to sending data to a subset of users or devices, whereas broadcast refers to sending data to all users or devices. A stock quote is disseminated to many receivers; a single e-mail is sent to many people on the network, each copy arriving at as close to the same exact time as possible; a video stream is delivered to many viewers; a system alert is sent to all users. These are examples of the one-to-many form of communication.

Many-to-many communication is a special case of one-to-many communication. In addition to the properties of one-to-many, each "one" can communicate with many. Chat rooms or interactive conferences spanning several locations are examples of many-to-many communication.

1.4 Examples of How We Use Networking Today

Networking has become an integral part of our business and personal lives. Client/server applications have an implicit network requirement, as they become the de facto information system for most businesses. We all take the phone network for granted to make and receive calls throughout the day, using both stationary and cellular phones. It is common for a person to have an Internet Service Provider (ISP) to access the World Wide Web (WWW) at home, to use a Local Area Network (LAN) at work, and to stop at a networked Automatic Teller Machine on the way home. The business traveler has a laptop computer and dials in remotely, connects directly to his office network with an Integrated Services Digital Network (ISDN) line at home, and plugs into an office network at different sites. Some computer/network enthusiasts go a step further by having a small repeater-based network at home to share a printer and files across multiple Personal Computers (PCs). Clearly networking has lost its luxury (optional) status and is a fundamental requirement of doing both personal and professional business. The following list captures a small sample of some of the many uses of networks today:

- Remote office connect from home, hotel, or another site
- Conference calling or video conferencing across distributed sites with ordinary use of the telephone
- Use of e-mail or beeper systems
- Searching the WWW for information and downloading information to a local site
- Use of the WWW for electronic commerce such as purchasing merchandise or trading stock
- Access to corporate databases on site and remotely
- Use of electronic bulletin boards for access to information or to download software updates
- Use of anonymous FTP to transfer files across the world or across a corporate campus
- Sharing of schedule information among many people or downloading and uploading from a handheld organizer
- Creation of a network at home or in office for sharing a printer and files across multiple PCs and/or workstations
- Use of the network to control a remote environment such as adjusting the thermostat or turning on one or more lights for security

1.5 Today's Networks

Information that can be networked comes in three fundamental forms: voice, video, and ordinary data. Today we have hundreds of WANs, millions of smaller LANs, and many interconnected private LANs that span the globe. One global network of today is the Internet that is designed to carry data; another is the telephone network that is designed to provide voice service; and private corporations use still many other global networks to construct their networks. These provide frame relay Permanent Virtual Circuits (PVCs) and may transparently connect across a large carrier's network using Asynchronous Transfer Mode (ATM). Local networks may be Metropolitan Area Networks (MANs) or LANs and vary in size and scope from a large network that spans a city to a small network within a private residence.

The Internet is a *connectionless* network, a packet-based network that provides a "best-effort" medium to send data between two endpoints. Data are broken into *packets* and sent to a destination without establishment of a connection. The route for each packet is determined in real time, unlike the telephone network that creates a dedicated connection prior to transmitting any information. In the Internet there are no guarantees that a packet will get to its final destination or that multiple packets will arrive in the same order in which they were sent.

A S I D E . . .

Transmission Control Protocol (TCP) provides a *connection-based* service on top of the connectionless Internet Protocol (IP) used within the Internet. TCP is widely used to provide reliable communication across the Internet. Chapter 2 has more information about TCP, IP, and layering of communication services.

The telephone network is *connection-oriented,* meaning that prior to communicating a connection, commonly called a *circuit,* is established. A circuit is a dedicated path or channel between two endpoints that enables data to flow in both directions across a predefined path, providing *full-duplex* communication. Connection-oriented networks can provide built-in service guarantees as they send data over a *dedicated* communication channel. The phone network enables us to carry on an interactive conversation with inaudible voice delays.

A N O T H E R   A S I D E . . .

Communication over very long distances sometimes uses satellite communications that have a built-in latency that can introduce an audible delay in a phone conversation.

One drawback of a connection-oriented service such as the telephone network is that access to the service may be denied due to limited resources. In the case of the telephone network, there are only a finite number of circuits that can be provided at any time. When there are no more circuits to hand out, service must be denied. This is why on holidays our phone service occasionally asks us to "try again at a later time" as all circuits are busy.

Both the telephone network and the Internet are being used for different purposes than those for which they were originally designed. The telephone network is often used to transmit other forms of data besides voice; perhaps the most common example is dialing in from a remote site over phone lines to check e-mail or to retrieve and send files. The Internet is starting to be used as a medium for interactive voice. Because interactive voice is delay-sensitive and the current packet-based Internet provides only a best-effort service, interactive voice over the Internet can be choppy with intermittent delays.

Today's local networks are predominantly packet-based like the Internet although some do employ connection-oriented technologies (like ATM) as well. Frame relay is a hybrid; its Permanent Virtual Circuits (PVCs) and Switched Virtual Circuits (SVCs) provide a path over which variable length frames are transmitted. Often local networks, sometimes called Intranets, are interconnected to other LANs using WAN services.

A S I D E . . .

Synchronous, asynchronous, and *isochronous* are three terms that are often used in networking literature and deserve extra mention.

- Synchronous is used to describe two or more processes (for example, data flowing between two systems) that use precise clocking to stay in unison or to work together.

- Asynchronous is the opposite of synchronous. With asynchronous transmission, clocking is not used; asynchronous transmissions are sent independently from each other without regulated intervals of time.

- Isochronous is used to describe data flow where there is always a constant number of unit intervals between subsequent transmissions. A normal voice conversation is isochronous.

1.6 Tomorrow's Networking Requirements

Let's enumerate some of the key challenges of tomorrow's networks:

- **The dependency on networks is increasing rapidly:** A few years ago, if the network was down for 15 minutes, no one complained. Now, if the network is down for a couple of minutes, the phone rings off the hook. Businesses are built around the network, which is becoming as fundamental as electricity and the phone.

- **Time is money:** A sluggish network costs businesses money. Think about having the trade of a plummeting stock postponed because of congestion. Waiting for a file transfer to complete, a Web graphic to download, or synchronization of e-mail files can send you for coffee, maybe even for lunch.

- **Best effort sometimes isn't good enough:** Have you ever had an important piece of e-mail get stuck in an Internet queue somewhere? Sometimes you want the network to guarantee delivery and prioritize your traffic ahead of the junk e-mail that floats about. Wouldn't it be nice to have a service guarantee similar to what FedEx will give you?

- **Real-time data networking isn't there yet:** Image file downloads are often sluggish, and interactive voice over the Internet is like speaking to someone who is continuously trying to catch his breath. Real-time video on the Internet is usually choppy, too.

- **Networks can be unreliable:** The number of times worldwide employees have made calls over the telephone network (a reliable service) to confirm or troubleshoot the delivery of a file (usually e-mail) over the Internet or their own corporate Intranet must be very high.

- **The 80 percent local, 20 percent remote rule is no longer applicable:** Networks were commonly built around the rule of thumb that 80 percent of the traffic stays local and 20 percent of the traffic travels remotely. With the advent of the WWW and globally distributed work environments, it is expected that the rule is now inverted with 20 percent of the traffic remaining local and 80 percent of the traffic remote.

1.7 The Main Goal of Networking

Networking is one of the fastest growing areas of technology. Networks provide the communication of information that has become a fundamental basis of our lives. Networks are creating new opportunities for businesses and personal use by reducing the apparent distance between sources and users of information. Figure 1.2 conceptually illustrates this main goal of networking.

Without a doubt our dependency on networking will further intensify over the next few years. Tomorrow's networks need to satiate our needs for

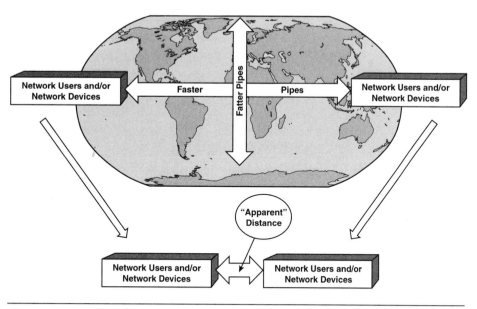

Figure 1.2 Reducing the "apparent" distance

speed, reliability, real-time support of voice and video, portability, and user customization. Cost is also a factor—networks must be affordable for everyone, yet they must provide premium performance (perhaps pay-per-usage) capabilities for those desiring these special services.

1.8 Incorporating Features of Phone Networks

It is expected that tomorrow's networks will be a hybrid of the best of the phone network *and* the data network. Ideally the result will be a new, more powerful Internet that applies the strong capabilities and features of the phone network to it. Some key features of phone networks need to be applied to the Internet; a phone network is:

- **Portable:** The cellular extension to a phone network has made it possible to make and receive calls from a phone number on the go.

- **Very reliable:** Unless there is a very bad storm or a catastrophic event somewhere in the world, you are able to make a call.

- **Customizable per phone number** (a phone number is like an Internet address): The phone network allows you to select services, such as call waiting or caller ID, and to pick from a variety of long distance companies (sometimes called carriers or telcos).

- **Able to support real-time conversations:** People expect a telephone call to be "the next best thing to being there"—to have no major, inconsistent delays. The phone network is not a best-effort service; it is a connection-oriented service that allocates a chunk of guaranteed bandwidth when a call is placed.

- **Extensible:** If you need one or more phone lines, you lease one or more phone numbers. The process is very simple, and for the most part, you can keep these leased phone numbers for a very long time. Occasionally the hierarchical structure of phone numbers used to represent countries and cities must change to facilitate growth. Overall though, phone companies do a good job of providing and servicing billions of users and keeping city and country codes as static as possible.

The phone network has a lot of built-in intelligence and is service rich. Use of the phone network requires only a very simple, inexpensive end-node device, namely the telephone. In contrast, the Internet expects that the end nodes are intelligent and its job is to provide only a lightweight, yet strong and dynamic infrastructure. For many applications though, the best-effort model that the current Internet employs is very useful. The Internet moves lots of data from many places in the world to many other places in a low-cost manner. Much communication (for example, e-mail, delivery of a stock quote, a Simple Network Management Protocol (SNMP) request or response) contains only a dozen or so packets, making it inefficient to incur the overhead of a dedicated connection. Much communication is not time sensitive; for this type of communication the Internet model is very strong. On the other hand, interactive video and voice are not best served over a best-effort, packet-based network.

Some believe that if the key characteristics of the mature phone network are applied to the growing Internet, we can converge on a multiservice network. Is this economically feasible? Does having discrete networks for different uses continue to make sense? Is partial convergence an option? These are the questions that need to be addressed over the next few years as our networking requirements drive the next generation networking infrastructure. It is always important to remember that *applications drive the network* and that we strengthen our network to service its application.

1.9 The Main Demands on Networking

If we had our complete preference, we would like a single, integrated, extensible, scalable network that is capable of

- true real-time transmission within a LAN and across WAN distances,
- plug-and-play portability and ease of use,
- customization as granular as an individual user,
- minimal propagation delay,[1] and
- providing 99.9 percent availability (still low when compared to the telephone network).

We would also like a network that is

- secure,
- accessible,
- compatible with any end-user piece of equipment,
- reasonably priced, and
- not controlled by any one organization.

In short we would like it all! Does this sound like an easy thing to create? This is hardly the case. However, these are the key characteristics of networking that everyone is looking for and the direction toward which we need to aim. We need *simple, transparent, customizable* ways to connect to the world.

Yes, networking is evolving rapidly, but there is no panacea to provide us with the ideal network overnight—and there never will be. In fact, once we think we have the ideal network, even for a fraction of a second, we will set our standards higher with a whole new set of features and requirements. Our demands are boundless because networking provides an infrastructure that is fundamental to our lives. As soon as we become comfortable with one level of life's basic needs, we will seek a higher level—this is human nature. We must

- be satisfied with *evolving* our network over time.
- build upon the infrastructure that we already have.
- continue to remember that networks are distributed and built of many expensive components; making extensive changes is costly and difficult to coordinate.

---

1. Signals in optical and electrical cables all travel at about 2/3 the speed of light. This is a delay that cannot be eliminated.

An advantage of an evolutionary model is that we are able to refine the direction along the way. Rather than having the entire solution worked out in advance, we can "try out" many technologies and converge on the few winners that satisfy our increasing dependency on networking.

1.10 Critical Components of Tomorrow

There are many emerging technologies, and thousands of Requests for Comments (RFCs) proposals have been submitted to the Internet Engineering Task Force (IETF). Only a subset of these proposals actually become standards, and of this subset, only a few become widespread technologies. TCP, SNMP, and 802.1d bridging are examples of standards that are widely deployed today.

A S I D E . . .

Some Internet standards are written in the form of RFCs, documents used by the Internet community initially to draft and later (optionally) to ratify a standard. RFCs are publicly available to anyone; look at the WWW site http://www.ietf.org. Other standards come from the Institute of Electrical and Electronics Engineers (IEEE) (http://www.ieee.org) and the Telecommunications Industry Association (TIA) (http://www.tiaonline.org). Both the IEEE and TIA charge for their standards.

This book presents many of the emerging technologies that are expected to help us move toward satisfying our demands of networking. Will all the technologies in this book become as ubiquitous as IP? Probably not. Will some of the technologies make the technology "top ten"? Probably so. What is important to realize, though, is that even if a technology does not become the next de facto standard, often its ideas and key features influence the next winner. This is all part of the evolutionary process leading to improved networking.

Switching is a fundamental technology that has experienced widespread growth and is evolving rapidly. Switching is well positioned to be the core of tomorrow's network within both the LAN and the WAN. When we talk about switching, we discuss switching in the LAN, ATM switching, frame relay switching, and switching at various International Standards Organization (ISO) reference model layers. (The concept of ISO layers is discussed in Chapter 2.) Switching provides the speed, integration of technologies, and sheer scalability requirements of tomorrow's networks. As a side benefit, certain layer-3 switching techniques provide the data to monitor data flows and to optimize the network around traffic patterns.

Quality of Service (QoS) and *Class of Service* (COS) are key requirements of tomorrow's network. QoS provides a prenegotiated service-level guarantee, and COS enables the network manager to prioritize traffic within a network based on corporate policies. Traffic such as interactive voice and real-time video is particularly time-sensitive, and the best-effort service provided by the Internet is not adequate for this type of traffic. To service interactive and real-time data better, we must either add traffic prioritization or dedicate resources to this delay-sensitive traffic.

IP multicast provides a way to save bandwidth throughout the network by transmitting only one copy of data to a rendezvous point and then fanning the data out to multiple destinations. It is expected that this conservation of bandwidth will be an important component of making our networks scale. Another key characteristic of IP multicast is the single-copy transmission of data resulting in the exact same update across many users at nearly the exact same time. This feature is essential with data like stock market updates; getting data even seconds ahead of a colleague may give a trader an advantage.

A S I D E . . .

Although having data arrive at many destinations at *exactly* the same time is an important goal for a multicasting technology, one must be aware that it is very difficult, if not impossible, to achieve. Even with multicast routing, different parts of the network will receive the data at different times. Nonetheless, it is worthwhile to reduce the disparity of delivery as much as possible.

IP multicast is expected to become the basis for transmission of data feeds to many users at the same time. It can be used to reduce significantly the amount of redundant traffic generated by "push" technologies that periodically flood the network with many copies of the same data to many end users. An example of a "push" technology is PointCast, a product that provides customized periodic news, sports, and stock market updates throughout the day.

Finally, service providers, such as Internet Service Providers (ISPs), are expected to provide future service differentiation by incorporating *policy-based* networking and offering stronger Service Level Agreements (SLAs). Virtual Private Networks (VPNs) and Voice over IP (VoIP) are two such emerging services that are expected to benefit greatly from customization and service-level guarantees. Policy may also be used within internal networks to control the prioritization of traffic of certain client/server applications. For example, customer sales and service-related applications may take precedence over internal "administrative" applications.

Policy-based solutions provide service providers with the built-in intelligence of knowing their customers and adjusting flow and resources accordingly. In the future, users within the company may have individual networking profiles that identify their network preferences, privileges, access rights, and resources. Or the profile granularity may be on a class basis giving certain users one of two or three priority levels of service. For example, the chief executive officer (CEO) of a company *may* just be given the highest-level priority.

1.11 Behind the Scene Network Needs

It is critical to understand what is important to network administrators; without these individuals there wouldn't be any networks at all. These individuals enable us to take the next steps in networking and to satisfy our networking demands. The following is an ordered list of priorities from a network manager's perspective:

1. **Manageability:** Management implies control; networks that are poorly managed are often out of control. Tools that enable configuration, performance monitoring, troubleshooting, security administration, and accounting are essential to network advancement, so new network equipment must be simple to set up and maintain.

2. **Robustness:** A robust network is resilient to unexpected change. Robustness implies minimum downtime and maximum availability, and one way to achieve this is with lots of network redundancy. Redundancy provides fault tolerance when equipment fails and a way to "hot swap" to new hardware or download new software without network disruption.

3. **Low Cost Migration:** Complete network replacements are costly in terms of money, training, and a lot of risk. It is important that networks and technologies evolve.

4. **Security:** As more and more networking goes in and out of the corporate LAN into the WAN, security becomes more of an issue. Maintaining the correct level of network security is a constant challenge; therefore network advances must allow for the correct level of security.

5. **Bandwidth Management:** Because WAN bandwidth is expensive and the use of the WWW has resulted in much more WAN traffic,

increased emphasis must be placed on managing this precious resource. In the WAN and LAN, bandwidth to critical resources must be constantly monitored to ensure availability.

6. **Traffic Prioritization:** Certain traffic is more important than other traffic. Clearly providing your customers with quick access to your Web site is more important than the response time workers get when they shop on their lunch hours. Tomorrow's networks must provide a way to prioritize traffic according to the needs of individual businesses.

A S I D E . . .

It is worth noting that the network manager's success is his undoing! When a LAN is running well, more workstations, PCs, and applications are added. These additions lead to the decline in service and often a scramble to resegment and fix the network. This cycle repeats as we continuously demand more and more of our networks.

1.12 Existing Patterns

Life is full of patterns and patterns can be used to influence and anticipate requirements and needs. By observing existing patterns, we can apply and build upon what we already know. Patterns, particularly patterns that are present to facilitate communication, are especially useful in networking.

The next time you are on an airplane, take a look at the world map in the flight magazine. Notice the concentration of airplane traffic and flight patterns. Then ask yourself, why do people travel? To communicate, of course! It seems as if the flight patterns and large city concentrations are *similar to* the data patterns of the Internet and phone networks. This inference is made because flight patterns are indicative of population concentrations—clumps of people that are probably on the network when they are not traveling, and even, in many cases (thanks to cellular communications), when they are traveling.

There is a heavy concentration of flight patterns (hence travel) to and from major cities. If the network is good enough to provide nearly the same communication as face-to-face people achieve by traveling, where do you think the network communication patterns will be? Local traffic patterns, train routes in Europe, and super highway layouts can be used to predict network needs between cities and within cities and towns. Existing physical traffic patterns are in place largely to facilitate communication and to give us a pretty good idea of where the traffic will be if networks can keep people at home—working from home, "visiting" friends and relatives from home, attending business meetings from home, shopping from home. It is too bad we can't distribute take-out ("take away" in Europe) food via the network!

1.13 Setting Expectations

It is important to note that because of the complexity of networks, the asynchronous updating of technologies across networks, the number of network devices, and the vast breadth of networks, our networks will have to *evolve* over time. Revolutionary replacement of networks is not an option. Technologies that are distributed across many vendors and network owners naturally evolve more slowly. Clearly you can mow your own lawn on Monday, but try to get everyone in your town or city to mow his or her lawn on Monday . . . not an easy coordination task to pull off.

In addition to coordination challenges, there are some significant technical challenges. Many technologies need to be integrated. Frame relay and ATM have a strong hold in the WAN; Ethernet dominates the LAN. The transparent integration of WAN and LAN, WAN and WAN (for example, frame relay and ATM), and LAN and remote LAN (for example, Ethernet and FDDI) technologies is critical to make progress at QoS, real-time transmission, and improved performance.

There are also physical limitations that are difficult to solve. Have you noticed how the maximum allowed distance for Ethernet keeps getting shorter due to speed increases and packet collision rules? Think of how nice it would be to have wireless setups everywhere but how limited the bandwidth would be. It is clearly easier to lay a cable in a building to extend a LAN than to lay one across an ocean for a WAN connection. Advances that surpass physical limitations continue to marvel us but often take considerable time.

Nonetheless, network progress continues to move very quickly. It is merely our insatiable daily appetite for more that makes networks appear to evolve slowly. It wasn't all that long ago that logging in remotely using a command line interface was considered adequate. Now people *have* networks in their homes and interact with the WWW across the world. Corporations have sophisticated Intranets across the world, and they use the WWW to administer paper-free benefit systems and corporatewide information systems.

It is an exciting time to be involved in networking. The challenge of making so many different technologies work together is the dream of many. Our network infrastructure is driven by work across many different companies, cultures, and geographical locations. It is this rich, diversified, distributed effort that brings so much information and so many people together.

1.14 Conclusions

The wide acceptance of networking has created some exciting challenges for technologists. Networking is now at the core of most businesses, and businesses are commonly using the network to span many different geographies, time zones, and cultures. The number of network users is increasing rapidly, as is the amount of information moving across our networks. These demands are placing many new requirements on networking.

The world is seeking networks that are secure, capable of real-time transmission, compatible with any end-user piece of equipment, and not controlled by any one organization. Networks must be plug-and-play; they must be customizable, offer minimal propagation delay, and must always be available. Networks must have all these characteristics—and all at a reasonable price.

Delivery guarantees and the ability to deliver real-time transmissions across the WAN are two important fundamental challenges of tomorrow. Multilayer switching, quality of service (QoS), class of service (COS), Resource ReSerVation Protocol (RSVP), ATM, Gigabit Ethernet, IP Multicast, network policy, and Service Level Agreements (SLAs) are strong possibilities for providing pieces of the solution. As these technologies emerge and are integrated into our networks, we will begin to see people and data get closer, even though physically they may be worlds apart.

CHAPTER 2

Our Networking Base

2.1 Introduction

One of the difficult things about learning new networking technologies is that you need to know a good deal of prerequisite information. Like many technical disciplines, networking builds off a rich core. Since this book spans the LAN and the WAN, the base material is vast.

This chapter provides a focused tour of background technology necessary to understand before reading the subsequent chapters. It covers the obligatory ISO Open Systems Interconnection (OSI) Reference Model, the fundamentals of bridging and routing, and some key TCP/IP concepts. It ties everything together by using the WWW and the HyperText Transfer Protocol (HTTP) to demonstrate how so many technologies work together to provide the most widely used network application to date—the common Web browser.

2.2 Key Solutions Offered

Networking has become a fundamental technology used across the world. Even though many important networking technologies are used to build networks, there are a few that are becoming the base upon which most networks are built. It is expected that the following technologies will persist over the next many years:

- Fiber and Twisted-Pair Media
- Ethernet in the LAN
- ATM in the LAN
- ATM, frame relay, and X.25 in the WAN[1]

---

1. Point-to-Point Protocol (PPP) over Synchronous Optical Network (SONET) is also a fundamental technology, although it is not emphasized in this text.

- TCP/IP
- Bridging, switching, and routing
- HTTP and the WWW

All the networking technologies presented in this chapter are based on existing standards. Standards are important as they enable multivendor interoperability.

2.3 The Prerequisite Information Challenge

One of the biggest challenges of writing a book is ensuring that your readers are "on the same page" with respect to prerequisite background material. Readers of varying background levels often use the same books, requiring a careful balance of background information without regurgitation of the same old stuff.

After a lot of thought, we decided to build this base chapter in a way that services

- the reader for whom the material is new,
- those needing a quick refresher of some or all of the base material, and
- the advanced reader who can "test out" part or all of the base material.

Now let's build a network from the ground up, highlighting the critical base components of switching solutions. Then we will take our network and perform a very common task showing how switching solutions are used throughout.

Note that each of these critical base components is presented in italic type and discussed in sections following this building exercise, giving you the option to read about one, some, all, or none of the base components depending on your level of expertise. If you have a good understanding about each base component, you "test out" and can proceed to Chapter 3. If you are hazy about some of the areas, read just those sections. Finally, if the text looks like Greek to you, read this chapter in its entirety.

2.3.1 The Chapter Two Road Map

Depending on your prerequisite knowledge, it may be a while before we talk about switching, which is covered in Chapter 3. So let's give a quick placeholder definition (also in the introduction) of switching solutions. You should keep this definition in the back of your head while reading this and other chapters, validating the definition as you learn more about the key switching solutions presented in this book.

Switching solutions help networks scale by addressing performance and robustness and encapsulating network intelligence.

Now let's look at a road map covering the Chapter 2 journey to determine which network cities you want to visit and which ones you have visited in the past.

We start off by learning about the *ISO OSI Reference Model,* which is key and core to networking. By understanding this model up front, we understand how networks *layer* functionality. Layering is a key concept in networking; it enables networks to scale and evolve from the simplest of networks to a large geographically distributed network.

We begin with the simplest of networks and grow from this rudimentary base—two PCs, each with a network interface card (NIC), connected by two links of *twisted-pair wiring* to a shared media hub. Both PCs are running Windows so we set up a simple Windows network as a network operating system (NOS). *Ethernet* is used to provide access to the shared media. We keep adding users until we get to sixteen. The network is slow, so we replace the shared media hub with a LAN layer-2 switch. At this point we are *bridging* traffic between users.

We continue to add users, which places more and more load on the network. If the network goes down, life goes down. We divide the network into two separate domains or *subnets,* purchase another switch, and plug in a LAN *routing switch* between the subnets. Routing enables us to scale beyond the capacity of the flat addresses tables maintained within layer-2 switches by introducing a hierarchical addressing scheme. Clearly a layer-2 switch cannot store (or swap in and out) every Ethernet address in the world! We offload the subnets by putting central database servers directly off the routing switch using *Fast Ethernet.* We are now heavily into *IP* with many addresses to manage, so we decide to use Dynamic Host Control Protocol (DHCP) for address management. Most of our client/server applications are based on *TCP* with an occasional use of User Data Protocol (UDP) for network management-related applications.

We solve the next growth spurt, moving to hundreds or perhaps a thousand users, by adding multiple router switches running *Gigabit Ethernet* between backbone switches or by introducing ATM switches and *ATM LAN Emulation* (LANE). One big difference between Ethernet and ATM is that Ethernet is *connectionless* and ATM is *connection-oriented.* Higher speed connections often use *fiber* instead of twisted-pair wiring.

While building the LAN, we then decide that being a LAN island isn't all that much fun. We want (need) Internet access to check stock quotes, shop, or just plain surf using the *HTTP* protocol over the *WWW*. We get a T-1 connection to a *frame relay switch* from an ISP. Although frame relay is a popular customer connection, the actual ISP network might be based on *ATM* or might even have segments of *X.25*.

It's now time to make a decision as to how you will proceed. Take another look at the above text and decide which topics are new, hazy, or "old hat" and adjust your chapter coverage accordingly.

2.4 The ISO OSI Reference Model

Layering, a key concept in networking, is used to reduce the complexity of networking and to enable simultaneous progression of technologies without widespread disruption when a single technology changes. Layering enables other technologies to depend on defined interfaces and blocks of functionality that can change independently. The ISO OSI Reference Model includes seven communication layers. This model is an attempt to divide and conquer the complexities of communication into manageable units, or layers. Although the seven-layer split may seem nebulous at times, the field of networking constantly references these layers. Subsequently, understanding the subdivision and the general motivation for these layers is fundamental to understanding networking.

Coupled with the reference model seven layers, you will see every communication stack "retrofitted" (they never fit exactly) along its side depicting the functional parallelisms. One stack, the TCP/UDP over IP communication stack, is popular and widely deployed. IP has gained a tremendous amount of popularity with the advent of the WWW. Table 2.1 shows each layer within the reference model, the approximate mapping to the TCP/IP layer, and the functional responsibility of the layer.

A S I D E . . .

Although Table 2.1 focuses on IP, it is worth pointing out that there are several other popular protocols that can be "fit" to the model. For example, Internetwork Packet Exchange (IPX) is a very popular layer-3 protocol that is used as an alternative to IP within LANs. In most cases, IPX runs over the same data link protocol examples as illustrated in Table 2.1 since most data link protocols support multiple network layers above them. In addition, AppleTalk and DecNET fit well into the ISO model.

Table 2.1 The ISO OSI Reference Model

No.	ISO 7 layers	TCP/IP layers	Responsibility
7	**Application**	There is no clear distinction between these layers in TCP/IP.	Applications running on a PC or work-station. (Some applications, like Telnet, FTP, HTTP, and e-mail span layers 5-7.)
6	**Presentation**		Provides an abstraction for data representation differences between applications.
5	**Session**		Offers an optional bidirectional or full-duplex service if not provided by transport layer.
4	**Transport**	**TCP, UDP, ICMP**[2]	Provides end-to-end management. For example, TCP provides flow control, acknowledgment, sequencing, and error correction; TCP also provides connection-oriented "reliable" communication. UDP provides connectless communication (datagram) service, a very thin layer on top of IP. However, it provides "unreliable" communication, that is, the data may get to its destination, or it may not.
3	**Network**	**IP, ARP**[3] (Address Resolution Protocol), **RARP** (reverse ARP)	Is responsible for routing of packets (which encapsulate frames) across the network.
2	**Data Link**	**data link** (Ethernet, ATM adaptation, FDDI, Fast Ethernet, Token Ring, Gigabit Ethernet *span both the **data link** and physical layers*)	Regulates access to the network. Provides point-to-point frame formation and management for various protocols. All frames contain source and destination addresses.
1	**Physical**	**physical**	Controls physical attachment, including wiring and signaling.

---

2. ICMP could be positioned at layer 3. However, it is positioned in layer 4 because it is an IP protocol and goes inside IP packets.

3. See Section 2.12 for more details on ARP (and RARP).

A S I D E . . .

It should be noted that layering within networking existed long before the ISO OSI reference model. In all actuality, the Internet is based on the Advanced Research Projects Agency NETwork (ARPANET) Reference Model (ARM) (see RFC 871). This model consists of three layers: the Network Interface layer, the Host-Host layer, and the Process Level/Applications layer. These layers are "logically" equivalent to layer 3, layer 4, and layers 5–7, respectively.

Layers 1, 2, 3, and 4 deserve extra attention, as these layers are where the core of networking takes place today.

2.4.1   Layer 1: Physical

Layer 1 is responsible for delivering data across a network link; think of it as providing a "stream of bits" across a wire. Layer 1 must regulate signaling and ensure that the signal stays strong. *Repeaters* and *concentrators* are network devices that operate at layer 1. Repeaters are used between two lengths of wire to regenerate a signal; concentrators (a special type of repeater) are used to share a single signal among many stations. It is important to follow the rules regarding the maximum span of wire and wire type associated with LAN technologies like Ethernet,[4] Token Ring, and FDDI. Examples of WAN layer-1 technologies are Plain Old Telephone Service (POTS) used to provide single-line telephones or the physical signaling used within a T-1 line.

2.4.2   Layer 2: Data Link

Layer 2 is responsible for transmitting frames of data across a layer-1 physical connection. Data frames are checked for errors and contain source and destination addresses. Two distinct layer-2 segments may be linked together with a bridge, which operates at the layer-2 level. LAN switches, sometimes referred to as *multiport bridges*,[5] operate at layer 2. Examples of WAN layer-2 technologies are T-1 links with a capacity of 1.544 Mbps, an E-1 link with a capacity of 2.048 Mbps, or Integrated Services Digital Network (ISDN).

---

4. Refer to Section 2.4 on Ethernet for more information on distance restrictions and general nomenclature. Ethernet is a very important LAN technology and is widely used in switched LAN environments. Having a firm grasp on how it works and its general terminology is important.

5. All bridges have at least two ports; LAN switches have multiple ports, typically 8 or 16.

2.4.3 Layer 3: Network

Layer 3 is responsible for routing packets (comprised of one or more individual frames) across one or more links, enabling stations to communicate across the network. Layer 3 has both a *data* path and a *control* path. The data path is used to send network data across the network; the control path is used to communicate error conditions and other information within the network.

The primary purpose of layer 3 is to determine the appropriate route between two end stations. This layer is also responsible for fragmentation and reassembly of data and network congestion. This following is a very subtle point, but one worth noting: *Network routers* operate at layer 3, although they may depend on protocols that update/maintain routing databases operating at a higher *application level.* Routers use routing protocols such as Routing Information Protocol (RIP) in the LAN, Open Shortest Path First (OSPF) in the LAN and WAN, and Border Gateway Protocol (BGP) in the WAN.

Routing protocols such as RIP, OSPF, and BGP use a combination of the control path and data path to communicate among peer routers. For example, BGP establishes an "application level" TCP session between peer routers, leveraging the data path for exchanging topology information. Another example of a control protocol is the Internet Group Management Protocol (IGMP); this protocol communicates group membership among routers supporting multicast communication. Multicast routers maintain tables of multicast groups so that they know where to send traffic for a particular multicast address.

The Internet Control Message Protocol (ICMP) is used as IP's network control protocol. Many ICMP message types are used to communicate error conditions and to make a network query. *Echo reply* and *echo request,* used by the Packet InterNetwork Groper (PING) protocol, determines if a network device is online, responding, and reachable. Host unreachable, destination unknown, and time exceeded are common control error messages that are sent back to the sender.

2.4.4 Layer 4: Transport

Layer 4 provides both an end-to-end reliable connection-oriented network connection protocol (TCP) and a connectionless, unreliable, unsequenced protocol (UDP). TCP enables applications to establish a communication session, exchange data, and tear down the session. The underpinnings of many client/server applications often build upon the reliable service provided by TCP using a network programming Application Programming Interface (API) for access. UDP provides a *low overhead* way to send and receive data as it does *not* set up a connection prior to communicating. Users of UDP are responsible for such things as packet reordering, general "timing out" when a reply is not returned within a certain time period, and duplicate packets. The Simple Network Management Protocol (SNMP) commonly runs on UDP.

A S I D E . . .

Most routers today also do *bidirectional* packet filtering (filtering out certain packets based on information in the packet header, like source or destination address). This is technically part of layer 4, assuming the filtering is done based on things like TCP/UDP port numbers.

2.4.5 Layers 1, 2, and 3

It is important to note that network layers conceptually exist on *each side* of network communication. Each layer "talks" with its counterpart, ignoring the "communication" of adjacent layers. Figure 2.1 depicts this communication for layers 1–3, combined with the common devices that facilitate connectivity. These network interconnection devices are the fundamental core of networks.

A N O T H E R   A S I D E . . .

The division also facilitates interoperability. For example, different physical implementations allow both Fiber Distributed Data Interface (FDDI) and Copper Distributed Data Interface (CDDI) to exist on the same ring.

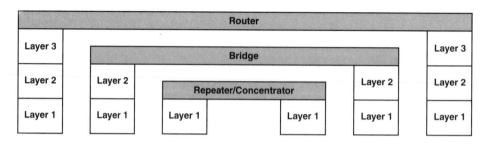

Figure 2.1 Relationship between network devices and OSI Reference Model

2.5 The Big Picture

At this point it makes sense to illustrate a high-level picture that justifies a significant portion of base technology by putting several components in context. This picture will provide an appreciation for needing so many technologies and the motivation necessary to push forward through a lot of concise text as we discuss each technology. Think of this illustration as the light at the end of the tunnel. Beginning with Section 2.6, we will go through components at each layer of networking. At the end of the chapter we will revisit this big picture.

Let's take an ordinary application that many use daily, a Web browser. You are looking for some new books, so you bring up your preferred browser and enter the Uniform Resource Locator (URL) of your favorite bookstore. Figure 2.2 shows all of the network devices (network equipment) and infrastructure that may be needed to do a simple Hypertext Transfer Protocol (HTTP) GET of the initial Web page. Yes, perhaps the example is slightly contrived to show off most of our technical base; however, it is not that far off. Even a simple request requires a *significant* amount of infrastructure, especially when going across both LANs and WANs.

Although we will not discuss each of the components in detail here, it is useful to have a simple key to explain each component with embedded acronyms in Figure 2.2. Table 2.2 provides this terminology key.

2.6 Twisted Pair and Fiber

There are two types of media commonly used in switched environments to interconnect network devices:

- **Unshielded Twisted Pair (UTP) and Shielded Twisted Pair:** 10baseT (10 Mbps baseT) and 100baseT (100 Mbps baseT)
- **Multimode and single-mode Fiber:** 10baseFL (10 Mbps baseFL), 100baseFL (100 Mbps baseFL), FDDI, and ATM

UTP, Shielded Twisted Pair, and multimode fiber dominate switched LANs and new installations; this is due largely to cost and ease of installation. Multimode fiber is used primarily in the LAN backbone whereas twisted pair is used out to the desktop. Single-mode fiber, used to span greater distances in the WAN, is more difficult to work with than multimode and is significantly more expensive.

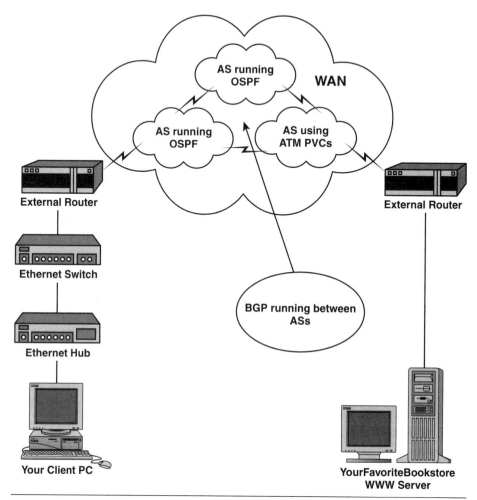

Figure 2.2 The big picture of your client PC connecting to
YourFavoriteBookstore WWW server

2.7 Connectionless versus Connection-Oriented

ATM is a connection-oriented protocol; that is, ATM sets up a *dedicated* pipe
prior to communicating. Connectionless technologies fire packets across the
network with the assumption that they'll eventually get to their destination.
ATM networks can guarantee a certain level of QoS or refuse the connection

Table 2.2 Terminology Key for Figure 2.2

Term	Description of Term
Your Client PC	A networked PC with a WWW browser. The PC depicted is connected to an Ethernet hub via twisted-pair wiring. Note that your client PC must have an IP address to utilize the WWW. This address may be assigned statically or dynamically via the Dynamic Host Control Protocol (DHCP) discussed later in this chapter.
Ethernet Hub	An inexpensive network device used to "fan out" a single 10 Mbps connection to several end stations.
Ethernet Switch	A LAN switch that bridges (switches) data across multiple 10 Mbps connections. In this example, data is switched to the external router.
External Router	The external router that connects the LAN to the Internet. The router has extensive firewall protection and may connect to the ISP's network with a frame relay link, perhaps over a fiber cable.
AS running OSPF	The ISP's Autonomous System (AS). The Internet is made up of many ASs that are interconnected via the Border Gateway Protocol (BGP). This AS is running Open Shortest Path First (OSPF) as an Interior Gateway Protocol (IGP).
AS using ATM PVCs	Another AS running BGP as an Exterior Gateway Protocol (EGP) but using ATM PVCs to switch traffic within the AS. This requires IP to ATM segmentation to convert frames to cells as data enters the ATM infrastructure and reassembles the converted cells to frames as data exits the ATM infrastructure.
BGP running between ASs	The Border Gateway Protocol (BGP) is the common protocol used between ASs.
YourFavoriteBookstore WWW Server	The WWW server that you connect to in order to download HTTP Web pages from the YourFavoriteBookStore site.
WAN	The Wide Area Network (WAN) made up of many ASs.

setup, since resources across the network are set up and dedicated to a particular session. ATM is sometimes criticized for the overhead involved for very short communication sessions. For example, setting up a dedicated connection to exchange a 10-packet or less e-mail is a lot of overhead to incur. On the other hand, longer communication sessions can benefit greatly from the dedicated connection: They have preallocated resources to use and are not impacted like connectionless networks by the sporadic congestion often found at peak network communication times.

Ethernet, Token Ring, and FDDI technologies provide connectionless networks and rely on packet-based networks. When a message is sent in a packet-based network, it is broken down into many individual packets (unless it is small enough to fit into one packet). These packets, which are a unit of data composed of a header to describe and control the data, the actual payload (data sent by the sender), and a trailer to terminate the packet and detect errors, are reassembled at the receiving end of the communication. The length of packets may vary, although they do have a minimum and maximum length. Packet ordering and congestion delays are two issues of packet networks; they may or may not arrive at their destination (higher-layer technologies take care of this problem), may take different routes to get to their destination, and may arrive out of order (that is, the end of a message may arrive before the middle). Packet networks have the obvious advantage of low overhead since no setup is required prior to transmitting data. However, repeated processing for packets destined to the same address is required, as each packet is *individually* routed through the network.

Ethernet is widely deployed in the LAN whereas ATM is widely used in the WAN. The majority of ATM used in the LAN serves as a fat pipe interconnecting Ethernet devices using ATM LAN Emulation (LANE). Sections 2.8 and 2.9 talk about Ethernet, ATM (as used in the WAN), and ATM LANE.

2.8 Ethernet

Ethernet is the oldest and most widely deployed shared-media LAN technology. It is popular because it is simple and efficient. However, a major criticism is that it is nondeterministic; that is, you cannot guarantee bandwidth to a user of a shared Ethernet segment, as only one device at a time can use the Ethernet media. Although there are many other Ethernet standards over different media using different connectors, Table 2.3 summarizes the most popular key characteristics of Ethernet.

Table 2.3 Key Characteristics of Ethernet

Ethernet Technology	10baseT	10baseF or Fiber Optic Inter Repeater Link (FOIRL)
Standard[6]	802.3i	802.3j
Speed	10 Mbps	10 Mbps
Medium	2-pair Category 3 Twisted Pair	2 strands single- or multi-mode fiber
Segment Length[7]	100 m (12 stations per segment)	2000 m
Frame Size	64 to 1518 8-bit bytes	64 to 1518 8-bit bytes
Topology	Star	Star

Standard Ethernet provides 10 Mbps aggregate bandwidth, which is shared among all users on a common communication channel called a *bus*. A bus is a segment of cable of a limited length to which many devices connect along the way, much like a string of decorative lights all sharing the same source of power. Only one user can use the bus at any given time, and therefore the bus is *shared.*

In a switched LAN, even though each switched port is an Ethernet bus, the physical topology used is a star. Star technology refers to a configuration in which all devices connect back to a common connection point using a separate length of cable. Figure 2.3 shows a simple traditional Ethernet bus transitioned to a switched star configuration.

Often star configurations "fan out" into *trees,* enabling you to split a single connection into multiple branches where each branch services a device. In

---

6. Over the years there have been several IEEE 802.3 standards to accommodate new mediums and speeds. To differentiate each standard, a lowercase letter is appended to 802.3. For example, the popular 10baseT standard is 802.3i.

7. In all actuality, the 10baseT Ethernet standard does not restrict segment length to 100m. By sticking with 100m, however, it is easy to upgrade later to Fast Ethernet, which does have a 100m restriction.

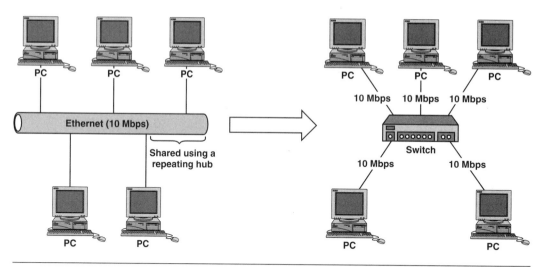

Figure 2.3 Traditional LAN segment (left) transitioned to a switched LAN (right)

essence, this forms a shared bus and enables you to attach many devices to a single switched port. A repeating hub fans out a single connection. Sometimes the combination of multiple trees attached to a star is called a *star of trees*. Figure 2.4 shows the use of a repeating hub to fan out a single switched port to many PCs.

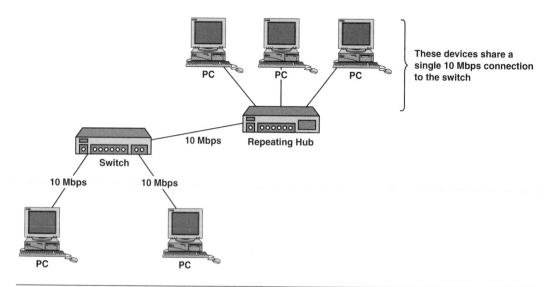

Figure 2.4 A switch with both dedicated devices and a hub fanning out to several PCs

A S I D E . . .

Although you can daisy chain hubs to hubs to fan out a single port several times, this may cause problems. *Cascading* often results in management headaches associated with disconnected cables, loose connections, and Ethernet signal problems.

Since Ethernet is a shared media, installations must obey strict distance restrictions so that the protocol can arbitrate who gets use of the cable at any time. Ethernet uses a Carrier Sense Multiple Access/Collision Detection (CSMA/CD) method for providing access to the cable. CSMA/CD specifies how an Ethernet station ("station" refers to any device connected to an Ethernet network) senses whether the cable is free and how to "back off" (how long to wait before retransmitting) if it is not free. Note that because of timing issues, even if an Ethernet station senses that the cable is free and puts a frame on it, another station could do the same causing a frame collision. CSMA/CD is quite involved, and the exact details go beyond the scope of this book; consult a book dedicated to Ethernet for more information.

When discussing switched Ethernet, you will often hear the term "collision domain." A collision domain is made up of a single CSMA/CD network. Each port on an Ethernet switch defines a single collision domain, implying that the collision domain is made up of all active users attached to a switched port at any given time. When a switched port is dedicated to a workstation, the user's collision domain is limited to the single workstation, called a point-to-point, dedicated connection. When a switched port is "fanned out" using a hub, the collision domain consists of all the devices to which the single network is fanned out. Naturally, a dedicated connection is better than a shared one and is more expensive as well. In fact, one common parameter used to decide upon a network configuration is cost per port. For obvious reasons, busy backbone and server connections should be always dedicated.

A nice feature in many switches is full-duplex Ethernet. It provides 20 Mbps aggregate bandwidth—10 Mbps in each direction. Full duplex is available only in point-to-point links using fiber or some twisted-pair media since each 10 Mbps channel is supported using a separate wire; that is, no "fanning out" with a hub is allowed. "Simplex" (half-duplex) is used to define bandwidth shared between both directions. When you run full-duplex Ethernet, CSMA/CD is disabled, allowing traffic to travel in both directions simultaneously by eliminating the possibility of collisions.

2.8.1 Fast Ethernet

Fast Ethernet is essentially the same as Ethernet, but ten times faster. Fast Ethernet achieves this speed by increasing the clock speed and using a different encoding scheme—both of which require a better grade of wire than standard Ethernet does. Two pairs (category 5) or 4 pairs (category 3/4/5) of wire are required. Category 3 wiring and connectors are designed to transmit up to 16 megahertz and works fine for 10 Mbps communication. Category 4 wiring is designed for up to 20 megahertz, so it really doesn't give you much over Category 3. Category 5 wiring and connectors are designed to transmit up to 100 megahertz and therefore is the most commonly used wire for Fast Ethernet and new twisted-pair installations (even if initially deploying 10 Mbps Ethernet).

As an alternative to twisted pair, you can use multimode fiber, which is much cheaper than single-mode fiber. Multimode fiber works for up to 2000m of distance whereas single-mode fiber is required for the long haul (up to 10km). Table 2.4 summarizes the key characteristics of the most popular Fast Ethernet configurations used within switched LANs.

Table 2.4 Key Characteristics of Fast Ethernet

Fast Ethernet Technology	Ethernet (100base-T)	Ethernet (100base-FX)
Standard	802.3u	802.3u
Speed	100 Mbps	100 Mbps
Medium	2 pairs Category 5 unshielded twisted pair (100base-TX) 4 pairs Category 3/4/5 twisted pair (100base-T4)	multimode and single-mide fiber
Segment Length	100m 2 pairs Category 5 or 4 pairs Categories 3/4/5 (1024 stations per collision domain)	2000m (multimode) 10km (single-mode)
Frame Size	64 to 1518 8-bit bytes	64 to 1518 8-bit bytes
Topology	Star	Star

Fast Ethernet also provides full-duplex communication that provides 200 Mbps aggregate bandwidth—100 Mbps in each direction. Like Ethernet, full-duplex Fast Ethernet is available only in point-to-point links using fiber or twisted-pair mediums since each 100 Mbps channel is supported using a separate wire.

One elegant feature of Fast Ethernet is autonegotiation, a scheme that facilitates automatic adaptation to the highest possible communication speed found at both ends of the cable. Assuming you originally installed data grade, category-5 UTP, this feature enables you to upgrade a 10 Mbps server connection to 100 Mbps within the wiring closet simply by moving the wire from a 10 Mbps port to a 100 Mbps Fast Ethernet port. Since 10/100 NICs are becoming less and less expensive, current trends are moving Fast Ethernet to the desktop.

2.8.2 Gigabit Ethernet

Gigabit Ethernet retains much of the simplicity of traditional Ethernet. It uses CSMA/CD, provides full- and possibly half-duplex communications at 1000 Mbps, and retains the frame format/size. It is designed to "drop in" to an existing Ethernet environment without much pain at all, enabling you to scale far beyond Fast Ethernet. Table 2.5 summarizes the key characteristics of Gigabit Ethernet.

Table 2.5 Key Characteristics of Gigabit Ethernet

Gigabit Ethernet Technology	
Standards	802.3z, 802.3ab
Speed	1000 Mbps (1 Gbps)
Medium	multimode or single-mode fiber (first-supported media, may support other media after initial standard)
Segment Length	500m
Frame Size	64 to 1518 8-bit bytes
Topology	Star

Gigabit Ethernet will place greater restrictions on wire spans; the Gigabit Ethernet committee is shot for spans of 500 meters of single-mode/multimode fiber, 25 meters for copper coaxial cable, and 100 meters for UTP Category 5. These shorter spans accommodate the CSMA/CD aspect of Ethernet. As with traditional Ethernet, use of a full-duplex repeater will allow you to increase the span. Gigabit Ethernet uses the Fibre Channel interconnection technology for its physical connection, yet it increases Fibre Channel's 800 Mbps signal rate to 1.24 Gbps for a throughput of 1 Gbps.

A S I D E . . .

Early implementations of Gigabit Ethernet experienced a 100m physical limitation on many existing multimode fiber installations. Gigabit Ethernet is now supported over multimode fiber up to 550m. Distances beyond 550m require single-mode fiber.

2.8.2.1 Interesting Facts about Gigabit Ethernet

Gigabit Ethernet is an exciting technology with a lot of potential. This section contains eight interesting facts about the technology that distinguish it from other Ethernet technologies.

1. Half-duplex Gigabit Ethernet supports *carrier extension* and *packet bursting*. Carrier extension increases the number of bits that travel across a connection without increasing the minimum frame length. This technique results in a performance hit for short frames. To solve this problem, packet bursting was introduced. It allows interconnection devices to send many short frames at once, increasing bandwidth efficiency. Carrier extension is a requirement for half-duplex Gigabit Ethernet; packet bursting is optional.

2. Gigabit Ethernet is positioned for deployment in the LAN backbone. Connecting a PC or workstation directly to a 1000 Mbps pipe is not necessary for some PCs and workstations as they cannot take advantage of the capacity.[8]

---

8. There are some PCs and workstations that max out the 100 Mbps Network Interface Cards (NICs) that are commonly and inexpensively available. It is expected that as Gigabit Ethernet NIC prices drop, we will start to see some users with Gigabit Ethernet at the desktop.

3. To get around the CSMA/CD distance restrictions, Gigabit Ethernet will be run mostly at full-duplex.

4. There are actually two standards for Gigabit Ethernet: 802.3z and 802.3ab. Gigabit Ethernet over UTP was broken off into a separate standard committee (802.3ab) in order to make the 802.3z standard move more quickly. Both standards are supplements to the 802.3 Ethernet standard.

5. Although Gigabit Ethernet has an autonegotiation protocol, it is limited to negotiating half- or full-duplex flow control and determining whether control frames are supported. Connecting a Gigabit Ethernet port to a Fast Ethernet port will just not work.

6. The physical layers of Gigabit Ethernet are based on layers FC-O and FC-1 of the Fibre Channel specification. As mentioned, Gigabit Ethernet increased the data rate of Fibre Channel.

7. Gigabit Ethernet disallows the interconnection of repeaters within the same collision domain due to high-speed data rate timing restrictions. It is expected that Gigabit Ethernet will be typically deployed from point-to-point or fanned out from a single hub.

8. Backpressure is a technique used to prevent network congestion. Simply stated, backpressure uses CSMA/CD to force collisions or make the wire appear to be busy. Since backpressure relies on CSMA/CD, it works in a half-duplex environment only. 802.3x is an official standard for implementing flow control across full-duplex connections.

2.9 ATM and ATM LANE

Asynchronous Transfer Mode (ATM) provides a common communication mechanism that simultaneously supports multiple types of data (that is, voice, video, text) at high transmission across switched WAN or LAN backbones. Unlike other LAN technologies, ATM cannot be a shared medium; hence the performance does not degrade as the number of users increases, as with Ethernet in shared (not full-duplex) mode. In the WAN, ATM is not vulnerable to loss due to congestion in a "bursty" traffic pattern, as IP is. (Bursty refers to when substantial data is transmitted at irregular intervals.) ATM is connection-oriented, meaning that an end-to-end connection is set up prior to communication. ATM differs from TCP (which is also connection-oriented); ATM sets up *dedicated* resources (much like a telephone call) that are used for the duration of a communication session, or it refuses the connection setup if sufficient resources are not available. With dedicated resources, ATM is able to provide a way to guarantee delivery with a negotiated set of parameters; this important feature is called Quality of Service (QoS). Table 2.6 summarizes the key characteristics of ATM.

ATM runs at many different speeds across all the popular media. Three popular speeds are 25 Mbps, 155.52 Mbps (OC-3), and 622 Mbps (OC-12). UTP and shielded twisted pair are typically used on the desktop in the LAN, whereas fiber is used in the backbone of both LANs and WANs. There is also a lot of 51.84 (OC-1) used in the WAN.

Table 2.6 Key Characteristics of ATM

Technology	ATM
Standard	Several B-ISDN/ATM Standards
Speed	25.6 Mbps 51.84 Mbps (Optical Carrier-1 (OC-1)) 100 Mbps 155.52 Mbps (Optical Carrier-3 (OC-3)) 622.08 Mbps (Optical Carrier-12 (OC-12))
Medium	Unshielded Twisted Pair (UTP) for 25.6 and 51.84 Mbps Multifiber or single-mode fiber primarily for 100+ Mbps[9]
Segment Length	N/A
Cell Size	53 bytes including a 5-byte header
Physical Topology	Star

---

9. Category 5 UTP and Category 1 STP may be used for higher speeds.

A S I D E . . .

Optical Carrier-n (OC-n), where n is 1, 3, 9, 12, 18, 24, 36, or 48, refers to the optical interface used within a Synchronous Optical NETwork (SONET). The basic rate of SONET is 51.84, and you can determine all other OC-n data rates simply by multiplying the "n" number by 51.84. For example, the data rate for OC-3 is 3 times 51.84 or 155.52; the data rate for OC-12 is 51.84 times 12 or 622.08.

ATM uses the notions of Permanent Virtual Connections/Circuits and Switched Virtual Circuits (PVCs and SVCs) to define communication paths. (Actually the abbreviation SVC can also stand for Signaling Virtual Channel, but its Switched Virtual Circuit use is more commonly used since it is more consistent with PVC.) PVCs are statically configured paths across network backbones; SVCs, set up dynamically on an as-needed basis, are set up and torn down via a signaling protocol. When a user wishes to establish a connection with another node, the user sends a message specifying the bandwidth and QoS desired. Simply stated, the signaling protocol "walks" through the network, keeping track of its path along the way to the desired destination. If the destination is successfully reached and the path satisfies the given QoS parameters, the switched connection is established and ready for use. There is a fair amount of overhead setting up a SVC; this is one disadvantage of a connection-oriented protocol, especially if the connection carries data for only a short period of time.

Unlike the variable packet sizes used within connectionless networks, ATM's basic transmission unit is a fixed-sized cell. A cell is a 53-byte unit with 5 bytes of header information that moves the cell to its destination and 48 bytes of payload (the actual data sent). ATM is often criticized for its *cell tax* since each 48 bytes of data requires 5 bytes (more than 10 percent) of overhead to send.

It is important to understand the use of Virtual Paths (VPs) and Virtual Channels (VCs) within ATM networks. A Virtual Path is composed of many VCs between two ATM switches. Each VC can be for a discrete communication session. Both the Virtual Path and the Virtual Channel have integer identifiers called Virtual Path Identifier (VPI) and Virtual Channel Identifier (VCI), respectively. VPI/VCI pairs are used as addresses to switch information across multiple hops in the network. When data flows through an ATM switch, the VPI is modified[10] to switch to the outgoing port. Hence the VPI is a link-by-link identifier used to direct cells to the next immediate destination. This pair is similar to the MAC addresses that are swapped by Ethernet switches to direct the frame to the next immediate destination.

---

10. Currently the VCI is ignored.

As expected, a VPI/VCI pair is part of every cell's header. The VPI/VCI is used to identify a communication session uniquely and is included in the header of each cell. Forget for a moment the dynamic nature of paths and circuits being virtual and coming and going. Think of a bundle of optic fibers contained in a plastic outer skin that can be thought of as the path identifier (or VPI) that contains many identifiable fibers (or VCIs). Now envision many such bundles used to create an ATM network. Each fiber strand can be identified by the bundle (path) and a strand (channel). This hierarchical identification scheme is a very powerful tool for multiplexing many communication sessions across a single path and many paths across an ATM network.

2.9.1 ATM LANE

To incorporate ATM in existing networks consisting of Ethernet and Token Ring, LAN Emulation (LANE) was created. LANE provides the normal connectionless, multicast service characteristic of traditional LANs and emulates the media access control (MAC) protocol used by connectionless technologies that enable you to support LAN technologies over ATM. FDDI over LANE and Fast Ethernet over LANE require translational bridging, which is commonly used to define an ATM pipe to bridge two LANs. The systems that participate in this emulated LAN across legacy LANs are said to be part of an Emulated LAN (ELAN). Often Virtual LANs (VLANs) are defined to overlap with ELANs. We will talk in-depth about VLANS in Chapter 3 because they are not just for ATM and they are a relatively new technology commonly integrated with switching.

2.9.2 Physical Topology in the LAN

In the LAN, ATM can be used to the desktop or, using LANE, only in the backbone. LANE is the most popular way ATM is deployed in the LAN, since it revolves around many concepts. First let's identify the component and then give a brief explanation of each. There are a lot of terms that are required to understand LANE. Here we go.

LANE involves setting up one or more ELANs; an ELAN consists of one or more LAN Emulation Clients (LECs) served by one LAN Emulation Server (LES). In addition we need:

- One LAN Emulation Configuration Server (LECS) shared across the entire ATM network, and
- One Broadcast and Unknown Server (BUS).

The interface between the LECs and the ATM network is called the LAN Emulation User to Network Interface (LUNI), and the interface between the BUSs and LESs (should you have many ELANs) is called the LAN Emulation Network to Network Interface (LNNI). Figure 2.5 illustrates all these terms in context.

LECs refer to the software that connects an end-node device such as a database server, PC, or workstation to the ATM network. A LEC's interface into the network is provided by the LUNI. Internetwork connections also use a LNNI. The LES provides such functionality as MAC to ATM address resolution (ATM uses 20-bit addressing, whereas traditional Ethernet LANs use 48-bit MAC addresses) and client registration to LECs. The BUS processes all broadcast, multicast, and unknown traffic into the ELAN. Remember, since ATM is a point-to-point technology, it has no built-in knowledge on how to generate broadcast and multicast traffic using built-in addressing procedures as they are found within connectionless networks. When you have many ELANs, you must have a single LECS that identifies each ELAN and its LES location.

A S I D E . . .

With ATM there can be more than one LEC associated with a switched port. This feature allows clients to be part of more than one Emulated LAN. However, there is generally a vendor-specific physical limit to the number of PVCs that a given switch may support—this, in turn, limits the number of LECs that can be supported.

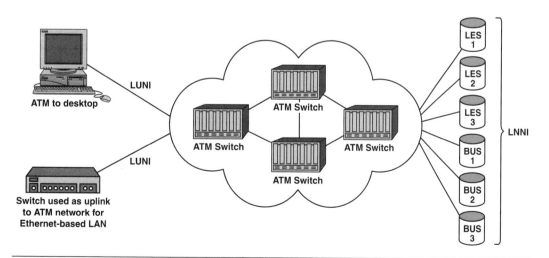

Figure 2.5 A LANE environment

An ATM trunk (sometimes called a fat pipe) is a high-speed (often 622 Mbps (OC-12)), permanent virtual circuit link between two switches in your network. ATM trunks may be used by traditional (non-ATM) LANs via LANE or in a pure ATM network where ATM goes out to the desktop. If LANE is employed, the "P to C" and "C to P" (packet-to-cell, cell-to-packet) conversions will happen inside of each switch on the alternate sides of the trunk. Because trunks are permanent, they are statically configured without needing to go through the signaling protocol. (This isn't to say that channels within the trunks may not come and go and be set up via signaling.) Use of trunks is popular with ATM in the LAN, because there was no other technology (albeit Fibre Channel isn't widely deployed as a data networking protocol) that comes close to the available bandwidth of 622 Mbps; Gigabit Ethernet, however, is rapidly becoming an alternative.

A S I D E . . .

ATM enables you to create a meshed network at layer 2—a network where each switch has a dedicated connection to other switches within your network. Meshes can be used to increase greatly the overall capacity and redundancy of your network. With Ethernet you cannot create a meshed network.

2.9.3 Physical Topology in the WAN

The telecommunication companies (telcos, for short) have made a large investment in deploying ATM PVCs across their WAN infrastructure. We can think of these PVCs as fat pipes that span long distances and enable telcos to pump lots of data. These pipes represent the telco's ATM-based Cell Relay Service (CRS). In 1995 CRS became publicly available; it used T-1,[11] T-3, and fiber-based lines. An interesting fact about ATM is that it is the only technology that can provide end-to-end communications across LAN *and* WAN with QoS guarantees. Delay-sensitive data (for example, interactive voice and real-time video) form a class of traffic that benefits from the ability to have "guaranteed QoS" since without it the quality of real-time traffic can degrade.

2.9.4 Operation

It is important to note a few key distinctions for the operation of ATM that distinguishes it from other technologies. The following summarizes ATM's operation:

---

11. T-1 and T-3 are North American standards for digital telephony data rates. T-1 provides a data rate of 1.544 Mbps, and T-3 provides a data rate of 44.736 Mbps.

- As mentioned previously, ATM is connection-oriented; an ATM circuit is set up either permanently or as needed via signaling.

- Because ATM is connection-oriented and allocates resources prior to communicating, ATM can provide QoS guarantees. This means ATM can guarantee delivery of data based on up-front negotiation. This guarantee is useful for time-sensitive data like interactive voice or real-time video. For example, you know how terrible it is to see a movie where the sound is out of synch with the picture; ATM's QoS is a powerful solution to guarantee that the sound arrives when the picture arrives. QoS (coupled with bandwidth) is the most important feature of ATM within a LAN environment; if you need guaranteed jitter-free, real-time video at low cost in a computer that has no RAM for buffering, you need ATM, end-to-end. Nearly jitter-free communication within a LAN can be achieved by significantly overprovisioning the network. (Chapter 5 talks about overprovisioning in length.) Note that overprovisioning bandwidth, buffers, and other resources may be expensive in the long run, especially in the WAN.

- As mentioned, ATM cells do not contain 48-bit MAC addresses (also know as LAN addresses), rather they contain path and channel identifiers (represented in 20 bits). LANE is used to map these path and circuit identifiers to MAC addresses.

- ATM literally works by pumping cells through a predefined mesh. Once a path is set up, ATM leverages switching to move data from source to destination at wire speeds. Switches use high-speed *switching fabrics* to route data. Switching fabrics, usually comprised of intricate, parallel interconnections built using very advanced ASIC (Application-Specific Integrated Circuit) technologies, refer to the hardware and software design of the switch.

2.10 Point-to-Point Connections and Cloud Technologies

Dedicated connections are typically used to link your LAN to another LAN across the WAN or to provide a link to the Internet. To make these connections, you need an external router. Note there are many types of routers, and external routers are a special breed. They come with all of the security and firewall features you need to protect your LAN. When you have private connections across a WAN to one or more sites, you have what is referred to as an *Intranet*—a private, corporate network. There are two options for dedicated WAN connections: the use of dedicated *point-to-point* leased lines or provider *cloud* services. The key distinction is that point-to-point lines are dedicated to one customer, whereas provider cloud services are owned and managed by a provider and are shared among many customers providing a meshed network, as already discussed.

The advantage of point-to-point leased lines is that they are private and are not shared with other users; the disadvantage is that they offer only point-to-point links. If you have lots of sites to connect, you have lots of lines to lease. For short distances (less than 1000 miles) they are often cheaper than using cloud technologies.

Cloud technologies are shared WAN technologies that allow you to connect from multiple points (or sites) without separate leased lines. For long distances (more than 1000 miles) they are often cheaper than leased lines. Use of cloud technologies is more popular when you have many sites to connect because of the flexibility they provide.

Regardless of whether you use dedicated leased lines or cloud technologies, they both use the same popular connections to connect you to your point at the other end or into the cloud: T-1, fractional T-1, or T-3. A T-1 line provides twenty-four 64 Kbps channels; this yields 1.544 Mbps of total bandwidth. A fractional T-1 line is a 64 incremental chunk of a T-1 line, anywhere from 64 Kbps to 1.472 Mbps (23/24 of a T-1). With fractional T-1s, the telco simply divides a T-1 among several different customers.

A T-3 is 28 T-1 lines or 45 Mbps (1.536 Mbps * 28, rounded up to the standard) of total bandwidth. For a WAN connection this is considered to be a pretty fat pipe and comes with a pretty fat monthly lease of several thousand dollars. There are three common cloud services:

- X.25 (the granddaddy)
- Frame relay (X.25 on steroids)
- ATM (emerging)

Since we have already covered ATM, we will discuss X.25 and frame relay.

2.10.1 X.25

Although no longer widely used in the United States, X.25 remains popular in Europe. X.25 provides a packet-switching data network with data rates up to 56 Kbps. With today's standards, this is relatively slow, but X.25 has lots of error detection and recovery built in. For example, packets are reassembled at each hop, verified for errors, and then passed along. Table 2.7 highlights key advantages and disadvantages of X.25.

Table 2.7 Key Advantages and Disadvantages of X.25

X.25 Advantages	X.25 Disadvantages
Since it is internationally deployed, in many cases X.25 is the only WAN technology available. It is popular in Europe.	The maximum rate is a slow 56 Kbps, making it unsuitable for voice or video; data rates are better served by frame relay.
Has built-in error correction, flow control, retransmission of lost packets make it highly reliable, and good for connections that span large distances over noisy lines.	There is high latency. Because packets are reassembled at each node along the way, packet throughput is low, and packet delay is high.

A S I D E . . .

X.25, like other packet-switching technologies, is often represented as a cloud. This is because X.25 provides the specifications at the connection points to the network but not to the network itself—what happens in the networking cloud is transparent to the user. As long as the service at the endpoints matches, X.25 or other packet-switching technologies may be used by a telco to provide the service.

2.10.2 Frame Relay

Frame relay service (FRS) is a widely deployed service that scales with the granularity of a T-1 line, from 56 Kbps to 1.544 Mbps. Up to T-3 (44.736) service is now available, although it is very expensive. Originally intended for data only, frame relay is used to carry interactive voice and, in fact, is becoming increasingly popular (see Chapter 7 for more information on services). When you set up your frame relay connection with your telco, you define a Committed Information Rate (CIR), a Committed Burst Size (CBS), and sometimes an Excess Burst Size (EBS). The CIR is the guaranteed average data rate that you need, and the Committed Burst Rate (CBR) is the maximum number of bits that can be transmitted over a time interval. If you select a CIR of 256 Kbps and a CBS of 1024 Kb, you are guaranteed to be able to transmit 1024 Kb of data over a 4-second period. (T= CBS/CIR $\Rightarrow$ 4 = 1024/256). This guarantee is a worst case scenario, that is, when the network is congested. If the network is not congested, the EBS comes into play. Given an EBS of 512 in the same example, you would be able to transmit 1536 (1024 + 512) Kbps more during the same time period. You should add a little fluff when specifying both the CIR and CBS for your frame relay connection. A good rule of thumb is to round up by about 10 percent. By overprovisioning by 10 percent you will have a bit of buffer for the inevitable growing network bandwidth requirements.

The tariff for frame relay is directly related to the distance the link must go and the bandwidth. Generally speaking the bigger the pipe and the longer the distance, the higher the cost. Telcos vary as to how they charge for your frame relay connection. Some carriers base the entire charge on usage; others offer a CIR at a fixed monthly fee. Table 2.8 presents key advantages and disadvantages of frame relay.

2.11 Bridging

Since LAN switching comes from bridging, bridging is a fundamental core LAN technology. This section provides a quick survey of the functionality of bridging, deferring a more detailed discussion of switching to the next chapter. Figure 2.6 provides a conceptual view of bridging within a LAN.

Table 2.8 Key Advantages and Disadvantages of Frame Relay

Frame Relay Advantages	Frame Relay Disadvantages
Frame relay is very fast, taking advantage of the cleaner signals in today's wide area connections by reducing error checking. Latency at intermediate nodes is far less than X.25.	There is an optional bit that may be set within a packet indicating that a packet may be dropped when the frame relay cloud is congested. Unfortunately it is rarely used. Subsequently frame relay is susceptible to congestion problems.
Variable-size frames work with any LAN packet or frame, for example TCP/IP, Ethernet, or Token Ring MAC, or even an X.25 packet. Frame relay thus provides transparency to the user.	There are no special provisions for time-sensitive, real-time traffic such as voice or video, even though a lot of voice is already transported over frame relay.
Frame relay provides bandwidth on demand, allowing you to exceed bandwidth to accommodate bursts.	Reduced error checking results in retransmissions when lines are noisy.

As Figure 2.6 shows, bridges have a forwarding table that contains Media Access Control (MAC)/Address/Age mappings and optional exchanges Spanning Tree Protocol (STP) and Bridge Protocol Data Units (BPDUs) to synchronize paths between bridges.

The following are key characteristics of bridges:

- Bridges forward frames (FDDI, Token Ring, Ethernet, and so on) at the data link layer, layer 2.

- Bridges forward frames based on the contents of their "learned" forwarding table. As mentioned, forwarding tables provide a "mapping" from a MAC address to a port on the bridge. A bridge's forwarding table may also contain entries that are statically entered by the network administrator.

- Bridges "learn" where MAC addresses are by monitoring the source addresses within frames. For example, if a frame comes from port 2 with a *source MAC address* of 02-60-8C-00-09-83, subsequent frames with a *destination MAC address* of 02-60-8C-00-09-83 are forwarded to this port. Figure 2.7 illustrates this important concept. Note that the forwarding table is only a conceptual view, as it will differ depending on vendor.

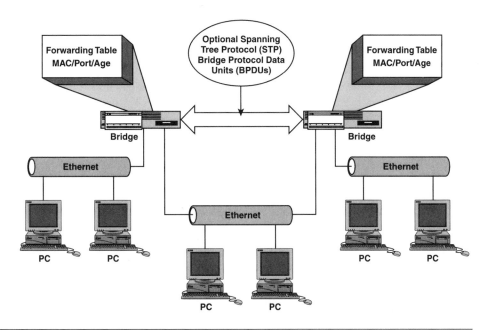

Figure 2.6 Conceptual representation of bridges within a LAN

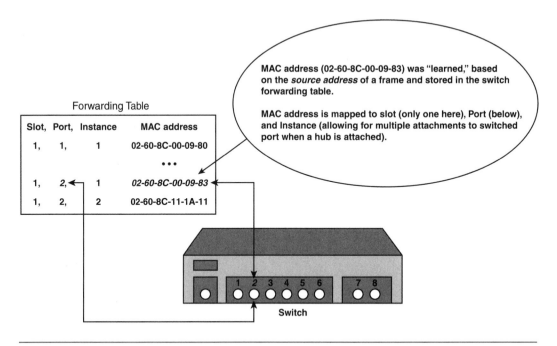

Figure 2.7 Relationship of MAC Addresses and switch forwarding table

- As shown conceptually in Figure 2.6, bridges optionally implement the Spanning Tree Protocol (STP). This protocol provides a mechanism for bridges to communicate with one another and to ensure that only one path exists between any two bridges. STP allows you to configure multiple paths between bridges for redundancy in the event that one port goes out, yet it eliminates bridge loops by having only one path open at any given time. If the open path goes down, the redundant path is opened up so that connectivity is retained. Bridge Protocol Data Units (BPDUs) by the STP are used to communicate between bridges.

- If a bridge does not have an entry for a destination address, the bridge "floods" the frame to all ports except the source port.

- If a bridge looks up the destination address and finds that it maps to the same port as the source port, it drops the frame, since it does not need to be bridged. This will happen if you have a number of devices that are attached to a concentrator or a hub that plugs into the bridge port.

- Over time bridges "age out" addresses from their forwarding tables to eliminate stale information and to keep the table from overflowing.

Typically a bridge forwarding table can hold only so many entries, for example, 1K (1024) to 8K (8192) entries. Entries are "aged out" of the table according to a timer that keeps track of when each entry was last updated. When the counter exceeds a preconfigured value, the entry is deleted from the table. As subsequent frames come in, their associated table entries are refreshed, that is, the counters are reset.

■ One noteworthy disadvantage of large bridged networks is the proliferation of broadcast traffic. Broadcast traffic, unlike unicast (traffic destined to a single destination), must be "read" by all network devices (including PCs, UNIX workstations, and so on) on your switched LAN. Lots of broadcast traffic can place significant overhead on each network device in a switched LAN. In addition, a broadcast storm (where a certain repeated broadcast uncontrollably floods the network) can be catastrophic. Routers and VLANs (discussed in Chapter 3) are used to "contain" broadcast traffic.

2.12 Important TCP/IP Concepts

TCP/IP combines the efforts of layers 3 (network layer) and 4 (transport layer) of the ISO Reference Model. It serves as the backbone to the Internet (and subsequently the WWW) and is widely used in LANs: There is a *lot* to TCP/IP. The following definitions provide you with the terms defined in Table 2.1 shown previously. These definitions give you a minimal working knowledge of TCP/IP.[12]

■ **TCP:** Transmission Control Protocol. TCP, designated as a connection-oriented service, provides reliable, end-to-end connections and is responsible for error control and recovery. Telnet, FTP, and remote log-in (rlogin) run on top of TCP ensuring a reliable terminal emulation session or file transfer session. TCP runs on top of IP, hence TCP/IP.

■ **UDP:** User Datagram Protocol. UDP provides a simple, connectionless service that does not establish a connection with its counterpart prior to communicating. UDP supports only limited optional error checking and is often designated as an unreliable connectionless service. SNMP normally runs on top of UDP, and UDP runs on top of IP. Sometimes you see UDP/IP in order to distinguish it from UDP/IPX, when you run Novell's Internet Packet Exchange (IPX).

---

12. Although this book does not provide comprehensive TCP/IP coverage, there are many fine books that do; please consult the bibliography for selected books.

- **IP:** Internet Protocol. IP provides connectionless routing service that is responsible for packet fragmentation and reassembly, routing, and data encapsulation. Each IP datagram has a 20-byte header (plus additional bytes for any options) tacked onto the front of each unit of data. This header includes things like type of service (TOS), total datagram length, time to live field (TTL), checksum, source address, and destination address.

- **ARP:** Address Resolution Protocol. ARP provides a mechanism to find a Media Access Control (MAC) physical address given an IP logical address. A MAC physical address is represented in a 6-byte format (xx-xx-xx-xx-xx-xx, where each "xx" represents the hexadecimal value of one of the six bytes, for example, 00-20-AF-12-34-56). An IP logical address is represented in a 4-byte format (xxx.xxx.xxx.xxx, where each "xxx" represents the decimal value of one of the four bytes, for example, 192.168.1.43). MAC addresses are typically burned into Network Interface Cards (NICs), hence physical addresses; IP addresses are assigned; hence they are logical addresses.

    ARP operates by broadcasting an IP address for which it wants to know the MAC address onto the network. The network node to which the IP address belongs replies to the ARP request with its MAC address; this MAC address is then used as the destination address of subsequent communication.

    The ARP command (`arp -a`) on a PC or UNIX workstation can be used to list the association between known MAC and IP addresses at any given time.

- **RARP:** Reverse Address Resolution Protocol. RARP, used by diskless workstations, provides a mechanism to find an IP address given a known network address (MAC).

- **TOS:** Type of Service. Within each IP packet is an 8-bit type of service field that includes a 3-bit precedence field, four TOS bits, and one unused bit that must be set to zero. The four TOS bits are minimize delay, maximize throughput, maximize reliability, and minimize monetary cost, respectively. Normal best-effort service has all bits set to zero. If TOS bits are used, only one bit may be set; the rest must be zero.

- **TTL:** Time to live. Within each IP packet is an 8-bit time to live field. The TTL defines the maximum number of routers through which a datagram can be sent before being discarded. It is initialized by the sender and decremented by one at each router through which it passes. If the field becomes zero, the datagram is dropped and the sender is notified with an ICMP message; this prevents datagrams from being propagated forever due to an inadvertent router loop.

A S I D E . . .

A MAC address is a unique (by design) address across your network, typically burned into the Network Interface Card (NIC) on your computer. The IP address is an assigned address that enables a network to be segmented based on traffic flow and other network management policy. Section 2.12.1 provides a brief introduction to TCP/IP addressing.

- **ICMP:** Internet Control Message Protocol (RFC 792). ICMP provides communication of control data (information and error recovery data) between IP nodes in the network. Error messages include such things as destination unreachable, echo request (ping), time exceeded, and parameter problem. Ping, a simple TCP/IP tool used to determine connectivity, is built on top of ICMP, an important part of the IP protocol.
- **DNS:** Domain Name System. DNS is a distributed name service used by TCP/IP to provide a mapping between host names and IP addresses.

2.12.1 IP Addressing

IP addressing is more complex than other addressing schemes largely because it is hierarchical. Hierarchical addressing provides needed scalability, although it includes one tradeoff—inadvertent addressing errors. In many cases it is the static configuration of TCP/IP addressing that is the root of networking problems. Duplicate IP addresses and incorrect subnet masks will often cause connectivity problems for those nodes or stations involved. It is therefore important to have a firm grasp of TCP/IP addressing.

Fundamental to TCP/IP's ability to span the world is its hierarchical addressing scheme. Version 4 (IPv4) addresses are 32 bits in length, are represented in dotted decimal notation (xxx.xxx.xxx.xxx, where each "xxx" represents each of the four 8-bit bytes of the address, for example, 192.168.1.27), and contain a network address (also known as a subnet) as well as a host address.

Subnets provide a way within TCP/IP to partition your network into logical entities and to contain broadcast traffic. Routing is required between subnets because broadcast traffic is not typically routed. A subnet mask is a 32-bit number that is represented by dotted decimal notation. This subnet mask is used to separate the network portion of an address (also known as the subnet) from the host portion. The mask contains "zero bits" to indicate the host portion and "one bits" for the subnet portion of the address.

2.13 What is DHCP?

TCP/IP address management can be a big challenge when running a network. TCP/IP's default behavior is *not* to learn a host's address automatically when a host boots; rather TCP/IP addresses are statically configured at each host in the network. This leaves lots of room for error. Dynamic Host Configuration Protocol (DHCP) provides a popular solution for automatic IP address assignment.

DHCP (RFCs 1533, 1541, and 1542) provides a general purpose client/server approach to IP address distribution. With DHCP, addresses are provided and managed by a central service, the DHCP server, in the network. If the network is small, there may be only one DHCP server. Larger networks tend to have several distributed DHCP servers that synchronize address assignment among them. Workstations and PCs are the clients of the DHCP server(s); they count on a DHCP server to provide them with their address.

DHCP servers maintain a range of addresses that may be distributed and *leased* to any device dynamically. Note that the lease period is configurable—from a few minutes to several months. Once a PC obtains a DHCP-served address, the address lease is refreshed, that is, once the lease is halfway to expiration. If the PC fails to refresh its lease within the lease period, the server may reclaim the address, and the PC is given a new address when it boots again.

Several DHCP solutions can be distributed across the enterprise, since they are able to manage many subnets simultaneously. Many DHCP servers integrate with a Domain Name Service (DNS) to provide name-based address management. It is often recommended that you install two DHCP servers for redundancy; one server remains in standby mode in case the primary server fails. DNS servers follow a similar redundancy model.

Clearly DHCP is an attractive alternative to the static, error-prone configuration characteristic of TCP/IP. All it takes is an incorrect subnet mask, invalid default gateway, or a duplicate IP address to cause a PC or workstation not to be networked and to prohibit anyone from remotely communicating to the system involved. If the system involved is a file server upon which multiple users depend, the problem becomes serious. Another benefit of DHCP is that the laptop meeting "goers" can "plug in" across your network campus at different locations and have a truly portable network.

A S I D E . . .

Many routers that are also communication servers provide DHCP. A caveat here is that some implementations (for example, Microsoft's DHCP) are often proprietary and may cause conflict.

2.14 Routing

Routing, the foundation of layer-3 switches, is a core technology used in both the LAN and the WAN. We will talk about layer-3 switches that perform both bridging and routing capabilities in the next chapter. Consequently a quick survey of the functionality that routing provides is presented in this section. Figure 2.8 provides a conceptual view of the synchronization of routing tables, a mechanism used to provide knowledge of how to navigate across a network connected by many routers. This synchronization process is fundamental to routing.

The following are key characteristics of routing:

- Routers route packets at the network layer, layer 3.

- Routers route packets based on the contents of a routing table.

- Routers *route* based on protocol. Examples of protocols that are routed are IP, IPX, AppleTalk, and DECnet. Although IP is the most popular routed protocol in the WAN and is quite common in the LAN,

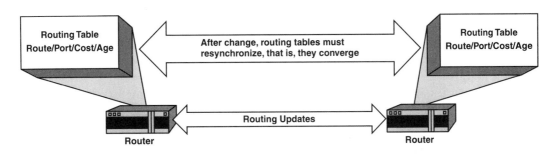

Figure 2.8 Conceptual representation of communication between multiple routers with a network

IPX (part of Novell's NetWare family) is still widely used and probably will be for quite some time.

- Routers (layer 3) route packets based on *logical* addresses, whereas bridges (layer 2) forward frames based on *physical* addresses. Logical addresses are protocol specific. For example, as previously discussed, IP, as well as IPX, has its own addressing scheme. Both IP and IPX addresses run on top of the same MAC addressing used to bridge packets at layer 2. The context of a physical address spans one hop (the destination physical address is changed at each intermediate hop), whereas the IP address goes end-to-end. The use of discrete addressing and layering is a very important concept in networking.

- Routing tables contain a mapping of destination to a port. Each table entry contains one or more metrics providing some indication of "cost." Thus if two or more routes exist for an entry, the router will pick the "least expensive" route. Note that some routers will load balance across multiple routes.

- Routers "learn" their routing table entries by communicating with their routing peers. Essentially each router has a set of preconfigured routes that it knows. By exchanging information at periodic intervals, routing peers can learn other routes provided by their peers.

- There are many routing protocols used to implement routing. For example, Open Shortest Path First (OSPF) and Routing Information Protocol (RIP) are particularly popular for TCP/IP implementations in LANs. OSPF is becoming widely used within ISP networks within the WAN, and Border Gateway Protocol (BGP) is used within the WAN as well.

- Each router is statically configured[13] with the networks to which it is directly attached. With bridges (and their respective forwarding tables) this is optional, with routers this is not. Preconfiguration is how routes are "seeded" for being "learned" by others. Somewhere in the network each route must be statically configured.

- Routers "age out" routes from their routing tables to eliminate stale information.

- Routers do not broadcast if they do not know where to forward a packet. Either the router will send the packet to a default gateway, or

---

13. Some LANs get by with only simple "static" routes, when the end user's workstations access only a few hosts.

the packet will be dropped. Packets have a built-in mechanism (for example, TCP/IP Time to Live (TTL)) that maintains the number of routers through which the packet has passed (also known as "hops"); once the TTL reaches a certain value, the packet is discarded, preventing the endless forwarding of "lost" packets.

- Certain protocols use underlying Logical Link Control (LLC) protocols that are not routable. For example, NetBIOS[14] Extended User Interface (NetBEUI) commonly used within LANs to network Windows-based PCs is not routable.

- Routers provide broadcast containment, because broadcast traffic is not typically routed. (Some routers can be configured to forward broadcast traffic; however, this is not recommended. Some switches can also filter broadcasts.)

- The key to routing is prompt updating and quick routing table convergence. If a route to a destination goes down, other routers must be notified as soon as possible, and the tables need to converge as soon as possible. Certain routing protocols converge more quickly than others; for example, OSPF converges faster than RIP.

2.14.1 Distance-Vector and Link-State Protocols

Routing protocols are classified as either distance vector or link state. Table 2.9 summarizes the key attributes of both protocol classifications.

Distance-vector protocols are based on the Bellman/Ford algorithm (see Bellman, *Dynamic Programming*) and use periodic updates containing neighbor vector of distances (that is, hop counts) between routers. Routes (or paths) are computed based exclusively on the fewest number of intermediate routers (or hops) between two network nodes. AppleTalk's Routing Table Maintenance Protocol (RTMP), IP's Routing Information Protocol (RIP), Enhanced Interior Gateway Routing Protocol (EIGRP) and IPX's RIP are all based on a distance-vector algorithm.

Distance vector has become popular because the algorithms are simple to implement and, developed by the University of California at Berkeley, are freely available to implementers. They do not require extensive computations to maintain the routing table, yet they do not converge (stabilize) quickly after a network change, especially as the network becomes large as when an adjacent

---

14. Network Basic Input Output System

Table 2.9 Key Characteristics of Distance-Vector and Link-State Protocols

Attributes	Protocol Classification: Distance Vector	Protocol Classification Link State
Basic Algorithm	Bellman-Ford algorithm (see Bellman, *Dynamic Programming*)	Dijkstra algorithm
Scalability	With large networks there is a tendency to break down (there is a lack of routing-table convergence).	Routing tables converge quickly even with larger networks.
Complexity	Implementation is simple and easy.	Implementation is complex, requiring lots of CPU cycles to calculate routes.
Bases Routes on	Least cost is determined by the fewest number of hops.[15]	The "lowest cost/shortest path" calculation is based on periodically running an algorithm on a topology database.
Advantages	Implementation is simple and easy.	Even with larger networks this scales well.
Disadvantages	• Routing tables are slow to converge on large networks. • There is a tendency to produce a lot of traffic for routing updates. (Note that Poison Reverse and Split Horizon address some of these problems in subsequent text.)	• This is complex and requires lots of CPU cycles and power to determine routes. • Routing updates can be minimized.

router goes up or down. Distance-vector algorithms also have the disadvantage that they generate lots of router-table update traffic, since routers periodically broadcast routing table updates to other routers (typically as often as every thirty seconds).

---

15. Although hop count is most common, some distance-vector protocols like Enhanced Interior Gateway Routing Protocol (EIGRP) use other "cost" metrics.

Split Horizon is a technique designed to minimize the amount of time it takes for the routing tables to converge. Essentially it modifies the update message *not* to include the same routing information it learned from each respective interface that it depends on for routes. In short, routes are not advertised on the ports on which the routes were learned. Split Horizon can have the side effect of preserving inaccurate information in a routing table longer since it suppresses some updates.

Poison Reverse augments Split Horizon by setting the hop count to infinity on destinations that are learned from adjacent routers, quickly eliminating potential routing loops. Poison Reverse greatly decreases convergence time to new routes since it immediately announces the old route with a metric of 16 (that is, infinity in RIP), avoiding the "counting to infinity" problem (discussed later in this chapter).

Link-state routing protocols exchange link states (whether a route is up or down) for each route between routers. These link states are used to construct a complete view or map of the network at each router. IP's Open Shortest Path First (OSPF) is an example of a link-state protocol.

In contrast to distance-vector algorithms, link-state algorithms are complex and require extensive computations to maintain the routing table, yet the routing tables converge very quickly. And, since link-state algorithms propagate only changes, they require far less network bandwidth to maintain. Quick convergence and less bandwidth for routing table maintenance are largely why link-state protocols such as OSPF are popular across WAN Intranet connections and large LAN installations. Link-state protocols scale better.

2.14.2 Routing in the LAN

Over the past few years with the advent of switching, there was a move away from routing within the LAN because routing was slower than switching at layer 2. With routing switches and layer-3 switching (discussed in Chapters 3 and 4), it is expected that routing will regain popularity within the LAN. As mentioned previously, RIP and OSPF are the two most popular routing protocols used within the LAN, but OSPF is also widely used by ISPs in the WAN. The next sections briefly discuss each of these protocols.

2.14.2.1 RIP

RIP (RFC 1058) is a widely used, simple routing protocol based on the Bellman-Ford distance-vector algorithm. Each router maintains a table of routes mapping an IP address to its corresponding IP gateway network address; this mapping tells the router the next hop address to use to forward packets destined for a particular range of addresses. When a packet comes in, the router uses the destination IP address to find the best match (lowest number of hops) within its routing table; this best match provides the gateway/port to route the packet out. Once found, the packet is routed accordingly. The router ages out each entry in the router table by maintaining a timer for each entry. *Entire* table updates are made by default every 30 seconds, although this varies by protocol, from neighboring routers to keep the routing tables up-to-date.

RIP's biggest shortcoming is that the routing tables tend to converge slowly when one or more routers go down, a route becomes disabled, or the network gets larger. By "converge" we mean to make adjustments based on changes so that packets are not misrouted. Several factors contribute to this sluggishness:

- Entire table updates by default happen every 30 seconds.

- Routes that do not receive updates are held for 180 seconds by default.

- A network can span up to 15 routers (not great for large networks), meaning that in the worst case it may take several 30-second intervals for a change at one end of your routers to propagate to the other end.

When your routing tables are out of sync, you end up with temporary routing loops, extra traffic congestion, and many dropped packets, obviously having a negative impact on your network. To address convergence, RIP employs Split Horizon and Poison Reverse as well as triggered updates. Triggered updates are much like SNMP traps (automatically generated events or messages sent by network devices) where a router sends out a table update as soon as it knows about a change rather than waiting for the next scheduled table update. Finally a technique called "count to infinity" is used to age out dangling paths gradually and to remove routes that, due to router disconnect or failure, are no longer available. Count to infinity works by incrementing unknown routes by two units at each routing table update, gradually getting these indeterminate routes up to a value of sixteen (infinity), which disables the route.

A S I D E . . .

To garbage collect packets that are looping endlessly throughout the network, IP maintains a hop count in the packet header (TTL). When the count decrements to zero, the destination is deemed to be unreachable, the packet is dropped, and a corresponding ICMP error message packet is returned to the sender.

RIP's simplicity has made it prevail, except when connecting two LAN islands (isolated LANs) across the WAN. Clearly the last thing you want to do is flood your precious WAN pipe with redundant routing updates. OSPF, an alternative routing protocol, reduces the updates, provides multiple metrics, and converges quickly. OSPF is used both within LANs and across Intranets that may span the WAN to connect two or more LAN islands.

2.14.2.2 OSPF

OSPF is a link-state protocol based on the Dijkstra algorithm (see Deering, "Multicast Routing in Internetworks and Extended LANs"). This routing algorithm supports multiple Type of Service (TOS) values, enabling the network manager to configure routes based on arbitrary metrics such as the largest capacity wire, the most fault-tolerant link, or the speed of transmission. This also provides a mechanism to associate several routes to a single destination that differs according to the TOS value.

OSPF routing tables are updated via Link State Advertisements (LSAs). In essence, each router maintains a virtual "map" of the network. Since each router constructs its map using the same algorithm and data, all routing maps are identical. After initial setup, the maps are maintained by updates of the changes only, not by entire table exchanges as with RIP. These reduced updates enable OSPF to converge quickly and eliminate routing loops. That OSPF uses multicast packets rather than broadcast packets (RIP) is beneficial because updates are directed at all routers participating in OSPF rather than at all networked devices (for example, PCs and workstations) on your network.

To eliminate redundant updates and reduce traffic, OSPF maintains versions of each route in a link-state database. When the timer goes off to refresh, a neighboring router sends its array of links with each link's corresponding version number. The recipient then requests information for only the "interesting" links, that is, the links that have different version numbers.

As a network becomes large, so does the respective link-state database at each router. In addition, the CPU and memory strain on each router participating in the OSPF network increase. To resolve this increased strain and to reduce traffic across OSPF networks spanning the WAN, OSPF has the concept of areas, illustrated in Figure 2.9.

Areas are essentially groupings of systems connected to a special backbone area that is designated as area 0. All areas *must* be connected to the backbone, often by using a dedicated virtual circuit (VC); there is no connecting an area to any area other than the backbone area, that is, adding another level of hierarchy. Routers within an area have an "area centric" view of the network;

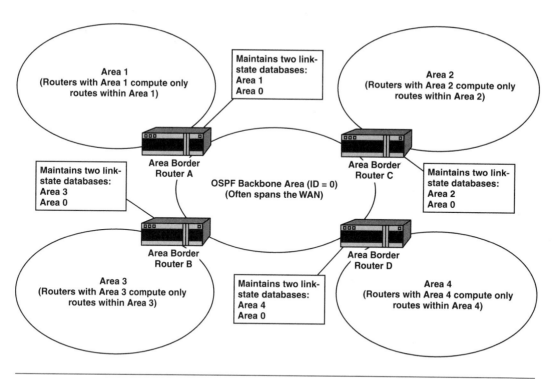

Figure 2.9 Conceptual example of OSPF areas

only the router that connects to the backbone area has knowledge beyond its area. This router is called the area border router and must maintain both local and remote link-state databases. In essence the area border router serves as the liaison to the rest of the network. Areas are ideal for connections that span the WAN as local router traffic stays local.

The two-level hierarchy provided by OSPF areas enables OSPF to scale to large networks. Suppose each area in Figure 2.9 (Areas 1, 2, 3, and 4) has 1000 end stations. If we had just one big OSPF routing domain, the routing table calculations would have to account for all 4000 end stations. However, because we have broken down the network into separate areas, routing table calculations of each area contain only 1000 end stations, with the notion of using the area border router to reach end stations outside of the local domain. The area border routers need to know only which represent addresses of certain address prefixes, not the details of each OSPF area. And, if an end station goes down in an area, only the local OSPF area needs to be concerned. Hierarchy provides an effective way to abstract away the routing details of each area and to grow the network without resulting in one massive single-level routing domain. Hierarchy is an important concept that is used in networking to make networks scale.

2.14.3 Routing in the WAN

Because routers rely on neighboring routers to direct traffic throughout a network, router synchronization is extremely important: Update timer mismatches and other inconsistent router configuration parameters can severely degrade the effectiveness of a network. Simple coordination of configuration information across large spans of distance among many different network managers can be problematic. As the number of routers increases within a network, router-based synchronization between the routers takes more and more time, resulting in misdirected and resent traffic. Routing must scale well in the Internet in order to deliver a reliable networking service that spans thousands of miles. To solve these problems, the IETF defined the Exterior Gateway Protocol (EGP). This protocol was later followed by the definition of the Border Gateway Protocol (BGP), which is still widely used today across the Internet.

2.14.3.1 Autonomous Systems (ASs)

The IETF solved the problem of having to synchronize the entire backbone of Internet routers simultaneously by defining autonomous systems as self-contained, independently managed routing systems. Think of an AS as a bubble of routers that intercommunicate using an interior gateway protocol (IGP) such as RIP or OSPF. Routing within a bubble happens independently from a routing occurring within another routing bubble. This means that routing updates within an AS are contained within that AS. ASs fix the problem of the ripple effect; one router going down causes a major exchange of routing updates to all routers. The Internet is a collection of ASs that communicate among themselves using an exterior routing protocol. Figure 2.10 shows three ASs, each with different internal routing protocols speaking a common routing protocol between themselves externally.

The difference between an OSPF area and an AS often causes confusion. OSPF is an interior routing protocol that runs completely inside an AS. If the AS is large, it may be desirable to create multiple, smaller, interconnected OSPF areas, the use of which reduces the size of link-state databases, since each area has its own. As mentioned previously, area border routers are used to interconnect OSPF areas within an AS.

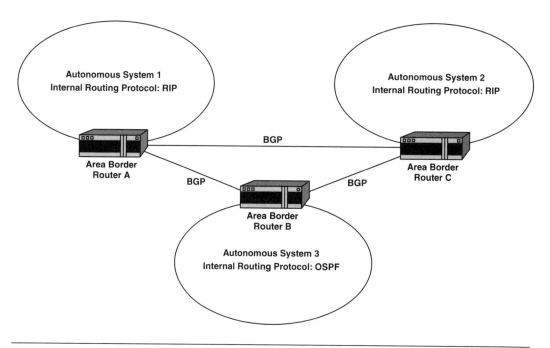

Figure 2.10 Conceptual view of autonomous systems

Discrete (at least logically) area border routers are used to connect one AS to other ASs; these routers are logically independent of the routers that are used to construct an OSPF area. In essence OSPF has its own two-level hierarchy, and the use of ASs is another discrete hierarchy. Think of OSPF area bubbles within an ASs bubble; then think of multiple AS bubbles within the Internet cloud. Figure 2.11 illustrates this bubble madness.

> **A S I D E . . .**
>
> It is possible to run RIP and OSPF simultaneously within a single AS. A group of routers running a common routing protocol is typically called a *routing domain*. When both RIP and OSPF are running you have multiple routing domains.

2.14.3.2 EGP

EGP, the first exterior routing protocol used between ASs with a routed infrastructure, is used to interconnect the routing bubbles so that data may be

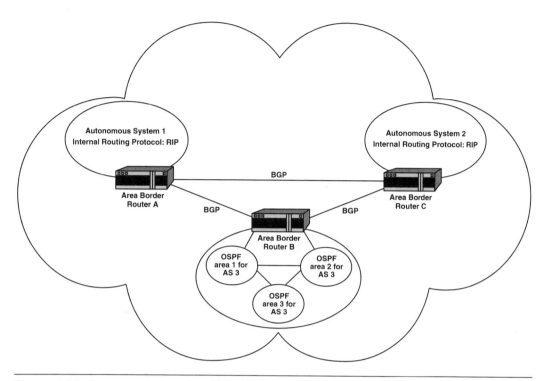

Figure 2.11 Conceptual view of multiple levels of hierarchy: OSPF areas within an AS, within the Internet

routed across one or more ASs. Each EGP has a unique 16-bit number that identifies the AS; two ASs first use an EGP two-way handshake to agree that they will exchange routing information. This handshake is followed by subsequent *neighbor reachability* request/response sequences to ensure link viability between ASs and *network reachability* exchanges to synchronize lists of reachable networks. A simple metric of 0 to 255 is used to determine the best route; a route metric value of 255 implies that the system is unreachable. Primary routes have lower metrics (See RFC 827 for more information).

As the number of ASs increases, EGP does not scale well. More ASs result in more updates and slower routing table convergence. Also, the metric of 255 is quite large for infinity, implying that catching a routing loop would take 255 iterations. Simply stated, the Internet outgrew the EGP and needed to define a new protocol, namely the BGP (Border Gateway Protocol).

2.14.3.3 BGP

BGP (Version 3, RFC 1267; Version 4, RFC 1467) is the routing protocol used today to exchange network reachability information between ASs within the Internet. BGP, designed to minimize routing traffic outside of ASs, enables ISPs to make more intelligent routing decisions as to the best path. Today's Internet is built as an interconnected mesh of ASs that use BGP as their exterior routing protocol in order to advertise routes to other ASs. An advertisement is a *serious* promise to deliver data to the IP space represented in the BGP advertisement since routers must be configured carefully to advertise only those routes to which they have a known connection. Incorrectly advertising another network's routes will cause some of the network's traffic to be directed to the offending router; this is not good to do in the global Internet space.

Like EGP, BGP employs a distance-vector algorithm. Unlike EGP, each router has enough information to build a graph of AS connectivity, represented as sequences of AS numbers, called *path vectors*. Via path vectors a router can "see" beyond its neighbors, enabling BGP routers to institute *policy-based* routing (routing based on multiple criteria rather than just on least cost to a router's neighbor). Since routing updates contain a complete, sequenced path of ASs between a source and destination, BGP helps prevent looping in complex topologies. For example, an AS that is listed twice within a path indicates that the path is in error. The disadvantage of maintaining path vectors for each destination is an increase in the size of routing messages and internal routing memory used to store the information.

To increase reliability and to leverage a well-understood, resilient protocol, BGP uses TCP as its transport protocol for exchanging routing information. Adjacent routers running BGP that connects two ASs set up a TCP connection to exchange entire routing tables. Every 30 seconds "keep alive" messages are sent between neighboring BGP routers, enabling the quick detection of link failures without the needless overhead of exchanging routing tables.

An external router can be either *single-homed* or *multihomed*. Single-homed routers have only one external connection, whereas multihomed routers have several. Single-homed routers need only to advertise their routes because maintaining the current routing state of the Internet's routes is pointless; data are always routed out via the single-homed path. Within an ISP multihomed routers that connect to the Internet need to advertise their routes and maintain the current routing state of the Internet routers. By maintaining this state, a multihomed router can make a decision as to the best route (currently one of about 50,000 routes) to the destination.

Another popular use of a single-homed router is one positioned on the edge of a corporate network, providing a connection to an ISP. Since there is no routing decision to be made, there is no need for the corporation to use BGP; it merely decides which portion of the address space it wants to make public and rolls this up to the ISP. Assuming this address space has been properly registered with the Internet Assigned Numbers Authority and is therefore unique, the ISP will amalgamate these advertisements into its own external BGP advertisements. When a corporate network goes down or becomes unreachable, the ISP can simply drop the incoming packets rather than injecting routing flap[16] into the Internet. This is particularly important with sporadic power outages and the inconsistent use of Uninterrupted Power Supplies (UPSs) in corporations today.

A S I D E . . .

It is important to note that corporate addresses that are "borrowed" (that is not registered, therefore someone else's addresses) will not be advertised by any ISP that wants to stay in business. It is critical that any address used externally is registered. See RFC 2050 for the Internet Registry IP Allocation Guidelines. Also, if you use addresses from your ISP, remember that these addresses are borrowed from the ISP and that if you switch ISPs, you will have to give back the addresses. One advantage of provider-based addressing is that it does help routing aggregation and leads to smaller routing tables.

Multihomed routers have multiple external connections; therefore a routing decision needs to be made. Routers that provide routes outside of an ISP's AS may be multihomed; multihomed routers use BGP to advertise their routes and to gain a view into the Internet of external routes.

A N O T H E R   A S I D E . . .

There is a big distinction between exterior gateway protocols and interior gateway protocols like OSPF and RIP. OSPF and RIP are focused on finding the "shortest" route to a destination. Exterior routing protocols are concerned with interconnecting ASs and managing the peering arrangements based on network policy between adjacent AS gateway routers.

---

16. *Route flap* is a popular term used to define the situation when the network is experiencing constant routing change. It comes from the term "flapping," which means to swing or sway loosely, indicating a general instability of routes. The routes keep flapping back and forth, resulting in misdirected packets and increased CPU load—because of recomputes due to constantly changing route tables.

A S I D E . . .

Perhaps one of the most interesting questions to ask a nonnetwork-savvy friend is what his or her vision of the Internet is. You may get answers ranging from something resembling a spider web to a huge information transfer station.

In all actuality the Internet is indeed a collection of networks (or ASs) that "connect" at only a few major points. There are four official Network Access Points (NAPs) across the United States and a handful of other connection points. There are many large ASs: some go from coast to coast; others go international. Vendors with large ASs will be able to keep certain traffic completely self-contained without entering the Internet or other networks. It is expected that maintaining a large network will become a Quality of Service (QoS) differentiator since, in many cases, the vendor will be completely able to manage and control the QoS of the traffic from end-to-end. QoS will be discussed in detail in Chapter 5.

2.14.3.4 CIDR and VLSM

Classless interdomain routing (CIDR) is the scheme used by BGP and other routing protocols (including RIP, version 2) to map a group of addresses to a single entry within a routing table. In fact, CIDR was the main motivation for coming out with BGP, version 4. Without it we would long ago have exhausted our Internet address space and have the constant challenge of minimizing the size of routing tables! CIDR significantly helps our Internet scale to meet the needs of explosive growth by reducing the size of routing tables.

With CIDR a group of class-C addresses with the same subnet mask can be combined into a large "supernet" or divided into smaller "subnets." This group of addresses can be handed out to an organization, providing a way to give the organization class-C addresses (the most commonly available address) yet exceed the class-C address limitation of 256. In short, CIDR provides a way to give an organization sufficient contiguous addresses space in addition to reducing the overall size of routing tables and the amount of routing changes that have to be propagated throughout the network.

Variable Length Subnet Masks (VLSM) extends the flexibility of which addresses belong to which subnet. VLSM allows the division of conventional class-A, class-B, and class-C addresses into subnets that vary in size, depending on the network need. This wastes far fewer addresses by allowing size to be subnet ranges that may be customized by the network manager.

2.15 WWW and HTTP

No one would disagree that the WWW (or the Web for short) has greatly increased the demand for easier networking. The Web's interface (the ubiquitous web browser) has earned the status of the "killer" application for the 1990s. With its many search engines, the WWW has become a vehicle for information searching, a fantastic tool for shopping, and a great infrastructure for corporate Intranets to share information among employees. The Web is a huge paradigm shift in our lives; it is clearly experiencing exponential growth throughout the world.

HTTP is the Web's custom protocol; it is used to retrieve graphics and text from Web sites around the world and runs on top of TCP. It nearly always connects from server to client over well-known port[17] 80. A Uniform Resource Locator (URL) is used to find a resource on the Web; URLs are the addresses of data and take the form of

```
http://www.myfavoritebookstore.com/computerbooks/
bestbook.html
```

where *http* represents the protocol, *www.myfavoritebookstore.com* is the name of the host, and *computerbooks/bestbook.html* is the path. The Domain Naming System (DNS) is a distributed service for converting the network name of the host into TCP/IP addresses.

HTTP's success is largely due to its small set of *simple* commands. As of this writing, HTTP supports the following set of five commands:

1. GET: used to retrieve a document
2. HEAD: used to get the header information for a document
3. POST: used to send data to the document
4. PUT: used to replace the contents of the document with data
5. DELETE: used to delete the document

GET is the most commonly used request; it retrieves information from the Web. POST provides an effective way to add context information to a document, and HEAD gives access to a document's header information. Most servers do not currently support PUT and DELETE, clearly indicating that these two commands will require password protection.

---

17. Well-known ports uniquely identify servers in TCP/IP. Well-known ports are assigned and managed by the Internet Assigned Numbers Authority (IANA).

A S I D E . . .

Browsers support services other than HTTP. You will often see URLs that begin with
the protocol `ftp` and `telnet` instead of `http`. Gopher and Usenet news (NNTP)
are two other protocols that browsers support.

2.16 Setting Expectations

There are many technologies that serve as the underpinnings of switched networks, and we didn't even touch upon routing protocols like IPX and AppleTalk
or data link protocols like FDDI and Token Ring or physical-layer technologies
like Synchronous Optical NETwork (SONET)! These technologies and many
others are used within switched network solutions to build on a very rich base
of existing and emerging technologies.

So you might ask why we covered this particular set of technologies as the
base for switched networks. We chose this set based on existing deployment,
the current level of enhancement activity for each technology, and the need to
cover a few important ideas that are influencing tomorrow's switched networks.
Everyone knows that Ethernet has a stronghold in the LAN—largely due to its
simplicity and its extensibility from 10 to 100 to 1000 Mbps. Likewise ATM
shines in the WAN as it is already widely deployed and endorsed by the telcos.
ATM QoS and the ability to integrate voice, video, and "bursty" data clearly set
ATM apart from connectless technologies.

Bridging and routing are complementary technologies and form the
underpinnings for switching and layer-3 switching. The WWW and HTML
have made IP deployment a technology winner across the LAN and WAN. In
fact, the WWW is one of the primary drivers of tomorrow's networks—the
need for a better networking infrastructure that the current Internet provides
today.

It is important to realize that tomorrow's switched networks build upon a
very solid base that has emerged over the last twenty or so years. Networks are
complex because they are distributed, and network devices need to interoperate in order to provide the desired networking services. Networks are self-
dependent; network devices use the network to exchange and synchronize
various data about the state of the network and path information. For these reasons, networks follow an evolutionary path rather than a revolutionary one;
next-generation networks respond to the increased needs and dependencies on
networking by extending the existing networking base.

2.17 Conclusions

For a moment, look back at Figure 2.2. Use this picture to reinforce the need for the base of technology represented in this chapter. It is pretty easy to gain an appreciation for just how many components need to work together in order to satisfy a single WWW request.

As we discussed at the beginning of the chapter, it is the notion of layering that facilitates interoperability of so many components and so many technologies. Layering is indeed fundamental to networking. The ISO OSI Reference Model has withstood the test of time in networking by providing our technical reference model for functional layering, the introduction of new networking technologies, and a good starting point for understanding the vast complexities of networking. Over the years many technologies have emerged to fulfill the functional requirements of the Reference Model:

- At layer 1: Fiber and Twisted-Pair Media
- At layer 2: Ethernet in the LAN; ATM, Frame Relay, and X.25 in the WAN; bridging and switching
- At layer 3: Routing and IP
- At layer 4: TCP
- At layers 5–7: Telnet, FTP, and HTTP

The fit to the model is not always a tight one; nonetheless the model gives us a reference point for building new networking services that satisfy a set of key functional networking requirements. Next-generation switched networks build on this solid base, addressing the key requirements of networks of tomorrow: networks that are capable of real-time data transmission, plug-and-play portability, minimal propagation delay, and 99.9 percent availability.

CHAPTER 3

Switching Technology

3.1 Introduction

As networking becomes an increasingly integral part of our lives, we see more and more networking functionality moving into hardware. By burning functionality into hardware,[1] vendors are able to reduce the overall latency of communication, improving the quality of networking and opening up networking to increasingly sophisticated network-dependent applications.

Loosely speaking, *switching* has become the term used to describe moving functionality into hardware. Switching uses header information (see Ethernet and bridging discussions in Chapter 2) in the data to take cells or frames from one or more *input(s)* and move the cells or packets to one or more *output(s)*.

Simply stated, switching is hardware-based, intelligent forwarding.

With the advent of switching in the LAN, Virtual LANs (VLANs) emerged. They provide broadcast containment within a flat, switched network. This chapter discusses the several types of VLANs, pointing out their advantages and disadvantages and the recent grouping technology standards.

This chapter is all about switching: We start by briefly identifying the origins of switching and then get into the application of switching both in the LAN and in the WAN. We discuss both packet-switching and cell-switching technologies and justify switching's popularity and bright future. We conclude by introducing VLANs and previewing the direction of switching over the next few years.

---

1. "Burning functionality into hardware" is an expression that means moving software-based solutions to hardware. Hardware-based solutions tend to execute significantly faster and are often fundamental to overall switch performance.

3.2 Key Solutions Offered

Fundamentally switching addresses network performance and network congestion, and switching technology moves more data to its desired location faster. A simple replacement of a LAN workgroup hub with a LAN switch can yield a significant increase in overall network performance. Many believe that in the WAN the deployment of ATM switches will significantly reduce the congestion of today's routed backbone. Frame relay switches already fulfill the interconnection of many Intranets.

Switching enables straightforward integration of many layer-2 technologies. It is not uncommon for a LAN switch to integrate FDDI, Fast Ethernet, Token Ring, Ethernet, and ATM (not strictly layer 2) into a single LAN switch. Frame relay and ATM are commonly supported in WAN switches. Multiprotocol switches are able to move data cleanly from one layer-2 technology to another.[2]

Many switches have plug-in modules (also called boards or blades) that enable the expansion of networking capabilities and integration of new technologies. Modules typically come in a variety of connector options. For example, boards with RJ-45 connectors for Ethernet, media interface connectors (MIC) for FDDI, and Bayonet-Neill-Concelman (BNC) connectors for coaxial cable are common board options. Modular architectures extend the useful life of the switch and allow for easy customization at installation.

Switched infrastructures in both the LAN and WAN are the future of networking. Switching will enable us to achieve the network performance, reliability, scalability, and end-to-end network solutions that will be required in the generations to come.

3.3 Switching Comes from the Telephone Network

Switching gets its roots from the circuit switching done by the telephone companies, which have been switching and multiplexing voice data across circuits for years. The telephone network includes a large mesh of switches that are fully interconnected. These interconnections are called trunks and each trunk is a pair of 64 Kbps time slices that can carry voice data in both directions. A widely used alternative to trunks is T-1 lines with *channelized T-1* lines delivering twenty-four 64 Kbps "channels." Both trunks and T-1 lines commonly use

---

2. Mixed packet sizes does present a problem that some switches solve by enforcing a uniform maximum packet size (typically Ethernet's maximum size of 1518 bytes) even when sending data across FDDI or Token Ring links capable of larger packet sizes.

single-mode fiber, as it is capable of spanning long distances without signal attenuation.

Sophisticated routing policies enable extremely reliable call setup, call transmission, and call tear down over the many available paths (that is, trunks between switches). Since voice traffic (and data, for that matter) is time-sensitive to where the sun is shining, selection of paths may dynamically adjust throughout the day. Thus the telephone switched network provides a highly reliable, scalable voice service.

A S I D E . . .

Routing in the telephone network is done based on the Signaling System 7 (SS7) protocol that runs in tandem to actual calls. When a call is placed, SS7 sets up the call; it is then "moved over" to circuits running in parallel to carry the call. SS7 is the brains of the telephone network and the underpinnings of popular services like caller ID, call forwarding, and call waiting. Advances are already being made to integrate SS7 technology into data networks; there are currently several IETF initiatives underway.

The telephone network is a connection-oriented switched network, providing sequencing of data and engineered with a very low initial error rate, enabling end stations (the common telephone) to be unsophisticated devices. Since bandwidth is reserved at call setup, the telephone network can provide a service-level guarantee after a call is set up.

It is anticipated that much of the telephone switched network will be replaced with an ATM mesh; significant activity is currently happening in parallel to maintain and enhance the current voice network. It is expected that once a pure ATM network replaces the network it will be less expensive to operate and capable of transporting a variety of traffic—exactly what ATM was designed for. Moving a carrier's mesh to an ATM network is a major undertaking, and the ATM network's reliability and scalability must be proven prior to moving off the current circuit switched infrastructure. This has resulted in many parallel networks with carefully planned and staged points where data is gradually shifted over to use these new infrastructures.

A N O T H E R   A S I D E . . .

At the time of this writing, ATM networks are mostly private and used by major carriers and ISPs.

There are options other than ATM that carriers may choose. Wavelength Division Multiplexing (WDM) is a technique used with fiber networks to increase the capacity of data that can be transferred by multiplexing multiple light wavelengths. Standards-based Synchronous Optical NETwork (SONET) provides multivendor networking and transmission rates from 51.84 Mbps to 13.22 Gbps over fiber-based links. Note that WDM and SONET are not necessarily independent; they can be and are used together.

We will see new carriers running IP over SONET and IP directly over WDM as the high-speed links make the latency insignificant—a necessary characteristic for running interactive voice over a packet-based network. Again this illustrates how the once clear demarcation of technology between the telephone network and data networks is blurring.

A S I D E . . .

Carriers or telcos—what is the difference? A carrier is a company, private or common, that provides communication services. Companies like AT&T, MCI, and Sprint are common carriers; they cannot refuse you service, whereas private carriers can. "Telco" is an Americanism for the local telephone company. "Carrier" is the more general-purpose term and is preferred over "telco" although you often hear the two terms used without distinction.

3.4 Switches Are "Designed" for the LAN or WAN

Switching outside of the telephone network has resulted in two distinctly customized solutions that, in essence, are "tuned" for their application. Although switching in the LAN is quite different than switching in the WAN, there is some overlap between the hardware switching techniques used.

LAN switching is predominantly based on connectionless technologies such as Ethernet, FDDI, and Token Ring. Switched LANs are often called best-effort networks because they provide no guarantee with respect to time of delivery or even that the data will get to its destination. Since packet ordering and error processing become the responsibility of the end nodes, the end nodes must be more intelligent devices (typically a PC or UNIX workstation) than a telephone. LAN switching also includes ATM and allows for PVCs to be set up in advance; in this case ATM usually serves as the cell backbone and is integrated with the connectionless services at the edges using LAN Emulation (LANE).

Not surprisingly, WAN switching more closely follows the circuit switch paradigm where a continuous path is set up prior to moving any data. ATM and frame relay are both WAN services that switch data across an existing permanent virtual circuit (PVC) or newly created switched virtual circuit (SVC). Today most available WAN services are PVCs; SVCs are largely internal or experimental. The predominate use of PVCs is because SVCs are significantly more complex to set up and administer and signaling protocols used to set up SVCs have been slow to execute. The execution speed of signaling protocols is being actively addressed.

ATM is the connection-oriented technology that has been positioned to span the LAN, the WAN, and interactive voice networks, unifying them all. In practical implementation, though, it is expected that there will be a well-integrated mix of our existing connectionless and connection-oriented technologies, enabling voice and data network convergence.

Both LAN and WAN switching are essential to achieving network scalability. This is demonstrated by observing trends in both LANs and WANs. In the LAN we are seeing widespread movement to switching from router-based or hub-based networks; in the WAN we are seeing similar movement to switching from router-based networks. Why? Because switches provide an infrastructure that scales, fundamental to satisfying today's ever-increasing LAN and WAN bandwidth needs. As the use of routing switches (covered in the next chapter) takes off, we will see the intelligence and scalability of routing put back into the networks while retaining the speed of switching. Switching is fundamentally becoming the base of our networks across LANs and WANs.

3.5 Switch Components

Regardless of whether a switch is "LANized" or "WANized," switches share a set of fundamental characteristics:

- Input ports and output ports
- A switching fabric that provides the intelligence between the input and output ports
- Built-in controller software/hardware that manages buffering, cell/frame processing, multiplexing, and de-multiplexing and signaling on some switches
- Built-in management software that enables custom configuration and monitoring of the switch

Figure 3.1 graphically depicts the components of a switch.

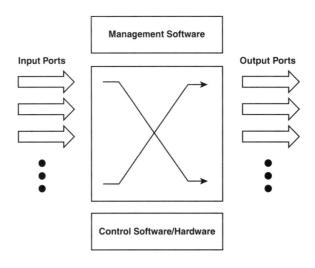

Figure 3.1 Components of a switch

3.6 Switch Implementations

Switch implementations vary greatly among switch vendors. Generally speaking switches leverage Application Specific Integrated Circuits (ASICs) to implement a high-end (core) switching "fabric" capable of moving large volumes of data quickly. Switching fabric refers to the hardware and software design of the switch; fabrics are usually comprised of intricate, parallel interconnections.

There are many other alternatives to ASICs used to build switches. For example, Digital Signal Processors (DSPs) are often used to build low-end (workgroup) switches. In addition, general-purpose CPUs, microprocessors, and routing-optimized switch processors are examples of other hardware used. However, in many cases, a switch is a hybrid of several technologies.

A S I D E . . .

As a rule of thumb, CPU-based software executes significantly slower than silicon-based firmware. For example, a CPU reading and executing a set of general-purpose software instructions is going to be slower than an integrated circuit (ASIC) that has functionality implemented in silicon. The advantage of CPU-based execution is the flexibility to modify and enhance functionality by downloading a new software image. It is often the careful combination of silicon- and imaged-based software that provides the speed and flexibility for the best switch implementations.

Switches that buffer data temporarily are called *store-and-forward switches*. They perform a cyclic redundancy check (CRC), checking the entire frame for errors as well as filtering out frames that are too short or long. After error checking, store-and-forward switches create the cross-connection.

Switch designs may be *cut-through;* a subset of the data (frame header with source and destination MAC addresses) is read and switched without temporarily buffering the data when "switching" it from the input interface to the output interface. *Modified cut-through* does not forward runts (packets that are too short because of collisions); it reads 64 bytes, buffers, and then forwards. The disadvantage of cut-through switching is that bad as well as good frames are switched. Because frames are switched prior to checksum validation, expect more FCS errors with cut-through switching. The advantage of cut-through designs is speed. Since cut-through is good for low-speed links, at 100 Mbps or Gbps the store-and-forward delay often becomes so small, as compared with the speed-of-light propagation delay, that doing all the work necessary for cut-through often makes less sense. Also cut-through works only if the output port is not busy.

Switches may have a *blocking* or *nonblocking* architecture. Blocking refers to having to wait when a particular data path is busy; nonblocking architectures handle moving data from input interface to output interfaces without delay. When a switch is nonblocking, it usually means that the switch's backplane is not oversubscribed (in a situation where it has more data than available backplane capacity) and therefore not subject to congestion. Generally speaking, a nonblocking architecture is significantly better than a blocking one, as blocking can kill performance by having to drop frames when the switch cannot keep up.

There are no specific rules as to which techniques a switch uses: A switch may use *both* cut-through and store-and-forward techniques in its implementation. Since performance is fundamental to switching, there are many creative, proprietary buffering schemes and hardware designs enabling products to switch at line speed[3] or as close to line speed as possible.

It is important to pay very careful attention to the internal capacity of a switch (also known as the backplane speed) and the amount of memory used for buffering of data. Ideally the internal capacity of a switch must exceed the summation of all the port capacities, otherwise there is going to be some blocking and frame dropping.[4] Likewise a memory-poor implementation may have

---

3. "Line speed" (or "wire speed") is a term used to indicate data transfer without interconnection (switch) device delay. Switches that can move incoming data to outgoing data without introducing any additional delay are often designated as being able to switch at line speed.

4. Some believe this is excessive overengineering. If *all* ports are saturated at the same time, it is indicative that you need a faster network, not a better switch.

to drop frames when traffic becomes heavy. These factors are particularly important when evaluating chassis architectures. A chassis with a low-capacity backplane architecture and/or minimal buffer space discounts the flexibility of swapping in new switching modules as the internal capacity and/or memory of the switch becomes quickly exceeded.

A S I D E . . .

When evaluating switches employing frame-based technologies, make certain the frames per second rate (or if the switch routes, the packets per second rate) are representative of *actual* networks in which frame and packet sizes vary dramatically. Impressive statistics based on purely minimal frame/packet size will not be so convincing when you introduce the switch into the real world where frame/packet sizes vary greatly. For example, many concurrent large file transfers (which use maximum packet size) forwarded by a substandard LAN switch may seriously degrade performance.

3.7 LAN Switching

LAN switching enables easy traffic segmentation of a traditional LAN by providing discrete "LAN" interfaces that are interconnected to form a bigger LAN. For example, an Ethernet port to which you connect as few as one user essentially results in a dedicated 10 Mbps pipe for that user—free of the frame collisions of others. Interconnection is through an intelligent switching fabric (massively parallel interconnection devices) that directs traffic to its destination, greatly reducing the contention characteristic of traditional Ethernet LANs. By using optimized buffering schemes, switching fabrics often switch at line speed. This, coupled with the reduced contention found within shared media, greatly reduces network bottlenecks.

LAN switches provide a *central integration point* (the switch) *for many separate LANs* (ports/interfaces on the switch). Each port is a separate LAN with its own dedicated pipe into the LAN; high-speed (typically many gigabits per second) backplanes are used to interconnect LANs. For example, an Ethernet switch may have several Ethernet ports (each providing a 10 Mbps dedicated bandwidth) that are switched across a 3-gigabit (3000 Mbps) switch backplane. LAN switches often "switch" together many technologies including Ethernet, Fast Ethernet, FDDI, and Token Ring, making it relatively simple to use a variety of technologies

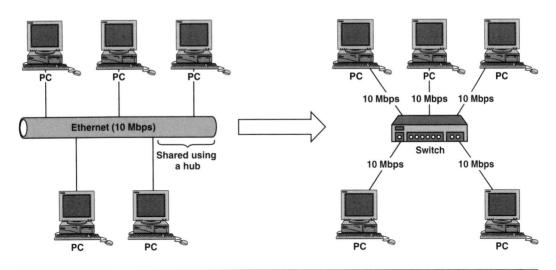

Figure 3.2 Traditional LAN segment (left) transitioned to several switched LAN segments (right)

in a LAN. Figure 3.2 depicts the transition of a single Ethernet segment to a switched LAN, where each PC has its own dedicated Ethernet segment.

3.7.1 Collision Domains and Broadcast Domains

One of the key things to understand about switching in the LAN is the difference between collision domains and broadcast domains. A collision domain is an Ethernet-centric term to describe a group of network devices (users) that share network access. In essence, only one device or user can communicate at any time; Ethernet's CSMA/CD, as discussed in Chapter 2, arbitrates network access. A simple Ethernet hub can be used to provide a network with a single collision domain. In an Ethernet LAN switch, each port maintains a separate collision domain, greatly reducing (especially in the case of one user or device per port) network access arbitration. Figure 3.2 illustrates several PCs sharing a single collision domain (on the left) transitioned to the same PCs connected by a switch, each with its own private collision domain (on the right).

A broadcast domain (often called a subnet in a TCP/IP network) defines a set of devices that hear the same periodic network broadcasts that are primarily used for network addressing. By definition a switch "switches" across a single broadcast domain, whereas a router "routes" across multiple broadcast domains or subnets.

A S I D E . . .

At first glance (Figure 3.2) it may appear that having a single PC on each switched port *eliminates* the collision domain. This is not the case: As long as the port is configured to run half-duplex, there is a collision domain. The collision domain includes the PC and the switch itself. Only if the port is configured to run full duplex is the collision domain eliminated.

3.7.2 Switched LANs

Switches "switch" all the current and emerging technologies: Ethernet, Fast Ethernet, FDDI, Token Ring, ATM, and Gigabit Ethernet. As technology advances, central switches can be upgraded to increase performance—again largely transparent to the user. If a user has a 10/100 Mbps NIC and Category 5 wiring, a central change from a 10 Mbps port to a 100 Mbps port will increase the user's bandwidth by a factor of 10 without even going to the user's office.

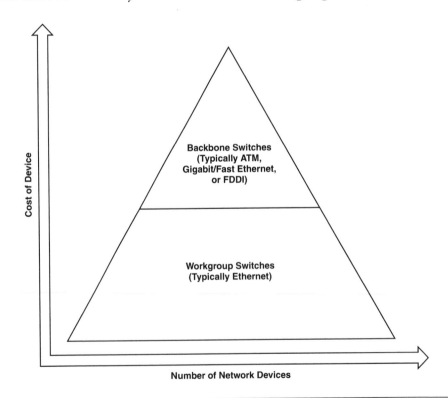

Figure 3.3 LAN switching hierarchy

Switching in the LAN can be depicted in the form of a hierarchy. In Figure 3.3, this hierarchy is ordered by power and price, least to most.

Backbone switches are high-end switches deployed in the core of a network. They aggregate data from hubs and workgroup switches, providing interconnection among these devices. Backbone switches typically accept cards that contain various network options. FDDI, Ethernet, Fast Ethernet, Token Ring, and ATM are usually supported by card options. These switches typically have one or more high-speed interconnections such as FDDI, Fast Ethernet, or ATM (often via LANE). Gigabit Ethernet will be initially deployed at the backbone.

Workgroup switches are lower-end devices that aggregate multiple shared segments by using switching technology. Workgroup switches are typically used to connect to the desktop or to lower-volume database servers. An example of a common switch is a 12-port Ethernet switch that provides 1.2 G aggregate bandwidth and can be thought of as 12 discrete Ethernet LANs. Often a workgroup switch switches onto a high-speed backbone connection such as FDDI or Fast Ethernet.

LAN switches are based on a very simple concept. They take frames from a source port and, based on the destination MAC address, *switch* the frame to the appropriate destination port at incredibly fast speeds. LAN switching combines advanced microprocessor technology with the concept of a layer-2 bridge. Like a bridge, a switch reads header information in a frame, and, based on source information, switches the frame to the appropriate port (or interface—many tend to use interface and port interchangeably although interface is a more generic term and port is somewhat Ethernet-centric). A switch also "learns" which source is where, based on the source address of incoming frames, and builds and maintains an address table. Finally it "floods" when it doesn't know where to send a frame—all characteristics of a bridge. *A LAN switch, then, is really a high-speed multiport bridge.*

Switches come in many configurations. There are dedicated boxes with 16 switched 10 Mbps ports; there are cards with eight 100 Mbps ports; there are cards that switch from FDDI to FDDI; there are cards with many Ethernet ports that switch to a FDDI ring. Nearly every useful combination has been made. Large switches can be configured with several cards, and since each card may have several interfaces (16 or more), a large switch can easily have more than 100 discrete interfaces.

3.7.3 Types of LAN Switches

Workgroup switches and backbone switches within the LAN fall into two types, in addition to a type that is not a switch at all—although it is often dubbed as one! Only LAN switches and layer-3 switches are actually switches that employ switching technology and can be positioned as workgroup or backbone switches.

1. **Port switch**[5] is a fancy name for a repeater or hub. (It does not really use switching technology because it is not a switch!) Essentially all ports share the same LAN segment and collision domain. Given an 8-port Ethernet port switch, all 8 ports would be sharing the same 10 Mbps Ethernet segment. Given an 8-port Token Ring Multistation Access Unit (MAU), all stations are connected to the same ring and share the same 4 Mbps or 16 Mbps ring.

2. **LAN switches** are network devices that operate at layer 2 of the ISO reference model. They are also known as LAN multiport bridges where all ports are discrete LAN segments. Given an 8-port Ethernet Port Switch, all 8 ports have their own 10 Mbps segment (or collision domain). Given an 8-port Token Ring switch, all ports are separate rings running at 4 Mbps or 16 Mbps. Ports bridged between each other provide communications among ports; typically one port provides a high-speed uplink (for example, FDDI or 100 Mbps Ethernet) to the backbone. Layer-2 switches leverage the concept of transparent bridging, connecting networks at layer 2, transparent to high-level protocols. This means that packets from TCP/IP, IPX, and AppleTalk can be bridged together using LAN switches.

3. **Layer-3 switches** are also known as multilayer switches or *routing switches* and include layers 2 and 3 of the ISO reference model (the data link and networking layers, respectively). They have the same layer-2 switch properties as a switch but also include some routing capabilities, although they are often more limited than those of a dedicated router. For example, you could assign ports to a certain IP subnet and a port to be the "default route" when packets need to be routed to a different subnet. You will often hear the adage, "Switch (bridge) where you can; route where you must." This saying focuses attention on speed[6] since the routing logic, which is significantly more complex than switching logic, is what slows down the process of routing packets. The amount of packet reading that must be done to route is far more than what must be read to switch frames.

---

5. Sometimes port switches consist of multiple repeaters with switching functionality between repeaters. One popular case is a 10/100 autosensing hub that has a 10baseT and a 100baseTX repeater with a switch between them. These types of hybrids sometimes make switch classification nebulous.

6. The simplicity of switching should not be underestimated. Many people like switching because it is easy to use. There is little configuration (and hence little misconfiguration); just plug it in.

A S I D E . . .

When using a switch as a router, make certain that you understand what the switch will do with a packet it cannot route. Will it be bridged or dropped?

A N O T H E R   A S I D E . . .

Some switch vendors also talk about "layer-4" switching where switching is based on layer-4 information, such as well-known port numbers, in the packet. There is more information on multilayer switching in the next chapter.

3.8 WAN Switching

WAN switching, like LAN switching, shares the common goal of providing increased overall network performance. Switching in the WAN has its own set of required switch services, breed of switches, and innovative solutions. It is connection-oriented and dominated by frame relay and ATM. These services are being used to replace router backbones within WANs. WAN switches usually operate on permanent virtual circuits (PVCs) or switched virtual circuits (SVCs).

This section discusses the required switch services and the characteristics of switches in the WAN. A discussion of emerging innovative switching solutions is deferred to Chapter 4 where layer-3 switching is covered in detail.

3.8.1 WAN Protocols

To put the WAN into perspective, it is useful to note the protocol options that are available today to get data across wide area connections. There are five major protocols used in the WAN: X.25, ISDN, frame relay, ATM, and PPP over Sonet.[7] X.25 and frame relay are both *packet-switched* protocols that "packet-ize" data at the source, transmit the data through the networking cloud, and "depacketize" the data at the other end. ISDN is a *circuit-switched* protocol that provides integrated voice, data, and low-end video service. Circuit switching involves setting up a dedicated connection at the start of communication, sending the data, and then tearing down the connection. ATM is a *cell-relay*

---

7. As mentioned in Chapter 2, PPP over Sonet is not emphasized in this text, although it is a widely deployed solution.

protocol that provides end-to-end integrated voice, data, and video service. The future of switching in the WAN revolves around frame relay and ATM. Therefore frame relay and ATM will be the focus of our discussion. SMDS is presented briefly since this technology may become important in ATM solutions.

As covered in Chapter 2, one of frame relay's advantages over X.25 packet switching is that it reduces the overall network latency by doing less error checking at intermediate nodes. Error checking can be reduced because signals are much cleaner in today's WAN networks. Frame relay also scales up with the granularity of a T-1 line—from 56 Kbps to 1.544 Mbps (or 2.048 Mbps over an E-1 European link), greatly exceeding the 56 Kbps limitation of X.25. And if you can afford it, frame relay will work over a T-3 line providing a speed of 45 Mbps. Frame relay allows variable sized frames of up to 4096 bytes per packet with only 6 bytes of overhead per packet. This enables frame transparency (no need to segment and reassemble as required by ATM) when connecting LANs across the WAN. Frame relay also provides bandwidth on demand by dynamically borrowing bandwidth from temporarily idle networks; this is easily facilitated since frame relay is a shared, switched network. Frame relay's focus is to move data, although it supports compressed and packetized voice and video.

ATM has been positioned as the future scalable protocol providing integrated voice, data, and video at speeds of 155 Mbps (OC-3), 622 Mbps (OC-12), 2.488 Gbps (OC-48), and 9.6 Gbps (OC-192). To date ATM has been deployed in carrier clouds but is yet to be offered to consumers as a service option like frame relay. Multivendor interoperability, convergence on standards, and flow control at high speeds are some of the challenges. ATM's QoS promise and support for interactive voice and real-time video continue to fuel deployment and investment in the technology.

Switched Multimegabit Data Service (SMDS) is a cell-switching service that provides a transparent interconnection between LANs within a metropolitan area. SMDS is connectionless and supports data units up to 9,188 bytes, although data is transmitted using the same 53-byte fixed-length packets used by ATM. This positions SMDS well for seamless integration with ATM WAN backbones in the future. Today SMDS supports mostly T-1 (1.5 Mbps) and T-3 (45 Mbps) connections but is positioned to support data rates of 155 Mbps (OC-3).

A S I D E . . .

SMDS was designed originally to connect LANs with bandwidth up to T-3 (45 Mbps). SMDS, which is rapidly being replaced by ATM and frame relay, employs cell switching using a 53-byte cell similar to that of ATM.

3.8.2 Types of WAN Switches

Essentially there are three classes of switches positioned at the carrier market: *access switches* that provide the point of presence entry from the enterprise into the service provider network; *edge switches* that provide the core intelligence within a carrier network; and large *core switches* that interconnect multiple edge switches into a high-speed trunk within a carrier's backbone network. Like LAN switches, switches in the WAN can be depicted in the form of a hierarchy. In Figure 3.4 WAN switches are ordered according to power and price, from the least at the bottom of the hierarchy to the most at the top of the hierarchy.

3.8.2.1 Access WAN Switches

Access switches, sometimes called *muxes* or *concentrators,* provide the connection from the carrier network to the private enterprise network via a data service

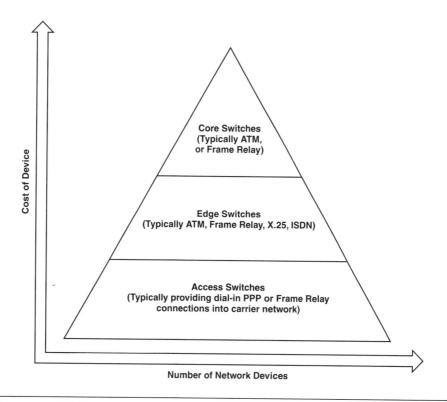

Figure 3.4 WAN switching hierarchy

unit (DSU). These switches will evolve to provide more services to the enterprise in the future with blurred distinction over edge WAN switches.

A S I D E . . .

WAN service providers (or carriers) supply DSUs that plug into channel service units (CSUs). Often the two are integrated and are called a CSU/DSU.[8] Together these devices form the end point of a digital channel on the customer's site. The channel service unit converts the LAN frames into a signal suitable for the WAN service provider and vice versa for the router used to export WAN traffic. The framing and line coding within the CSU and the router must match.

3.8.2.2 Edge WAN Switches

Edge switches typically provide multiple services. Consequently many vendors call these switches *multi service edge switches*. It is not uncommon for a WAN edge switch to include support for many of the following: IP, frame relay, ISDN, SMDS, voice, and ATM. In addition, LAN bridging and circuit emulation are two other services that may be provided. Support for multiple protocols and services is not unusual since edge switches typically service many diverse enterprise customers—all with various WAN connection needs.

Edge switches tend to be a lot more expensive than their LAN counterparts. They typically have a large per port buffering capacity to handle WAN signal delays and retransmissions and often feature redundancy for fault tolerance. Edge switches typically have a throughput capacity of 5–10 Gbps and have built-in traffic management necessary for providing QoS guarantees as discussed in Chapter 5. Carrier providers offer service-level guarantees, hence these switches tend to be fault-tolerant. Proactive, well-integrated network management is also extremely important since an edge switch may provide service to many corporate enterprises at once. These capabilities tend to increase the overall cost of the switch.

Today most public services provide only permanent virtual circuits (PVCs) with guaranteed bandwidth. Perhaps the most popular data service is frame relay. Since PVC-based service is constant, metering cost is easy. PVCs are in essence endless phone calls, that is, dedicated connections (often called a

---

8. WAN monopoly restrictions from years ago forced a physical separation between CSU and DSU functionality, hence the two devices. Currently, in these less-regulated times, the devices are usually combined as one.

data pipe) between two points that are manually set up and left intact as long as the subscriber pays the bill!

Switched virtual circuits (SVCs) offer an alternative to PVCs. They provide service dynamically by using a signaling protocol to set up a connection prior to communicating. SVCs follow the model of our phone system today where a connection to a "callee" is made after the caller dials the number. When switched virtual circuits are provided, billing will become more of a challenge. Next generation edge switches must be prepared to provide manageable, consolidated voice, video, and data networks over SVCs. Q.933 is the signaling standard for frame relay. Private Network-Network Interface (PNNI) is a signaling protocol used for both routing of topology information and signaling of SVCs set up across a large multivendor ATM switched network. PNNI provides the mechanism to set up a connection according to a certain desired QoS.

3.8.2.3 Core WAN Switches

If you think of edge switches as aggregating many different types of secondary roads, then core WAN switches would be the major, multilane highways that interconnect the edge switches. Core switches

- provide gargantuan amounts of bandwidth (tens of gigabits, greater than 20 Gbps is not uncommon).
- have large amounts of memory used for buffers and table management.
- have switch fabrics that are nonblocking.
- tend to process only one protocol (for example, ATM or frame relay) resulting in a simpler, reduced amount of embedded code that can run faster.
- are fully redundant.
- are scalable suitable for large aggregation points.
- are produced by only a few vendors.
- are very expensive, secure, and reliable.

Core switches are positioned to provide the replacement for the core routers that currently exist in the WAN. In actuality, routing technology is being integrated into switches (see layer-3 switching in the next chapter).

Some vendors are starting to offer voice and data integration in their edge and core switches. It is expected that this trend will continue as businesses push for integration and cost savings. Concurrent developments of voice over ATM, frame relay, and IP provide alternative software solutions to the same business demand.

The importance of *scalability* within WAN switches (both edge and core) cannot be underestimated. In the LAN the number of connections is in the thousands; in the WAN, tens of thousands and hundreds of thousands of simultaneous connections are common. A WAN switch must be capable of supporting a large number of virtual circuits (VCs) to handle many simultaneous end-user connections. If SVCs are supported, the switch must be capable of handling the "bursty" traffic which is characteristic of data networking. Sophisticated techniques, such as temporarily borrowing from an idle PVC to satisfy an SVC request, are being explored by many vendors. Scalability, the requirement of service-level agreements and QoS, the expense of making the long-area connections, and multivendor interoperability requirements provide WAN switch vendors with significant challenges.

Last it should be no surprise that *reliability* is a fundamental requirement of WAN switches. When you have tens of thousands of users, the cost of down time is extremely high—hence the need for highly redundant architectures, sophisticated network management that scales, and minimal downtime guarantees. Being able to swap out boards without bringing down the switch (sometimes called "hot swappable") and download new software images while the switch is running are important.

3.9 Packet and Cell Switching Technologies

When technologists talk about switching, they refer to switched networks as having either a cell or a packet core. This section briefly identifies the only cell core technology (ATM) and some of the many packet-based technologies (or technically frame-based, since frames are switched and packets are routed) commonly used in the WAN and LAN today.

3.9.1 ATM Switching

ATM switching is a cell switching technology positioned for both the LAN and the WAN. In the LAN ATM is most commonly used with LANE by establishing an ATM cell backbone that fans out to a connection-free media like Ethernet at the edges using LAN Emulation. In the WAN ATM is positioned to support both high-speed PVCs and SVCs, across which all types of data can travel simultaneously. The promise of QoS is the predominant feature that makes ATM so attractive.

It is expected that many protocols will travel across ATM switch WAN backbones. The following list only touches upon the many emerging areas of development:

- RFC 1932 provides a framework document for IP over ATM.

- ATM Internetworking provides a solution for frame relay and ATM mixing.

- Some of the key aspects of multiprotocol over ATM (MPOA) are to provide a solution for legacy LAN support, layer-3 switching/protocols, and running conventional routers across WAN ATM backbones.

- Interactive voice over ATM is actively pursued.

- Traffic management integration with the IETF's Resource ReSerVation Protocol (RSVP) is being investigated.

- Work on RFC 1577 attempts to provide a multicast solution for ATM.

This list is not intended to be an exhaustive list of all ATM activities to date. That list would be quite long and out of context. However, it is intended to show with just a few bullets the trends of convergence—ATM convergence with IP and voice and data convergence. We are seeing a hybrid solution emerge, one that takes the best characteristics of multiple solutions and results in even better solutions. And what is the common technology integrator? The powerful switch, of course!

3.9.2 Frame Relay Switching

Frame relay switching is positioned for the WAN and provides a frame relay service (FRS) across long distances. FRS is often used to connect many distributed sites within a corporate enterprise.

FRS has been extraordinarily successful and is widely deployed today. It provides economical, reliable WAN connectivity with minimal delay at T-1 or fractional T-1 speeds; in fact higher speeds are currently being evaluated. Many carriers deploy frame relay instead of ATM, as it is simpler to implement and requires less disruption to an existing network. The interconnection of frame relay and ATM is important, since many frame relay and ATM networks run as discrete implementations. Using frame relay over ATM is another area actively being pursued.

Today frame relay is still primarily a PVC-based environment without any end-to-end QoS guarantee. As frame relay is expanded to voice (although not a standard, voice over frame relay is working today) and other services, it is expected that SVC-based services will be provided to the customer. Providing QoS in a frame relay-pure network and running frame relay over ATM are other challenges; some argue that frame relay's ability to support a committed information rate (CIR) with a committed burst rate (CBR) provides many of the benefits of an SVC and QoS. Offering a true SVC and QoS is a challenge for service providers because SVCs and QoS solutions must work across many switch implementations. Standards help greatly here, but there are always vendor idiosyncrasies around which the ISP must work. Getting multiple switches from different vendors to interoperate and provide a consistent service across a WAN is the ultimate challenge.

A S I D E . . .

One common criticism of ATM is that each 53-byte cell has a 5-byte overhead with it. Frame relay, on the other hand, allows for variable length packets up to 4096 bytes with only 6 bytes of total overhead. You can easily see how ATM's 5-byte overhead for each 48 bytes of payload can add up, especially with file transfers with maximum packet sizes.

3.9.3 FDDI and Token Ring Switching

FDDI and token ring switching are positioned for the LAN. Like other switching technologies, FDDI and token ring switches provide a way to divide a network into dedicated switched segments, enabling you to interconnect several token ring- or FDDI-based rings and "switch" data between the rings.

FDDI and token ring switching provides increased performance and flexible installations. For example, putting a busy FDDI-based server on its own switched segment can often provide a significant network performance boost. In the case of Token Ring, switching enables you to establish both 4 Mbps and 16 Mbps rings and to interconnect stations using different media speeds. (Recall that mixing speeds on the same ring is a no-no!) Many vendors provide a way to mix and match FDDI and token ring switching with ATM and/or Ethernet; this often enables you to grow legacy installations without total upheaval.

3.9.4 Ethernet, Fast Ethernet, and Gigabit Switching

Ethernet switching is positioned for the LAN. The 10/100/1000 Mbps Ethernet switch hierarchy provides an excellent scalable solution in the campus environment. Ethernet's simplicity and ease of deployment have made this technology pervasive within the LAN environment.

The one drawback of Ethernet (and all connectionless technologies, for that matter) is its inability to provide QoS. Resource ReSerVation Protocol

(RSVP) is the protocol positioned to enable IP to provide some level of service guarantee over connectionless technologies like Ethernet. Priority queuing (also known as Class of Service, or COS) is another technique being deployed to ensure a better level of service for critical traffic. Last, overprovisioning (simply throwing more bandwidth through the enterprise) is a very popular means of mitigating network delays. Chapter 5 discusses these approaches in detail.

A S I D E . . .

When deploying Ethernet, pay careful attention to segment lengths, wire types, and wire grades. Ignoring these standards is one of the biggest problems causing network failure within a LAN.

3.10 Gigabit Ethernet and ATM

No discussion on switching in the LAN would be complete without a discussion that compares Gigabit Ethernet and ATM switching. Because Gigabit Ethernet is the first technology that rivals both 155 Mbps and 622 Mbps ATM connections, Gigabit Ethernet is often compared head-to-head with ATM.

In small to medium-size sites, Ethernet is more widespread than ATM in the LAN. This may be because it has been around a lot longer and it is simple to deploy. It is estimated that about 80 percent of all desktops and servers within LANs use Ethernet.

In many larger LAN sites, ATM is prevalent as a backbone as it provides a more *trustworthy* network. ATM facilitates creation of redundant links, a fully meshed network, and traffic management; these features justify the extra expertise necessary to manage ATM's complexities.

One of ATM's strengths is its built-in QoS, enabling it to offer performance guarantees when communication is established (remember, unlike other LAN technologies ATM is connection-oriented and uses signaling to negotiate a connection with certain bandwidth requirements), and making it very attractive for real-time data. Note, though, that ATM QoS can be difficult and expensive to implement and that *for QoS to work it must be end-to-end*, not just in the backbone as ATM is commonly deployed today. ATM is enormously complex; just understanding it well enough to deploy it is an undertaking.

As we discussed previously, Ethernet has no guaranteed QoS; it must rely on the layers above to provide any kind of traffic management. Ethernet allows frames of variable length (unlike the fixed 53-byte ATM cells); use of variable frames makes it difficult to regulate real-time flows that might get caught in the middle of a file transfer of consecutive 1500+ byte frames. Many of the topics discussed in a subsequent chapter, such as RSVP (Resource Reservation Protocol) and COS (Class of Service), provide mechanisms to aid QoS across Ethernet.

In addition, Gigabit Ethernet is still Ethernet and is therefore vulnerable to the problems and limitations of CSMA/CD as discussed in Chapter 2. Performance of Ethernet typically suffers after sustained 40 to 50 percent utilization, so Gigabit Ethernet is roughly equivalent to 500 Mbps. Obviously the more dedicated an Ethernet connection is, the fewer problems with performance due to CSMA/CD there are.

Proponents of Ethernet tend to leverage the overengineering (or overprovisioning) approach to reduce possible congestion and provide comfort with respect to good response times. Remember Gigabit Ethernet is a fat pipe; it will take considerable traffic to saturate a Gigabit Ethernet link. Subsequently overengineering will provide the low latency connections necessary to support delay-sensitive applications over Ethernet.

Finally, Gigabit Ethernet is expected to be less expensive than 622 Mbps ATM; the ballpark figure is around 50 percent cheaper. This, coupled with the fact that Ethernet is well understood and simple, makes Gigabit Ethernet very attractive as an alternative to ATM in the LAN.

A S I D E . . .

Overengineering in this context refers to applying more technology to an anticipated problem without completely analyzing the problem space. In many cases this provides a great safety net, although you run the risk of adding technology that is not really necessary in certain areas of your network. The cost is the initial cost and maintenance of the technology. Proponents of overengineering in high growth networks often believe that the gains clearly outweigh any cost, especially in the LAN.

3.11 What is a VLAN?

Flattening a LAN by primarily using layer 2 (switching) rather than layer 3 (routing) can dramatically improve overall network performance. Traditional layer-2 LAN switching advocates flattening your network and taking advantage of the line-speed switching capabilities to move traffic rather than the slow path offered by traditional routers.

At the same time, having a large, flat network that is subject to an excessive amount of broadcasting and sporadic broadcast storms sweeping across your network can be detrimental to performance. In the past your only option was to divide your network into smaller pieces and route, since routers typically do not route broadcasts. VLANs provide another alternative.

The new VLAN standard is 802.1Q, discussed later in this chapter. Be careful though, because not all VLANs are standard. They have been around for a few years, and the standard is new as of 1998. This means that many VLANs are proprietary in nature and usually work with equipment only across a single vendor. An example of a proprietary solution is the use of the 802.1g option frame header defined for security. Some vendors (for example, Cisco) have overloaded this optional header for VLAN tagging purposes.

802.1Q is a standard for frame tagging. It is hoped that 802.IQ will remove the proprietary nature of VLANs and make them work across many vendors and network devices that don't support VLANs. Standards facilitate networkwide solutions, ensuring the interoperability across a diverse enterprise.

VLANs enable you to create logical groups of network devices *across* your LAN. These logical groups might span one or more layer-2 switches, or they might be done on a switch-by-switch basis. Within these logical groups, you can contain broadcast traffic. *A VLAN defines a broadcast domain; it is as simple as that.*

You may recall that the conventional way to form a broadcast domain is by forming an IP subnet. The big difference between a VLAN and an IP subnet is that an IP subnet is based exclusively on an IP address; a VLAN is a logical grouping based on many varied attributes. Recall though that all hosts in an IP "subnet" have to be in the same broadcast domain or ARP will not work—don't create a network that will not work! Section 3.12 details the various attributes used to create VLANs.

ASIDE...

Note that your network may use VLANs and contain some routers or bridges, although these devices do not usually participate directly in VLANs. There are two reasons for this:

- Switches are replacing bridges, so there is not a lot of activity on new bridge development. Nothing precludes VLAN participation for bridges; there just isn't much going on here.

- Routers do not operate at layer 2; layer 2 is the main focus of VLANs, and both the new standards (802.1Q and 802.1p) extend the core layer-2 bridging standard (802.1d).

There has been some activity on layer-3 VLANs, and this may become an area of interest over the next few years; Chapter 4 may provide the "VLAN solution" for routers.

A S I D E . . .

A VLAN can span the WAN if you tell you router to forward layer-2 traffic. This has the negative side effect of forwarding lots of broadcast traffic (such as that used for address resolution for ARP by IP or for advertising networking services by NetWare) across your expensive WAN link.

VLANs form software-controlled virtual groups that can assist in network security, improve overall bandwidth utilization, and be managed without going to the wiring closet. For example, you can create a VLAN consisting of all accounting personnel across your enterprise. This group doesn't physically have to sit close together (as VLANs can span network devices); it is uninterrupted by broadcasts from other VLANs and can have exclusive access to a database server with important restrictive financial data.

3.12 VLAN Creation Techniques

There are many techniques used to partition a flat, bridged physical topology into a collection of VLANs across your network:

Protocol Grouping: This technique includes groups based on protocol type (IP, IPX, or AppleTalk) or network address (given IP subnet).

MAC Address Grouping: The MAC address of the network device determines VLAN membership.

Port Grouping: VLAN is a collection of ports across one or more switches. Devices attached to ports within the VLAN collection are members of the VLAN.

Table 3.1 enumerates some of the strengths and weakness of each VLAN technique. Figures 3.5, 3.6, and 3.7 show simple protocol, MAC, and port-based VLANs, respectively.

Table 3.1 Strengths and Weaknesses of VLAN Techniques

VLAN Technique	Strengths	Weaknesses
Protocol Grouping	• It allows partitioning by protocol type. • A single port can participate in multiple VLANs. • There is no need for frame tagging. • It is particularly good in conjunction with IP subnets (it can assign VLANs by subnet and eliminate granularity of assigning individual users to specific VLANs).	• It can be a performance hit. It must read layer-3 addresses in packets. • It does not work with "unrouted" protocols like NetBIOS. • It cannot configure a port to support multiple subnets on some switches. If supported, it may conflict with DHCP solution that dynamically assigns IP addresses, as addressing may need to be "hard-coded."
MAC Address Grouping	• VLAN membership moves with a device that has MAC embedded, so there is no need to reconfigure.	• It has performance degradation on ports with several MACs on different VLANSs due to excessive switch processing that is required to filter traffic properly. • VLAN membership is tied to network device—it cannot use any PC to attach to the network and be in your VLAN. • All users must be configured to be on at least one VLAN. • Replacing a NIC requires VLAN reconfiguration.
Port Grouping	• It is easy to understand and administer. • There is a common methodology across vendors. • It can be used to create a logical group of users connected to different switches across the enterprise. • Since a single port may be connected to a hub that supports a shared-media, multi-user network, port grouping can be used to group two or more shared-media networks.	• It must reconfigure the user when a workstation moves to a new port. • It cannot have a single port in more than one VLAN.

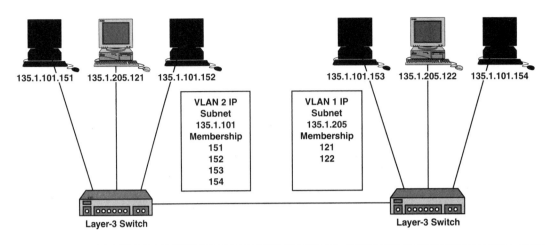

Figure 3.5 Two simple protocol-based (IP subnets) VLANs

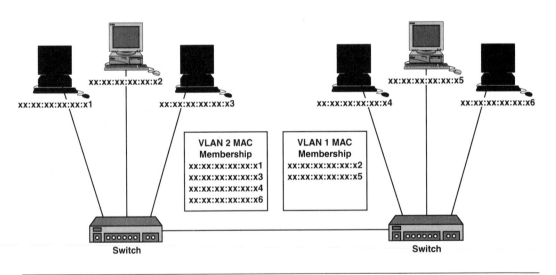

Figure 3.6 Two simple MAC-based VLANs

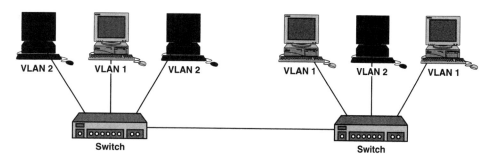

Figure 3.7 Two simple port-based VLANs

3.13 **VLAN Advantages**

The biggest advantage of VLANs is *broadcast containment*. With a set of well-defined VLANs you can retain the speed of a flat, bridged network while eliminating the broadcasts that slow the network. (Remember that each broadcast must be accepted and acted upon optionally by each device in a broadcast domain.) In addition to broadcast containment, VLANs also reduce the impact of a broadcast storm. Because you retain your layer-2 network, you don't need to segment with routers (introducing increased latency) to fix the broadcast problem.

VLANs allow you to define your own private and secure networks across your switched network. If security is important, this may be a viable solution for your LAN.

VLANs are purported to reduce the effort of adds, moves, and changes that add significant overhead to network management, and this might very well be true for VLANs based on protocol grouping and to some degree on MAC address grouping, since MAC addresses tend to stay with workstations and PCs. (With the exception of Personal Computer Memory Card International Association (PCMCIA) Ethernet cards used in laptops and upgrades, you don't often see exchanges of Network Interface Cards (NICs).) Port grouping, however, definitely has serious reconfiguration costs.

3.14 **VLAN Disadvantages**

Like filtering or any other management technique that restricts traffic flow, it is critical that you confirm that your VLAN actually works the way you think it is working. An invalid "secure" VLAN may have serious consequences.

It is important that you understand the performance both before and after VLAN segmentation. If the VLANs are not properly defined, performance can actually degrade. If you define too many VLANs that need to communicate between one another, performance might worsen. If this oversegmentation into VLANs causes the traffic to be routed rather than switched, performance can suffer. Of course, you could argue that with the advent of routing switches this will not be a problem. However, as a counter argument, why do you need VLANs with routing switches, anyway? It is therefore important that you ensure that you do not become overly granular with your VLANs.

One of the techniques widely used to troubleshoot network problems is having a mental picture of your network. Obviously as your network becomes very big, you tend to rely on network management platforms to provide most of this picture.

With VLANs, network managers no longer can associate the physical layout of the network with its absolute operation.

This logical view makes it more difficult to pinpoint a problem on a VLAN, such as finding a failing device. Just because you know the physical connectivity of a network device, you don't necessarily know the logical network connectivity. Even if something is physically connected, it may not be logically connected. For example, if you have two nonoverlapping VLANs with a user on one and a printer on the other, the user will not be able to send a print job to the printer, even though the printer and the user are both physically connected to the same switch. This adds a level of abstraction to the network and increases the dependency on strong network management tools. VLANs add a software view or *logical view* of your LAN that you must use in association with your *physical view.*

Since VLANs that span many devices depend on network connections for broadcast containment, VLANs add traffic to your network backbone. In a sense you are taking the traffic containment provided by a single switch in your network and *spreading it out over your network* to create a virtual switch. The result is additional traffic through your backbone as you move traffic that is normally contained within a high-speed backplane to use the bandwidth on your network as the "backbone." In a sense *your backbone becomes a virtual backplane.* Make certain that your backbone connecting your VLANs is sized appropriately to deal with the extra VLAN traffic.

Last, VLANs are still largely proprietary. Most networks are made up of equipment from a variety of vendors, making it difficult to define viable VLANs.

A S I D E . . .

It is important to be aware of the notion of closed and open VLANs:

- A closed VLAN is what you might expect—a VLAN that limits the broadcast domain to elements only within the VLAN definition. For example, if you define a port-based VLAN to contain ports 3, 4, and 8 on a switch and the VLAN is closed, only frames contained within this small port group (ports 3, 4, and 8) are switched together.

- Open VLANs may see additional traffic beyond the VLAN definition. This often happens when you have overlapping VLANs where a single port may be servicing more than one VLAN. Since ports on a switch often share a *single bridge forwarding table,* two or more VLANs containing the same port will see frames from the other VLANs. Sometimes open VLANs are said to "leak."

3.15 What is Tagging?

We're all familiar with the UPC-based destination strips that airlines use to route luggage from one city to another. By applying a destination tag at the source airport, a ticket agent can automatically sort and direct luggage to the appropriate series of planes necessary to reach the desired destination without actually looking at the true destination address. This sorting happens quickly without much user intervention, without baggage "routers." In much the same way, layer-2 tagging and filtering provides a way to switch frames that are sorted by priority.

The current 802.1d bridge specification, which is the foundation for switching, defines a rather simple forwarding process. Recall that the bridge (switch) "learns" where destination MACs are by associating the source MAC address found within the frame header with a port on the bridge. These table entries are automatically "aged out" or deleted from the table after a certain period of time without traffic from a source address. Likewise these table entries are refreshed (resetting the aging timer) as new traffic is seen. Static entries may also be configured and may be exempt from the aging process. 802.1Q and 802.1p build upon the 802.1d bridging foundation.

The 802.1Q and 802.1p are IEEE standards that add significant intelligence to the current 802.1d-based bridge frame forwarding process. Note that it is impossible to talk about one of the specifications without the other, so we will start with the tag header that is fundamental to both. Then we will zoom in on the specifics of each in its own section.

3.15.1 Tag Header Organization

The Tag Header that is added to the frame directly after the destination and source MAC addresses (and routing, if present) is the fundamental component used to filter traffic. The tag header contains a Tag Protocol Identifier (TPID), indicating that it is a tagged frame, and Tag Control Information (TCI). Figure 3.8 illustrates a tagged header. Within the TCI there is

- a *user priority* (a number from 0 to 7, represented in 3 bits) that designates the priority of the frame.

- a single bit *Token Ring encapsulation flag* used to designate whether the frame is in IEEE 802.5 Token Ring native format. (This flag is important in the frame translation process.)

- a *VLAN identifier* (a VLAN ID represented in 12 bits) that associates the frame with VLAN membership.

This information enables a bridge to restrict frame forwarding to ports associated with the particular VLAN ID and to prioritize traffic forwarding based on the priority value. More important, this tag is preserved between switches; even though bridging is still point-to-point, the tag adds information used to help "route" frames through the network without routing. Figure 3.9 provides a conceptual view of 802.1Q and 802.1p VLAN and priority tagging.

A S I D E . . .

The twelve-bit VLAN ID may be set to two special values. If it is set to 0, it implies that the Tag Header does not contain VLAN identifier information. If it is set to 1, the frame is associated with the default VLAN; the default VLAN is inclusive of all nodes.

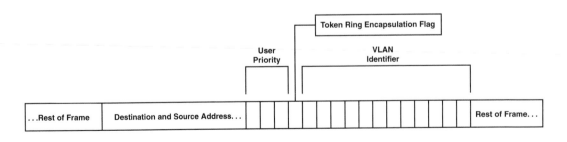

Figure 3.8 Tag header frame format

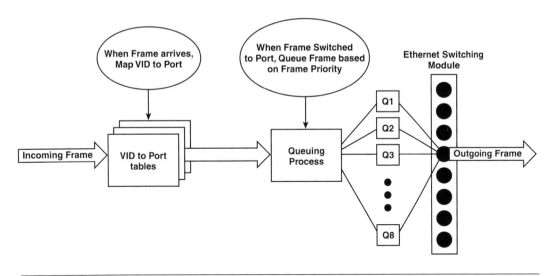

Figure 3.9 Conceptual use of 802.1Q and 802.1p VLAN and priority tagging

The 802.1Q specification provides some nomenclature that is useful to know when discussing tagging:

- **Tagged frame:** frames with tagging information
- **Untagged frame:** frames without tagging information
- **VLAN-tagged frame:** frames that contain VLAN information in the tag header
- **Priority-tagged frame:** frames that contain priority information in the tag header
- **Tag-aware regions:** portions of your LAN that utilize tagging for bridging frames
- **Tag-aware bridges:** bridges that recognize and utilize tagging

It is important to realize that when you introduce new technologies into your LAN, you should be prepared to deal with mixing the old with the new. When both untagged and tagged frames are in your network, there will be areas that leverage tagging (tag-aware regions) and new bridges (or switches) that recognize and utilize tagging. In certain cases the old and the new will coexist well; in other cases, the hybrid will cause problems, such as network congestion. Be aware that often when a new technology such as this one is introduced, you have interoperability problems among various vendors' implementations. This is especially the case for tagging since there are already quite a few instances of proprietary solutions that overload the frame field for VLAN support; few (if any) are capable of coexisting with one another.

3.15.2 802.1Q

The focus of 802.1Q is the formalization of VLANs. Essentially, by using the VLAN identifier, packets may be filtered to go to a particular group of destination addresses (VLAN) rather than flooded to the world. Group Address Resolution Protocol (GARP), defined in the 802.1p emerging standard, is used to manage group membership and to distribute group membership among the bridges (or switches) in the LAN.

The initial version of 802.1Q is defined to work over a single spanning tree, even though it is conceivable that it could have a spanning tree defined per VLAN. The committee felt that having a spanning tree per VLAN was overly complex and would have too much overhead associated with it. You can only imagine all the traffic generated by bridges to keep the spanning trees up-to-date! Nothing in the standard precludes having multiple spanning trees in the future.

Bridges supporting 802.1Q are designated as VLAN-aware bridges. These bridges can coexist with non-VLAN-aware bridges for backward compatibility. According to the specification, control frames addressed to higher-layer entities in bridges, like spanning tree Bridge Protocol Data Units (BPDUs), GARP PDUs (802.1p), and other management PDUs, do not go through the same filtering process. This leaves existing assumptions about these frames unchanged when using 802.1Q.

Associated with each bridge port may be a set of ingress rules (used to define which frames will be filtered when a frame enters a port) and a set of egress rules (used to define which frames will be filtered when a frame exits a port). These lists, maintained to designate VLAN membership, may be autoconfigured by using the VLAN membership resolution protocol (VMRP). VMRP is modeled after the GARP protocol defined in 802.1p. Both end stations and bridges use the VMRP to communicate VLAN membership among neighboring bridges. A 12-bit VID (VLAN ID) is used to designate each VLAN.

A S I D E . . .

One concern with 802.1Q tagging is how to tag a full-length packet. Since tagging relies on adding additional bytes to the packet, tagging can exceed the total size of the packet. If you exceed the MTU throughout the network, packets may be dropped. Full-length packets are used by default for *any* TCP bulk transfer. The IEEE 802.3ac draft standard allows for larger packets necessary to implement VLANs properly.

3.15.3 802.1p

The 802.1p specification standardizes prioritization of traffic across a LAN, which serves the need for delay-sensitive traffic. 802.1p employs frame filtering to achieve a level of QoS regarding latency, overall frame priority, and throughput. Filtering adds intelligence to the existing bridge forwarding process by limiting frame distribution to portions of the network where there is a high probability of finding the destination rather than just flooding the frame throughout all ports.

802.1p uses GARP to communicate groupings of MACs that are associated with a certain traffic priority. A GARP PDU has a unique MAC address; when a bridge receives a frame with this MAC address as the source, it knows that this is a GARP packet providing information about group membership. 802.1p also defines port modes that are associated with each bridge port. GARP is used to communicate port modes that may be set to one of three modes:

- **mode 1:** forward all addresses (ignore filtering database).
- **mode 2:** forward all unregistered addresses, but use group registration entries to filter out frames to only those in the group.
- **mode 3:** filter all unregistered frames—require an explicit filter to get to port.

Like entries in the bridge, forwarding table filters may be dynamically or statically configured. GARP provides automatic learning of dynamic filtering information via GARP protocol exchanges. Removal of dynamic filter information is also accomplished via GARP exchanges.

Each group has priority characteristics. Based on this priority, the frame is queued at the exit port. A bridge may have up to eight queues associated with eight traffic classes to prioritize traffic. Priorities may be as granular on a port basis—each port may have x traffic classes numbered from 0 to N-1. It is not a requirement that all ports in a bridge have the same number of traffic classes and queues.

You can think of each switched port as having eight separate queues. As an example, high-priority traffic waits in queues 7 and 8, medium priority is in queues 5 and 6, and low-priority in the remaining queues. Traffic is serviced in a round-robin fashion by favoring the high-priority queues (taking more frames from them) or by some other algorithm. Regardless of the algorithm, higher-priority traffic on the average waits less time in the queue. By sorting traffic by priority, the switch can better service time-sensitive traffic.

There are several good examples of situations in which you may want to adjust the priority of certain traffic. For example, you may want to give broadcast traffic or IP multicast traffic a lower priority than IP point-to-point (unicast) traffic, or you may decide to reduce the priority of IPX broadcast traffic or AppleTalk traffic. Traffic prioritization gives you a way to "tune" your network traffic around your corporate policies. If your corporate policy is to limit web use during the workday, you can provide some control by merely giving external HTTP traffic (WWW traffic) a lower priority than other traffic from 9 AM to 5 PM.

3.16 Setting Expectations

Switching in the LAN has clearly brought together many technologies. It is not uncommon to see a LAN with a cell ATM core that fans out to Fast Ethernet and Ethernet. Likewise FDDI may be at the core with Ethernet and Token Ring at the edges. Gigabit Ethernet is positioned at the core of the LAN, providing a packet-based (or more correctly frame-based) core. Switching has enabled protection of legacy investment of Ethernet and Token Ring topologies and has provided easy ways to extend and grow the LAN.

Tomorrow's LAN switches have new challenges: priority queuing, service-level guarantees, and tighter integration with the WAN. Tomorrow's switches will be smarter and will bring us closer to end-to-end services within a LAN— from a LAN to a destination in the WAN and from a LAN through the WAN to another LAN. LAN switches will need to improve WAN integration, focusing not on basic connectivity confined to the LAN but rather on service-level, end-to-end connectivity regardless of where the two ends may be.

Tomorrow's WANs must go from being discrete ATM and frame relay networks to networks that better share resources and provide extensive mix-and-match services that are well integrated with LANs. Moving beyond the predominance of PVCs and enabling dynamic allocation of bandwidth, WANs must realize support for SVCs. Even PVCs must become more dynamic allowing for time-based transitioning of usage perhaps from voice during business hours to data during off-hours. WAN switch implementations must provide multiple services, allowing for the natural integration of all forms of data, and enabling complete communication solutions.

Switching is the future of networking. Our switch infrastructure has the challenges of

- handling bursty traffic via smart traffic management—congestion control and flow control.
- supporting multiple protocols and services.
- providing seamless integration across multiple vendors.
- disruption-free scaling to meet the needs of the next day.
- fault tolerance and reliability.
- increased performance portability, customization, and simplicity.
- decreased cost, network delay, plug-and-play, and guaranteed delivery.
- adequate and flexible security.
- support of both PVCs and SVCs.
- better (more transparent) integration of the LAN and WAN.

Switching must employ smart buffering and queuing techniques that will result in minimal data loss, nonblocking flows, and minimal resource contention and low latency. Switching must allow for priority queuing and tagging optimizations that will enable more predictability and line speed service. Switching must continue to complement routing and ease congestion in both LANs and WANs.

VLAN technology provides a solid idea base for tagging and grouping solutions, even though, with the advent of wire speed routing, VLAN deployment and popularity are challenged in certain installations. However, it may be the combination of VLAN (801.1Q tagging) and high-speed routing that allows traffic to be prioritized based on a set of customized queuing rules (Class of Service (COS)) and still travel at line speed.

Pressure will continue to be placed on switching to provide more integrated solutions that span the LAN *and* the WAN. The convergence of LAN and WAN switching and the provision of end-to-end services will take time. Even though it makes sense to optimize a switch implementation around a WAN or LAN deployment, care must be taken to ensure that switches can become part of an end-to-end solution that spans both the WAN and LAN.

3.17 Conclusions

Switching has become *the* fundamental component of networking. It provides a flexible, modular way to move data from one or more inputs to one or more outputs. The interconnection of many switches enables communication solutions spanning from meters to kilometers.

It is useful to look at where switching has taken us. Circuit switching deployed in our telephone network enables billions of calls per day with unprecedented reliability. LAN switching has resulted in tremendous performance increases while simultaneously protecting investment in legacy equipment. Frame relay switching in the WAN has provided an economical alternative to leased lines and is exhibiting explosive growth. ATM infrastructures are in place at all the major carriers and are expected by many to deliver integrated voice, video, and data with guaranteed performance. We are seeing more and more intelligence incorporated into switching, especially better integration with routing.

In the LAN we predominantly see Ethernet and ATM (via LANE) switching. FDDI also has a large presence where fault tolerance is important, since FDDI provides built-in redundancy. Token Ring switching solutions are in place and provide a means to integrate legacy Token Ring networks into ATM or Ethernet backbones. In the LAN we have also seen VLANs emerge. Although VLANs provide a way to achieve broadcast containment, they introduce a logical aspect to networks that can be difficult to manage. Fortunately with the advent of layer-3 switching we can achieve router-based broadcast containment without severe performance degradation and the introduction of "logical" LANs.

In the WAN we predominantly see switches that provide frame relay or ATM services. ISDN, X.25, and SMDS also have a presence in some WAN edge switches. Frame relay is widely deployed in North America and is seeing some strong penetration internationally. X.25 is still popular internationally although it has lost much of its appeal in North America because of its limited bandwidth.

The distinctions and lines between the LAN and the WAN are becoming blurry and will continue to do so. Customers are demanding preassembled networks providing end-to-end services that span from LAN to WAN to LAN rather than the "assembly-required" components of today. Switches that can be easily integrated to work together as a service-providing network will become the solutions of choice. The next step for switching is to provide LAN/WAN convergence by increasing the amount of intelligence within switches, making them capable of becoming the building blocks of end-to-end communication services across the LAN and WAN.

CHAPTER 4

Multilayer Switching

4.1 Introduction

Clearly, switching provides a powerful solution set for layer-2 performance problems. In the LAN, switching allows networks to be segmented cleanly, eliminating Ethernet contention and reducing the number of devices sharing the same token across the ring technologies. In the WAN, frame relay switches offer a low-cost, simple means for interconnecting remote LANs. Frame relay links facilitate both a committed information rate (CIR) and a committed burst rate (CBR). Both of these features have worked well with the "bursty" traffic characteristic of data networking. ATM switches are deployed in the WAN to provide multiservice networks capable of integrating voice, video, and data.

Multilayer switching addresses the problem of traffic bottlenecks at the higher layers by improving performance and adding more intelligence to higher-layer devices, namely to routers. Switching traffic at line speed only to have it wait in an ever-increasing router queue is a performance problem, and solving this performance problem and incorporating more routing intelligence across the network are the main targets of multilayer switching.

Marketing organizations have gone crazy trying to ride the wave of a very successful infiltration of switching technology. Layer-3 switching, layer-4 switching, Tag Switching, IP Switching, network layer switching, multilayer switching, and Multiprotocol Label Switching (MPLS) are terms that have been used by various marketing teams across the globe. Ignoring the fact that *layer-x switching* where *x* is anything but layer-2 is a contradiction of terms, many of the techniques and emerging products will become an important part of tomorrow's networking solution set. Fundamentally all of these new *switching* technologies address the routing aspect of networking, with a focus on getting more performance out of the network and, ultimately, enabling networks to scale better.

This chapter starts by concisely mapping the array of terminology used to describe multilayer switching to the actual functionality that each technology addresses. We discuss switching at all the layers and the many proprietary solutions. We also spend a good deal of time on MPLS, the emerging standard for label-based switching. The goal of this chapter is to provide a comprehensive survey of multilayer switching across the LAN and WAN, clearly identifying areas of overlap and convergence.

Before we get started, though, heed the following caveat: A small portion of the factual material for this chapter comes from Internet-Drafts. Internet-Drafts are not standards and therefore can change at any time. Although it is unlikely that there will be radical change, some change is inevitable, and any factual information derived from an Internet-Draft is clearly pointed out in the text as "work in progress."

4.2 Key Solutions Offered

Simply stated, multilayer switching addresses network performance and scalability which are interrelated. If performance is poor with 10 nodes, it is most likely worse with 100 nodes. As traffic becomes less and less localized, more and more traffic is routed. Traditional routers require a significant amount of packet processing for each packet they route, largely because they are very rich in functionality and they service so many protocols simultaneously. Unfortunately though, traditional routers go through the same amount of packet processing for *each* packet, even when there is a stream of packets going to the exact same destination!

Multilayer switching attacks routing bottlenecks with two discrete approaches:

1. **hardware-based routing** (speeding up the process of routing) and
2. **flow- or label-based routing** (optimizing route determination based on traffic patterns and use of short, fixed-length labels to route packets instead of requiring repeated packet interpretation).

Both approaches have merit: They complement each other and may be used in tandem to improve the overall performance and scaling needs of our networks. There are a variety of emerging techniques that are aimed at speeding up routing in both the LAN and the WAN. Within the LAN, IP subnets are created to contain broadcasting and to facilitate management, a necessary requirement of scaling any LAN. IP subnets are interconnected with routers; therefore "line speed" routing (or layer-3 switching) becomes an attractive solution. Layer-3 switches still process every packet, but they do so at line speed. Layer-3 switches that are capable of multiprotocol (particularly IP and IPX) switching are even better since most LANs are still multiprotocol. Layer-4 switches read more of the packet, such as TCP session-related information, enabling routing optimization based on common port numbers such as Web-based HTTP or file transfers with FTP. Although layer-3 or layer-4 switching was initially targeted at the LAN, nothing precludes using them in the WAN. Other LAN techniques like Fast IP provide a way to "route once, switch many" by first learning the route and then diverting traffic to a faster switched path.

In the WAN, techniques like Tag Switching map fixed-length tags (or labels) to intermediate routing hops, reducing the amount of packet processing at each hop, and enabling routing based on network policy. Tag Switching also provides a strong base for introducing differential packet handling. Other techniques like IP Switching divert routed traffic to an ATM PVC, again optimizing the amount of processing necessary to move traffic to its destination. MPLS is the emerging standard for label-based routing that incorporates the efforts of the many proprietary label-switching approaches.

A S I D E . . .

Is switching really faster than routing? At the lowest level of routing we have a 4-byte destination address lookup versus a 6-byte destination address lookup (the destination MAC address) on a switch. If both address tables are in memory, which lookup is faster?

As mentioned, traditional routers perform a significant amount of packet processing for each packet they route. This is largely because traditional routers are very rich in functionality and they service many different protocols simultaneously. This richness is typically satisfied by software-based solutions that execute more slowly than hardware-based solutions. Layer-3 switches provide hardware-based solutions of a reduced set of processing. This results in significantly faster routing with significantly less functionality than a traditional router that usually supports only one protocol—IP.

4.3 Routers Can Be Traffic Bottlenecks

Over the years more and more intelligence has been incorporated into traditional routers. Routers support multiple protocols, span the WAN and LAN, have hundreds of configurable parameters, allow for sophisticated packet filtering, and provide a way to add significant control to a network. Thanks to faster processors and RAM capacities, increased functionality has been possible without denigrating performance. Unfortunately though, as networks attempt to service more and more traffic, congestion becomes the common, ugly word used to describe the clogged data pipes.

Visualize a popular grocery store on a Saturday afternoon. There are too many groceries (packets) to ring up and too few cashiers (routers), resulting in spending too much of your time in line. Simply stated, congestion occurs when the sum of the traffic from multiple input streams exceeds the forwarding capacity of the router(s). Traditional routers are required to read parts of the layer-3 header in order to make a routing decision. Traditional routers must also manipulate the header in every packet, that is, decrement the TTL field and generate ICMP messages (TTL exceeded, MTU mismatch, network unreachable) with error conditions. All of the duties of a router increase the time that is needed to get packets on their way.

Congestion, too, exacerbates delay. Because routers discard packets when congested, retransmission places additional strain on the network. TCP's slow start and back-off algorithms help some, but they are not enough. So how do we resolve the situation? How do we provide a solution for the congestion of today and the increased congestion of tomorrow due to exponential network growth? The past is full of routing optimizations that just don't scale. Sophisticated caching schemes, increased memory for buffers, and marginally faster processors are all techniques that offer only small gains at high costs. Yes, there are some very large routers that do scale, but these are often prohibitively expensive. So how is this problem fixed?

Enter bar code (label) readers in the grocery store; enter label-based switching in the network. Enter faster cashiers (routers) in the grocery store; enter line-speed routers in the network. Label-based switches and line-speed routers provide the foundation for our next generation networks. Multilayer switching provides a creative, powerful foundation for tomorrow's ever-growing networks.

4.4 Multilayer Switching in a Nutshell

There are many techniques for multilayer switching, and it helps to be able to compare and contrast the techniques in a simple chart (see Table 4.1). Following this chart we will go into detail about each technique, including how it works and the advantages and disadvantages of its deployment.

Table 4.1 Various Multilayer Switching Techniques

Technique	Vendor or Standard	Positioning	Summary
Layer-2 Switching	Many vendor solutions	LAN and WAN	This is true switching and includes hardware-based forwarding of various data link protocols—Ethernet or FDDI—in the LAN and switching over VCs—frame relay and ATM—in the WAN.
Layer-3 Switching	Many vendor solutions	The initial focus is LAN, but it will be seen in WAN.	This hardware-based forwarding is based on routing information in the layer-3 packet header. IP is the most common and often the only protocol that vendors support in layer-3 switches.
Layer-4 Switching	Many vendor solutions	The initial focus is LAN, but it will be seen in WAN.	This hardware-based forwarding is based on transport information in the header. Forwarding based on port number is especially popular, since there are various well-known port numbers that can be used to influence the forwarding decision.
Fast IP and NHRP	3Com	LAN	This "route once, switch many" technique is used to provide cut-through forwarding of packets. The initial request is routed; subsequent requests are switched over a fast (layer-2) switched path.
Multiprotocol over ATM (MPOA)	IETF standards (NHRP, LANE bridging)	LAN and WAN	This technique includes a standard's based approach to forwarding network layer packets over an ATM backbone. MPOA alleviates performance bottlenecks in router backbones by taking advantage of high-performance ATM switching. It follows the "route once, switch many" technique.

continued

Table 4.1 Various Multilayer Switching Techniques (continued)

Technique	Vendor or Standard	Positioning	Summary
Multiprotocol Label Switching (MPLS)	IETF Standard	WAN	This emerging standard provides packet forwarding based on fixed-length labels. It is positioned to support multiple protocols and to facilitate • Explicit routing • Traffic engineering • Service differentiation • Network scalability MPLS is derived from features in IP Navigator, ARIS, and Tag Switching.
Tag Switching	Cisco	WAN	This packet forwarding approach is based on fixed length tags. Like MPLS, Tag Switching is positioned to support multiple protocols and to facilitate • Explicit routing • Traffic engineering • Service differentiation • Network scalability
IP Navigator	Ascend (Cascade)	WAN	This packet forwarding approach is based on fixed-length labels. Like MPLS, IP Navigator is positioned to support multiple protocols and to facilitate • Explicit routing • Traffic engineering • Service differentiation • Network scalability
Aggregate Route-based IP Switching (ARIS)	IBM	WAN	This packet forwarding approach is based on fixed-length labels. Like MPLS, ARIS is positioned to support multiple protocols and to facilitate

continued

Table 4.1 Various Multilayer Switching Techniques (continued)

Technique	Vendor or Standard	Positioning	Summary
			<ul><li>Explicit routing</li><li>Traffic engineering</li><li>Service differentiation</li><li>Network scalability</li></ul>
IP Switching	Nokia (Ipsilon)	LAN and WAN	This technique converts IP packets into ATM cells to route them over ATM VCs. It follows the "route once, switch many" paradigm but may not scale well in the WAN.
Cell-Switched Routers	Toshiba	LAN and WAN	The "route once, switch many" approach is designed to accelerate forwarding and take advantage of ATM's high performance switching. This approach monitors for long-term router flows and dynamically creates "cut-through" paths across ATM switches. It may not scale well in the WAN.

4.5 Layer-2 Switching

One type of layer-2 switch is the classic LAN multiport bridge that enables simple network segmentation often resulting in significant performance improvements. Layer-2 switching is also present in the WAN with frame relay and ATM switches.

A S I D E . . .

ATM does not map exactly to layer 2 as it has attributes from layers 3 and 4 of the ISO reference model. Nonetheless, ATM is often loosely classified as a layer-2 protocol. As mentioned in Chapter 2, the ISO Reference Model provides only an approximate mapping—especially since it preceded ATM!

Layer-2 switching is *switching in the traditional sense.* The previous chapter focused on switching; this section is included largely for completeness. The popularity of layer-2 switching has led to the layer-3 and layer-4 switching market; these switches use network and transport layer packet information to forward packets at line speeds. The next few sections discuss these switching solutions.

4.6 Layer-3 Switching

There are many vendors with fast router solutions. These switches have all the capabilities of layer-2 switches combined with integrated routing. Key and paramount to layer-3 switches is moving data at *line-speed* (or *wire-speed*) across many ports simultaneously. Layer-3 switches are positioned to give you the best of both worlds: the *speed* of a flat, switched network with the *control* of a routed network.

Layer-3 switches typically used Application Specific Integrated Circuits (ASIC) technology to burn functionality into hardware that was formally done as software. Digital Signal Processors (DSPs) are sometimes used instead of ASIC technology in low-end layer-2 switches; most layer-3 switches (perhaps because of the required complexity of routing software) are built with ASICs. Some vendors use *several* ASICs to achieve parallelism within the switch; this is an effective way to achieve line-speed data rates across many ports. One layer-3 switch vendor actually has a dedicated ASIC per port, clearly demonstrating simultaneous processing.

Another characteristic of layer-3 switches is that they tend to support only a subset of the features of a fully functional router. Reduced functionality usually means less code to run through and therefore faster performance. For example, many layer-3 switches are aimed at providing an IP routing solution, but not a multiprotocol solution. This can make it difficult to replace existing routers with a layer-3 switch in environments that are protocol rich. It is expected that more functionality will be included in future releases of layer-3 switches with convergence toward full functional routing. Again, though, trade-offs may be made with respect to functionality, speed, and simplicity.

Beyond the performance of forwarding packets, the next most important characteristic of layer-3 switches is the ability to do automatic flow classification. Flow classification or class of service (COS) provides a form of QoS that enables packet queuing into a few distinct classes of service based on a priority. (Chapter 5 discusses COS and QoS in detail.) In typical nonconnection-oriented LAN environments like Ethernet, COS can be used as an extremely powerful way to ensure that high-priority traffic gets precedence over lower-priority traffic. COS coupled with traffic monitoring—perhaps using Remote Network Monitor Version 2 (RMON2)—can be used to *tune* a network and improve overall predictability without moving to a connection-oriented technology like ATM.

Some other features that vendors include in layer-3 switches are

- the ability to extend the firmware with programmable additions such as IPv6 support.
- support of RMON2 for network management and traffic monitoring.
- support of standard-based traffic prioritization as defined by 802.1Q and 802.1p.
- VLAN integration.
- sophisticated packet filtering for security and traffic management.
- support of RSVP flows and IP multicast trees.
- support of Ethernet, Fast Ethernet, Gigabit Ethernet, FDDI, and ATM.
- support of one or more routing protocols such as RIP or OSPF.
- creative buffering and pipelining solutions to achieve maximum performance.

4.7 Layer-4 Switching

Layer-4 extends layer-3 and layer-2 switching by enabling fine-grained network tuning and prioritization based on traffic flows. Whereas layer-2 switching (traditional switching at layer 2 of the ISO reference model) switches on MAC addresses and layer-3 switching (routing at layer 3 of the ISO reference model) routes according to destination address, layer-4 switching (policy-based routing at layer 4 of the ISO reference model) uses layer-4 information. For example, the TCP/UDP application port number is commonly used to refine further how traffic is forwarded.

Layer-4 switching enables prioritization of traffic based on applications; this gives the network manager the ability to limit certain application-specific traffic during the day and dedicate a certain level of bandwidth for mission critical applications. In essence layer-4 switching provides a way to implement COS across a network. For example, a corporation may decide to reduce the amount of WWW traffic or FTP traffic while giving more priority to e-mail or telnet traffic.

A S I D E . . .

Recall that with TCP port numbers 0–1023 are registered, well-known port numbers used by applications across the network. Telnet sessions use port 23, HTTP sessions use port 80, and SNMP uses ports 161 and 162. The combination of two IP addresses and two port numbers is called a TCP socket. Network applications commonly use sockets to communicate across the network, and this information can be used to control bandwidth allocated to applications (for example, Web traffic comes in via HTTP) and users (IP addresses). Consult a good book on TCP (see Bibliography) for more information on port numbers.

4.8 Fast IP and NHRP

Fast IP (a solution provided by 3Com) is a technique that provides high-speed switched connections across many hops without the need to route data. Fast IP puts "routing" in the hands of end nodes and Fast IP-capable switches. With Fast IP, "routing" is not done in the traditional sense; rather Fast IP leverages three standards: 802.1Q, 802.1p, and the Next Hop Resolution Protocol (NHRP). (802.1Q and 802.1p were discussed in Chapter 3.) In essence after initially routing data via layer 3, data can "shortcut" through the layer-2 path of the switch. Often this process occurs in the same layer-3 switch, because layer-3 switches also support layer-2 switching. To better illustrate this technique, let's walk through the example illustrated in Figure 4.1.

A N O T H E R   A S I D E . . .

The NHRP is an IETF protocol that uses a Next Hop Server (NHS) instead of traditional routing to determine the next hop. This provides a mechanism that extends address resolution beyond the boundaries of subnets.

Suppose User A wants to accelerate data sent to User B located two hops away. An NHRP request that contains the source, the destination MAC (an intermediate bridge as the final destination is unknown), the IP source and destination addresses, and the frame type is sent. The NHRP data includes the source end station's MAC address (important, because along the way the header's source address will change to the destination to reflect the required point-to-point hops)

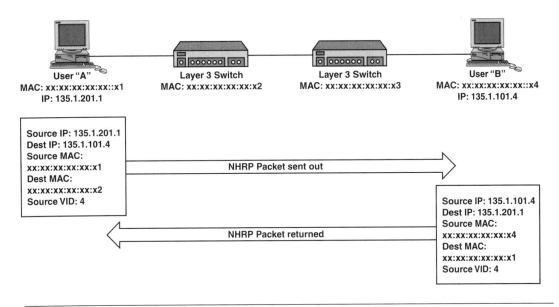

Figure 4.1 Fast IP Next Hop Resolution Protocol (NHRP)

and the VLAN ID.[1] The NHRP is forwarded to the destination end system through the routers. Note that this packet obeys all the normal routing policy, such as filtering in place between A and B. The destination returns an NHRP response using the *source MAC address* and *VLAN ID* found in the data portion of the packet. The destination also sends its MAC address so that data from the original source can use the same technique when it goes in the other direction. Switches between them use layer-2 switching to bridge the data using either the MAC address, if it is in the bridging table (that is, directly connected) or the VLAN ID, if the MAC address is not found. Once the packet returns, subsequent data can be "switched" through multiple hops. Fast IP results in a very high-speed pipe that does not require layer-3 routing table lookup—rather it utilizes the new features that extend traditional bridging with tagging.

Fast IP does not have to be used for every packet; it can be triggered based on the amount of data flowing from A to B or some other frequency measurement. Fast IP is fault tolerant in that, if a response NHRP packet is not received upon sending an NHRP request packet, communication will continue as normal. Fast IP is vulnerable to GARP-based VLAN ID management working

---

1. VLAN IDs have to be assigned by someone, so this is a companywide (not worldwide) solution.

properly and VLAN ID change. (Recall from Chapter 3 that Group Address Resolution Protocol—GARP—is defined in 802.1p and is used to manage and distribute group membership information.) If a Fast IP "connection" times out after establishment, the NHRP will have to be used again, possibly to locate another path. While this happens, nothing precludes communication to continue with the normal routed mechanisms. From a management perspective, it would be interesting to have a count of the number of NHRP requests made over time, the frequency of like NHRP requests, and the number of NHRP retries from an end node perspective as well as from an intermediate switch perspective.

4.9 Multiprotocol over ATM (MPOA)

Multiprotocol over ATM (MPOA) is a standard-based solution that opens up the speed and QoS of an ATM core to IP and other protocols. MPOA is positioned at providing an effective relief for the congestion of traditional routers, primarily in the LAN. Using the same virtual subnetting as ATM LANE, packets are forwarded to destinations without the need to route every packet.

MPOA is a cut-through routing approach, sometimes referred to as following an *overlay* model. Overlay implies that there are separate layer-3 and layer-2 addressing and discrete paths. Figure 4.2 illustrates MPOA's overlay model.

A S I D E . . .

Private Network-Network Interface (PNNI) (as shown in Figure 4.2) is ATM's standard-based routing protocol. It enables ATM switches from many different vendors to interoperate within the same network.

One important requirement of mixing ATM with IP is address management. MPOA does address management by designating an MPOA (route) server (MPS) to be the keeper of address information source for edge and ATM switches. The Next-Hop Routing Protocol (NHRP) is used to map between ATM addresses and layer-3 addresses.

MPOA has some distinct advantages that have already made a significant ATM investment, especially in LAN environments.

- It is standard-based, so interoperability between different vendors' equipment should be possible.
- It is currently shipped by many vendors.

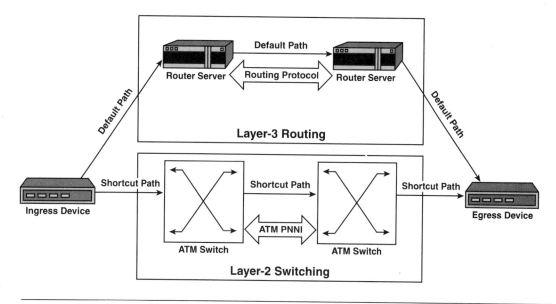

Figure 4.2 MPOA's overlay model

- It provides an infrastructure for building Virtual Private Networks (VPNs). A VPN becomes a virtual subnet.

- It improves on the ATM LANE solution. For example, ATM LANE requires routing hops for connections between VLANs. This can become a traffic bottleneck.

- It improves on Classical IP over ATM (RFC 1577), which is IP-centric.

- It will enable multiple protocols to take advantage of ATM-based QoS.

- It can coexist with traditional ATM.

It is questionable, however, how well MPOA will scale beyond the LAN. Clearly setting up communication based on flow with shortcut granularity of one shortcut per flow results in scaling problems. In addition, it is likely that the signaling overhead associated with call setup will introduce too much latency for short-lived communication.

4.10 Routing Combined with Connection-Oriented Services

We're all familiar with pure packet-based networks. Traditional routers create a networking mesh that provides an effective connectionless datagram service. Routers learn the topology across wide areas and stay current with respect to topology changes. Routers correctly route datagrams between multiple sources and destinations by doing explicit, individual, "longest match" lookup at each interconnection point. Longest match lookups means that every packet's destination address is individually examined at each router against the current contents of the routing table in order to find the best match. This match tells the router which port to send the packet out, that is, the next hop. Packets are filtered for security purposes based on many different items within the packet header; for example, source, destination address, and port number (layer-4) filtering are quite common. Packets that loop are effectively dropped when the time to live (TTL) in the packet becomes zero. As the network increases in size, so do the routing tables and routing table churn (routing flap); these factors tend to slow down the routing process. Traditional packet-based routers make no attempt to "learn" common communication paths or packet flows as packets are routed individually, based on destination address, and handled individually, making it very difficult to do traffic engineering.

ATM and frame relay use permanent virtual circuits (PVCs) identified by Virtual Path Identifier/Virtual Channel Identifier (VPI/VCI) pairs and Data Link Connection Identifiers (DLCIs), respectively, to get data to its desired location. In the case of an ATM switch, the "next hop" of every cell is determined by reading the VPI/VCI pair; these identifiers enable intermediate switches to "route" data from an input port to the correct output port. DLCIs provide frame relay with the locally significant information necessary to "route" data to its next destination. Both ATM and frame relay are connection-oriented technologies. Paths of how to route the data are set up a priori, greatly reducing the processing necessary to route the data. In addition, it provides a framework for traffic management, a necessary component of making networks scale.

Label-based switching technologies attempt to *combine the best of these connectionless and connection-oriented technologies.* Let's enumerate some of the strengths and weaknesses of connectionless and connection-oriented technologies. We will use this list as a way to transition into our discussion of MPLS and to demonstrate how attractive it is to combine the best features of both approaches.

- First and foremost, routing was designed for fault tolerance. You can literally power-cycle a stateless Ethernet hub without losing any TCP connections. The Internet was designed to withstand nuclear attack.

- Routing allows for *variable-size packets*. This minimizes the amount of overhead required to do large file transfers. ATM uses fixed-size (53-byte) cells; each cell has 5 bytes of overhead. ATM is often criticized for the amount of cell tax one must pay to do the equivalent large file transfer as done in a packet world. Frame relay allows for variable-size frames, each with only 6 bytes of overhead. Low overhead is considered to be a very attractive feature of frame relay.

- ATM provides a strong infrastructure for *traffic engineering*. Because ATM maintains tables of where traffic is headed at any time, traffic can be easily load balanced across multiple circuits, and QoS can be maintained and ensured. Since routing doesn't maintain any state on communication flows, it is difficult to load balance a pure router-based network and impossible to offer packet performance guarantees.

- Packet-by-packet routing requires a significant amount of *processing overhead*. Each packet must be individually examined at each router before it is routed to its next hop. Line speed routers (also known as layer-3 or routing switches) alleviate much of the pain here, although much of the traditional functionality of a router is often limited. For example, line speed routers often route only one protocol, such as IP. Connection-oriented technologies make the routing decision at the beginning of a communication session by setting up an SVC (or using an existing PVC). Setting up an SVC is a significant overhead for small transfers.

- ATM includes sophisticated traffic management that facilitates congestion management. Currently router-based networks typically do not have integrated traffic management. In fact, TCP uses heuristics to detect loss due to congestion and reacts to it by adjusting traffic.

- ATM provides an infrastructure for voice, video, and data and therefore *multiple communication services*. Router-based networks were originally designed for transmission of data only.

4.11 Label-Based Switching

Label-based switching (LBS) is all about moving repetitive and high-priority data flows from a packet-by-packet routing paradigm to a virtual circuit (VC) switching paradigm. This hybrid leverages the best features of packet-based and ATM networks. LBS facilitates overall network scalability, improves overall network predictability, and provides a way to guarantee network service levels across the network.

LBS uses short, fixed-length tags to encapsulate the routing semantics of the packet forwarding process (See Figure 4.3). At first glance it might seem that this is done to speed things up. Clearly, looking up a label is faster than routing that is based on reading and interpreting the entire layer-3 header for each packet. *Speed, however, is not the motivation for LBS.* LBS provides technology integration—combining the best of connectionless and connection-oriented networking that enables our future WAN networks to scale and provide multiple concurrent services.

LBS provides the means for communication of variable-sized multiprotocol packets across a combined router *and* ATM core network. In essence LBS abstracts away the specifics of cell-based and packet-based switching into a higher layer based on labels. It is this abstraction in particular that is so powerful and important to LBS; by switching based on a label, LBS is able to provide a clean convergence of these two very different technologies, taking advantage of the features of both. LBS leverages the notion of topology-based routing of variable-size packets from the router world with scalability, and QoS, labeling, and traffic engineering from the ATM world. Label-based switching provides us with a way to provide scalable, tuned, multiservice networks.

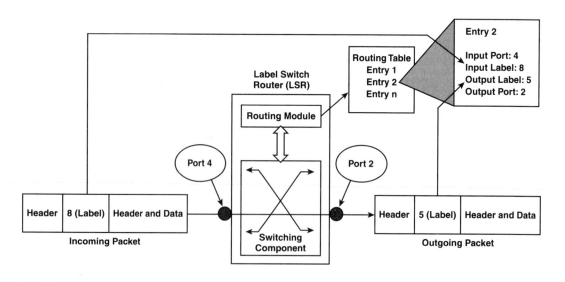

Figure 4.3 Label swapping

In summary, LBS facilitates *explicit routing (routing based on many factors) without the heavy overhead of putting the explicit route in each header.* Rather, the label can be used as a pointer into the explicit routing policy (more about this in Chapter 7). Label-based switching also enables

- Traffic Engineering,
- IP QoS over ATM,
- Service Differentiation, and
- Scalability.

We will discuss each of these key features in subsequent sections.

4.11.1 The IETF MPLS Effort

Like many other emerging standards, the ideas behind MPLS come from many technical experts across the industry. Representatives from several vendors have been very active members of the MPLS working group. Often the ideas from many converge on the best overall solutions.

At the time of this writing there were several IETF draft documents that discussed different aspects of MPLS.[2] Much of the factual material presented in this chapter comes from these "work in progress" documents and is therefore subject to change.

MPLS has a few straightforward goals:

- To improve price, performance, and overall network scalability.
- To be link layer independent.
- To be network layer independent. MPLS is designed to be network layer independent, although initially it is positioned at IPv4 and IPv6. It is expected that other protocols like IPX, AppleTalk, DECnet, and Connectionless Network Protocol (CLNP) may be supported in subsequent versions.
- To coexist with native ATM and native routing services.
- To facilitate support for multiservice networks, that is, networks capable of services far beyond conventional best-effort service.

---

2. "A Framework for Multiprotocol Label Switching" by R. Callon of Ascend Communications, Inc., P. Doolan of Ennovate Networks, N. Feldman of IBM Corporation, A. Fredette of Nortel Networks, G. Swallow of Cisco Systems, Inc., and A. Viswanathan of IBM Corporation. (November 1997) and "A Proposed Architecture for MPLS" by E. C. Rosen of Cisco Systems, Inc., A. Viswanathan of IBM Corporation, and R. Callon of Ascend Communications, Inc. (August 1997) are two key MPLS Internet-Drafts.

There are many proprietary label-based switching solutions, and they all have their advantages. For example, the MPLS standard attempts to combine the best ideas from each. After discussing the MPLS standard, we will cover the proprietary solutions that are emerging concurrent to MPLS.

4.11.2 MPLS Functional Requirements

The MPLS working group has defined several functional requirements for the efforts. The following requirements come from both framework and architecture specifications:

- MPLS must not be tied to any one routing protocol; it must work with many. There are several routing protocols that are used today, and if MPLS is to be widely deployed, it must fit into existing network structures rather than require widespread replacement. *Evolution* rather than *revolution* is a requirement.

- The MPLS solution must address loop prevention and elimination. Packet loops can result in significant bursts of traffic causing dropped packets and moments of network "brownout." This problem will clearly exacerbate, as the network becomes more loaded with multicast traffic.

- "Aggregate forwarding" must be supported. It enables streams of data to be forwarded as a single entity between Label Switch Routers (LSRs), facilitating multicast traffic as well as efficiency and scalability.

- MPLS must be manageable and not impede the existing use of current IP tools. Traceroute, which depends on the time to live (TTL) field in IP packets, must somehow be supported across ATM switches. (Recall that ATM headers do not have a TTL field.) We will discuss this topic later.

- MPLS must be compatible with existing network equipment that will not support MPLS.

- MPLS must work transparently and simultaneously with existing layer-2 switching protocols. In the industry this requirement is often referred to as "ships in the night."

- Both topology-driven and traffic/request-driven label assignment must be supported. Topology-driven label assignment refers to having the labels determined by integrating with the layer-3 generated topology; traffic/request-driven label assignment refers to assigning labels based on flows. In large core networks, topology-driven assignment is the preferred solution as it scales better. You can imagine how many flows come and go across the Internet and how big the MPLS tables would have to be to store labels! Traffic/request-driven labels may, however, work very well in an enterprise (or LAN) or may be appropriate for certain long-term traffic across the network that has stringent performance requirements.

- MPLS must be compatible with the Integrated Services (IS) Model proposed by the IETF. This includes the RSVP specification discussed in Chapter 6.

4.11.3 Important MPLS Terminology

Like most new technologies, MPLS has a lot of new terms and concepts. Table 4.2 includes the most important new terms and a few other acronyms that are important to know when discussing MPLS.

4.11.4 Key Features of MPLS

There are a few key features discussed in the framework document that have the potential to help us *significantly* converge toward meeting tomorrow's networking requirements as discussed in Chapter 1. The list of MPLS offerings that are explained in subsequent paragraphs are

- simplified forwarding,
- a unified forwarding paradigm,
- efficient explicit routing,
- service-level differentiation,
- QoS-based routing, and
- straightforward traffic engineering.

Labels facilitate *simplified forwarding*. Once labels are established and a label (or optionally a stack of labels for explicit routing) is assigned at the ingress node, a packet can traverse the network quickly. Forwarding is based on label lookup, similar to what is done by layer-2 switches with MAC address tables and ATM with VPI/VCI pairs. This is simpler than reading, interpreting, and acting on the header contents (for example, IP address and TTL) of *each* packet at *each* router. LSRs can focus their attention on topology and label synchronization since forwarding software is significantly simpler. This does not, however, eliminate the need for the traditional router, particularly at the ingress and the egress points of the MPLS network.

Table 4.2 MPLS and Related Terminology

Term	Definition
Data Link Connection Identifier (DLCI)	The identifier used by frame relay networks to identify a particular circuit.
Egress Node	A point of exit (edge node) out of the MPLS-based network.
Flow	A single host-to-host or application-to-application exchange of data.
Frame Merge	Same as stream merge (see below) but applied to frame-based data. Addresses the potential problem of ATM cell interleave.
Forwarding Equivalence Class (FEC)	A group of packets that share a set of common characteristics (for example, destination, source, priority) and hence are forwarded using the same stream. FECs provide the mapping of "packet type" to stream.
Ingress Node	The point of entry (an edge node) into the MPLS-based network.
Label	A short, fixed-length tag used to identify a path.
Label Information Base (LIB)	A database of label bindings.
Label Swap	The forwarding operation done at each network interconnection. The incoming label is used to determine the outgoing label, necessary encapsulation, and port. This process is similar to what ATM does with VCI/VPI identifiers.
Label Distribution Protocol (LDP)	Protocol used to distribute labels among LSR, Egress Nodes, and Ingress Nodes in the network.
Label Switched Hop (LSH)	The hop between two MPLS nodes that utilizes label-based forwarding.
Label Switched Path (LSP)	A path created by concatenation of many LSHs. This enables a packet to be forwarded by swapping labels from an MPLS node to another MPLS node.

continued

Table 4.2 MPLS and Related Terminology (continued)

Term	Definition
Label Switch Router (LSR)	Router knowledgeable of routing and MPLS. Typically at the Egress and Ingress of the MPLS-based network.
Loop Detection	A methodology for determining the existence of a loop and subsequent loop elimination. TTL decrement is the methodology used by IP to eliminate loops.
Loop Prevention	A methodology for eliminating transmission of packets over a loop.
Label Stack	An ordered set of labels possibly forming an explicit route.
Merge Point	A point at which multiple streams and switched paths are combined into a single stream.
Multiprotocol Label Switching (MPLS)	A draft standard for label-based routing.
Next Hop Label Forwarding Entry (NHLFE)	An entry within a LSR's Label Information Base.
Stream	A group of packets that is forwarded on the same path with the same level of service. Streams are made up of many flows.
Stream Merge	The process of aggregation of one or more flows into a single stream, also known as an aggregate stream.
VP merge	The process of merging several Virtual Paths (VPs) into one single VP. VCIs must be unique, allowing for cells from different sources to be distinguishable.
VPI/VCI	The Virtual Path Identifier/Virtual Circuit Identifier is the unique identifier of a connection on an ATM network. The VPI portion of the identifier is an 8-bit field, and the VCI is a 16-bit field.

Labels result in a single, *uniformed forwarding paradigm.* Frame relay traffic, ATM traffic, IP traffic, IP tunneling, and perhaps IPX and AppleTalk may all be routed across the network using the same labeling scheme and the same routing paradigm. This is particularly critical in the WAN where integration of the most prevalent technologies (IP, ATM, and frame relay) is so important. It is expected that this uniformity and integration will help lower costs.

Often packets have to travel through many routers to get to their destinations, particularly in the Internet. Simply stated, *explicit routing* concatenates together an ordered list of address hops directing a packet across the network, in essence, encapsulating the path. This is like putting explicit travel directions (turn left at the stop sign, take a right at the next traffic light) in each packet. With traditional routing, it takes a lot of extra bytes to add explicit routing to each packet, making explicit routing prohibitively expensive. Because labels are short, fixed-length tags, with MPLS explicit routing via defining an ordered label stack becomes a possibility. In fact, each label within the stack can be associated with more than just the next hop; it can be associated with many other attributes allowing for service-level differentiation.

Service-level differentiation refers to using a label as a key into a table containing many detailed attributes about how traffic with a certain label should be routed. For example, a label can be used to distinguish a virtual private network (VPN) or to indicate a priority level. Class of service (COS) and security provisioning are also possibilities. All of these topics will be discussed in Chapter 5.

One desirable feature of next generation networks is the ability to support a certain QoS for a specific stream of data. This may be used to provide a certain service-level guarantee since bandwidth is explicitly allocated to a particular communication stream. Although QoS is explicitly built into ATM, there is currently no way to make a service-level guarantee on a packet-based network. *QoS routing* refers to the notion of selecting a particular stream based on a certain level of QoS required. Typically QoS routing can take advantage of the ability to specify an explicit path, enabling nodes along the path to be knowledgeable about the flow and to account for the required bandwidth. QoS routing also can be used to refuse a flow, if adequate resources are not available.

Traffic engineering refers to the process of monitoring network flow and making flow adjustments across the network to load-balance traffic evenly across the network. With traditional packet-based routing, traffic engineering is very difficult since the only way to redirect traffic is to adjust the metrics associated with each link. This is an effective way to do some load balancing between certain individual hops, but it does not consider the entire network (the whole picture) and hence may be only marginally effective. Worse yet, it can actually cause congestion elsewhere in the network. It is the difference between a driver unable to see beyond his local proximity and caught in a traffic jam taking a few shortcuts and a helicopter that can see overall traffic patterns and make *entire* alternative route suggestions. MPLS provides a straightforward means to do traffic engineering. Measurement and adjustments are quite simple to make, since streams between nodes are individually identifiable by their labels. With explicit path routing it is also easy to ensure that data takes the preferred path.

4.11.5 How MPLS Works

Normal operation of MPLS is straightforward. MPLS relies on

- traditional IP forwarding at the edge and label forwarding in core;
- topology-based label assignment;
- flow, streams, forward equivalence class, label-switched path, and labels; and
- Label swapping at each switch.

The following four steps illustrate the simplicity of MPLS. See Figure 4.4 for an illustration of some of the MPLS components in context.

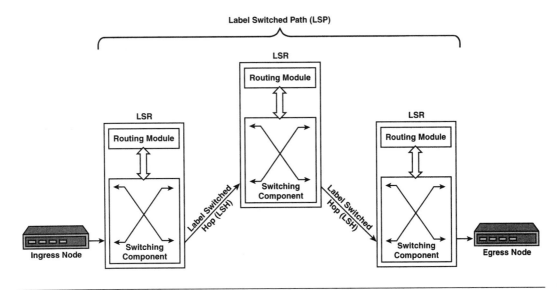

Figure 4.4 Label-based switching

Step 1: MPLS Setup and Label Maintenance. At MPLS initiation, interconnection network entities—*ingress nodes, egress nodes,* and *Label Switch Routers* (LSRs)—use standard routing protocols (BGP, OSPF) to determine routes through the network. Routes between any two network entities are associated with short, fixed-length labels that are distributed throughout the network. Labels at each LSR are stored in a Label Information Base (LIB) and are periodically refreshed and distributed using the Label Distribution Protocol (LDP). To represent an explicit route, labels are concatenated together in the form of a *label stack;* they are associated with a Forwarding Equivalence Class (FEC) that associates a group of packets with a set of common characteristics (for example, destination, source, and priority). Ingress nodes and egress nodes use FECs to provide the mapping of "packet type" to stream.

Step 2: Packet Entry. Packets enter the label-based switched network via an Ingress Node. At entry each packet is associated with a FEC that provides the instruction set on how to forward the packet base on the destination address and possibly other header information. If a FEC is found, the appropriate label (or label stack for explicit routing) is shimmed into the packet between the network and data link packet headers. If a FEC for the packet is not present, the packet is routed using conventional routing. This facilitates interoperability with conventional routing and provides a method for forwarding packets while MPLS is initializing.

Step 3: Network Hopping. At each intermediate hop, the label is used to look up the next label within the LIB. If an entry is found, the label is replaced and the packet is sent on its way; if an entry is not found, the packet is routed by reading the layer-3 header using conventional routing. If the packet has an explicit route (that is, a label stack), the label of the current LSR is popped off and the packet is sent on its way without needing to do a table lookup.

Step 4: Packet Exit. When the packet gets to the end of its label stack (there are no more labels) or when an entry is not found in the LIB, the packet is ready to exit the label-switched network. The label is stripped off and the packet is either routed to the next hop conventionally or sent to its final destination. Packet exit happens at the egress node; the egress node must strip off the tag so that the packet can be conventionally routed or directly delivered to the end node.

4.11.6 Label Management

There are many options for the location of the label within the packet. As mentioned, MPLS labels may be sandwiched between the data link layer and the network layer as a "shim" or embedded within the network or data link layer headers. Naturally, though, there must be agreement across all LSRs as to where the label is and how it is encoded.

The MPLS architecture specification proposes that any "shim" header contain the following:

- A *label stack* component: one or more labels that follow a push and pop metaphor to get a packet to its final destination. Since multiple labels can be pushed (and popped), the label stack facilitates explicit routing.

- A *Time-to-Live (TTL) field:* an explicit TTL outside of the one in the layer-3 header enables loop prevention across all LSRs, even across ATM switches that currently do not have a TTL within the ATM cell header.

- A *Class of Service (COS) field:* a field allowing MPLS to assign packet processing priorities.

A S I D E . . .

When you add an MPLS shim header, the maximum packet size may be exceeded. When a packet size is exceeded, packets must be fragmented.

Labels are synchronized between LSRs using the Label Distribution Protocol (LDP). Labels may be a single label (one hop) or a label stack (two or more labels). A label stack can be thought of as an ordered series of hops that a packet must traverse in the direction of a packet's destination; label stacks enable support of explicit routing, tunneling, and partial explicit routing toward a destination.

The LDP must be a reliable protocol that ensures proper sequencing of protocol messages. One option for the LDP is to use a transport protocol like TCP. At the time of this writing the MPLS committee is still working on the exact specifications for the LDP.

Entries within the Label Information Base (LIB) are called Next Hop Label Forwarding Entries (NHLFEs), and each NHLFE contains

- the next hop,
- a data link encapsulation used for the packet,

- the label stack encoding, and
- guides on handling the label stack (simple pop, replace the label, and so on).

A S I D E . . .

There may be an NHLFE at the LSR Egress even though there is no further LSR to switch to. The specification points out that this enables the label to contain other information like packet priority of a Virtual Private Network (VPN) encoding.

4.11.7 Label Assignment: Local versus Egress Control

Label assignment and distribution are important aspects of MPLS. MPLS provides two choices for assignment and distribution: distribution by the local nodes (or ingress nodes) fanning out to the egress nodes, or distribution by the egress nodes back toward the local or ingress nodes.

The advantage of local assignment is that labels are distributed quickly, enabling label-based switching to be activated sooner. The big disadvantage of the local approach is that it easily allows for inconsistent routing decisions. With local control, each LSR makes decisions on how to forward FECs independently; this almost guarantees that some LSRs will treat flows more granularly than others, resulting in the need to do a lot of label adjustment. Mapping a "course" flow (mapping multiple IP address prefixes to a single label) to a "fine" flow (mapping each individual IP address to a separate label) results in a subsequent need to adjust the labels. Adjusting many labels at many points in the network can result in label churn across the network. Label churn is as undesirable as routing table churn found in conventional routing.

Churn can be significantly reduced with egress control label distribution. Egress control works in the reverse of local control: labels are distributed by the egresses in the direction toward the local nodes. Nodes upstream must wait until they get a label from a downstream neighbor before passing a label to the next node upstream. This results in consistent granularity across the network.

An easy way to understand the difference between local and egress control is to think of a typical river. If you walk along the river against the flow, from the destination to the source, you know precisely what to expect downstream because you can "record" where you have been. On the other hand, when you navigate in the direction of the flow of the river, from the source to the destination, every river bend may reveal another surprise requiring you to adjust how you would navigate the river the next time. For example, if the river branches into a narrow flow, you might not end up where you wanted to go since you have no way of anticipating the final destination.

Egress control is criticized for its initial delay in distributing labels. It is believed that this initial delay is well worth the wait as egress control is expected to result in far less need to make LIB changes after initialization. Label churn can also happen under egress control if downstream nodes need to change their granularity of labels or if an LSR goes down. Churn is expected, however, to occur far less frequently than with local control.

4.11.8 Tunneling

Tunneling is an important and powerful technique in networking; essentially it provides a means to pass foreign packets through one or more devices without interpretation of their encapsulated headers. In MPLS, tunnels may be implemented using label switched paths (LSPs) instead of traditional header encapsulation. Two labels at each end of the tunnel are used to define an LSP tunnel. Packets use an LSP to tunnel through and then "pop off" the "label stack" at the ends of the tunnel. LSR provides a very simple, natural way to tunnel. We will further discuss the use of tunneling in Chapter 6 and in the Chapter 7 discussion on Virtual Private Networks (VPNs).

4.11.9 MPLS Challenges

With every new technology come challenges. The following sections highlight the most important challenges and the current solutions that MPLS has.

4.11.9.1 Merging Streams: VC and VP Merge

As the draft architecture points out, LSR may or may not support data stream merging. Merging facilitates multicast traffic by allowing traffic destined for a particular egress node to be merged into one stream and to use the same label. This has the obvious advantage of reducing the number of labels that need to be maintained as well as requiring only a single flow of packets to traverse the network and be "fanned out" to many nodes at the end.

Merging on ATM switches presents the potential problem of interleaving cells of different packets without having any way to reassemble the packets at the egress nodes. There are three solutions for ATM vendors. They may

- explicitly not support merging,
- support Virtual Path Merge (VP Merge), or
- support Virtual Circuit Merge (VC Merge).

Virtual Path Merge (VP Merge) takes advantage of the VPI/VCI address hierarchy built into ATM. VP Merge enables multiple virtual paths to be merged and uses the VCI to distinguish between the multiple paths. VP Merge is compatible with most ATM implementations, does not require extra buffer space, and will not result in transmission delays incurred by having to reassemble packets at the ATM switch. It does, however, require that all ATM switches synchronize on the VCI space used within each VP.

On the other hand, VC Merge requires explicit buffering of cells from one packet at each ATM switch before the packet goes on to the next hop. The draft standard suggests that the end-of-frame indicator may be used to distinguish the end of the packet. VC merge nodes need only a single VPI/VCI pair since data is mapped to a single VC. Nodes that do not support merging would pass through any request they get from above and optionally obtain a VPI/VCI for traffic that they originate.

4.11.9.2 Support for Multicast Traffic

The MPLS architecture specification states that MPLS intends to support multicast routing fully. Unfortunately, at the time of this writing, most of the details are not given. It is expected that the NHLFE for a multicast label packet will contain the outgoing label and a set of output interfaces for the packet. The packet can then be distributed out one or more ports using the same label encoding.

4.11.9.3 Supporting Traceroute

Time-to-live (TTL) is a field within the IP header; it is used to limit the lifetime of a datagram within the network. When a packet is sent, the field is set to a value (often 32 or 64). As the packet traverses each router, the field is decremented. If the packet's TTL field reaches 0 before getting to the receiver, the packet is dropped and the sender is notified with an IP Internet Control Protocol (ICMP) message. TTL eliminates the routing of packets in endless loops.

Traceroute, a program to determine the route of a packet, uses a succession of packets with incrementally larger TTLs. It starts off by sending a packet with a TTL of 1; the first router throws away the packet and returns an ICMP message. Traceroute now knows the first hop of the path. It then sends a packet with a TTL of 2 and so on until the end destination is reached, recording each intermediate hop along the way.

Traceroute is a very useful tool for determining the path of IP packets. As mentioned, it depends on the time-to-live (TTL) field in IP packets to determine the path. The 5-byte ATM cell header has no knowledge of TTL; therefore, when label switching through ATM switches, there is nothing to decrement. The MPLS committee has proposed putting a TTL in any "shim" MPLS header to be used to support traceroute and to eliminate loops even across ATM switches.

A S I D E . . .

Traceroute has some inherent built-in unreliability since IP allows packets to take different routes each time they are sent. The results of a traceroute (the paths between hops) may be different, especially the later hops that are several hops away.

4.11.9.4 Loop Prevention and Avoidance

Loop prevention is an extremely important requirement of MPLS since it provides the "routing" function of the network. Routing loops waste bandwidth, exacerbate congestion, and consequently affect overall network performance. Because of ATM, the conventional TTL mechanism used in traditional routing is of limited use, leaving MPLS to devise other techniques.

The first measure to take for loop prevention is validation that every Link Switched Path (LSP) identification list that enters an LSR does not contain the LSR's own identification. (Recall that periodically LSP identification lists are exchanged to keep label tables up-to-date.) If the ID of the LSR is contained, the current labels are retained and the LSP is dropped, as it would introduce an obvious loop. Eventually the routing protocols will break the loop and send a new LSP facilitating a loop-free path change.

The second measure to take for loop prevention is a "diffusion computation" prior to updating an LSP. The MPLS architecture specification describes this as a pruning process of any upstream tree branches that would introduce a loop. It is safe to activate the new path only after a route has been completely validated by a series of neighbor queries and "OK" responses have been received. Query messages are "timed out" after a reasonable amount of time so that new routes can be introduced, even if one of the paths becomes temporarily or permanently inoperable. Temporary or permanent inoperable branches are pruned. Note that even when a branch is pruned, the upstream path remains intact, allowing for reconnection at a later time.

It is expected that more energy will be placed on loop prevention and elimination in the immediate future. As networks become larger and traffic greater, looping becomes more prevalent and problematic. Loops are especially troublesome with multicast traffic since so much data is replicated, increasing the impact of a loop. It is believed that the shim header proposed by the MPLS draft architecture specification contains a TTL first for loop prevention and second for the support of traceroute.

> ### A S I D E . . .
>
> Loop prevention is an optional feature of an LSR. Nodes that elect not to do loop prevention do not propagate loop information upstream. This may seriously limit the effectiveness of MPLS's loop prevention.

4.12 Tag Switching

Tag Switching (RFC 2105 contains an overview), a technology developed by Cisco Systems, Inc., shares many characteristics with MPLS. This is not surprising since Cisco actively participates in the MPLS standard and Tag Switching has many fundamentally strong ideas. Like MPLS, the information here is based on Internet-Drafts[3] and is therefore subject to change.

Tag Switching comes with a few new terms that are useful to know; Table 4.3 includes the most important terms used.

Tag Switching thrives on simplicity. In a nutshell, Tag Switching uses tags assigned at the network edges to route packets across a WAN network. When a packet arrives at a switch, the tag is used to index into a Tag Information Base (TIB), a database of tags that is constructed and maintained by routing protocols like OSPF. Each entry in the TIB contains an outgoing tag, an outgoing interface, and link status. When a packet comes in, the packet's tag is compared against the contents of the TIB. If there is an exact match and the link status for the outgoing interface is okay, the packet tag is changed to the outgoing tag and pushed out the outgoing interface. The power of this level of simplicity cannot be underestimated.

Tag Switching divides the routing process into two fundamental components: a *forwarding* component and a *control* component. The forwarding component uses label-swapping techniques to modify tags within headers, and the control component uses existing routing protocols to do tag binding and tag

---

3. The Internet-Draft, "Use of Tag Switching with ATM" (January 1997) by B. Davie, P. Doolan, J. Lawrence, K. McCloghrie, Y. Rekhter, E. Rosen, and G. Swallow of Cisco Systems, Inc. and the Internet-Draft, "Tag Distribution Protocol" (May 1997) by P. Doolan, B. Davie, Y. Rekhter, and E. Rosen of Cisco Systems, Inc. and D. Katz of Juniper Networks provide the background material for Tag Switching.

Table 4.3 Tag Switching Terminology

Term	Definition
Tag Information Base (TIB)	This table entity associates incoming tag with one or more subentries containing outgoing tag, interface, and other link level information.
Tag Distribution Protocol (TDP)	Inter router protocol is used to distribute and manage tags.
Tag Edge Routers (TER)	Routers located at the boundaries of the Internet perform value-added network layer services; they also apply tags. These routers must be fully capable of traditional routing and Tag Switching.
Tag Switches	These switches switch packets or cells based on tags. Many of these switches also support full layer-3 and/or layer-2 switching.

distribution. This division of labor provides Tag Switching with a flexible and powerful framework for controlling how traffic is routed while preserving existing routing environments. For instance, a conventional routing-forwarding component can be used with or to replace the label-swapping forwarding component without changing the control component.

Tag Switching utilizes existing knowledge of routing topology and the simplicity of label swapping to create an evolutionary approach to routing that will scale. For example, when ATM is in the picture, Tag Switching uses native ATM VPI/VCI pairs as the tag. Keeping technology simple and leveraging existing infrastructures cannot be underestimated as being *key* to the acceptance of a new technology.

Like MPLS, Tag Switching

- supports explicit routing.
- is complementary and works concurrently with conventional routing.
- allows for a graceful evolution of better traffic management and Internet scalability.
- has no reliance on ATM, but it does provide integration with ATM.
- is positioned to be multiprotocol, although IP is the initial focus.

- supports many forwarding granularities; for example, routing is based on the final destination (unicast or multicast), preserving existing routing environments.
- utilizes topology-based label assignment.
- allows for multipoint-to-point trees.
- relies on IP forwarding at the edge and label forwarding in core.

A S I D E . . .

Tag Switching supports ATM with VC Merge and uses Protocol Independent Multicast (PIM) for multicast label exchange. (See Chapter 6 for a discussion on PIM.)

Since the Tag Information Base (TIB) is central to Tag Switching, it deserves extra mention. The TIB is constructed based on information from routing protocols such as OSPF, BGP, or the Enhanced Interior Gateway Protocol (EIGRP). When a packet comes into a tag switch, the tag is used as an index into the TIB. If an entry in the TIB is found, the tag switch obtains one or more subentries for the tag. The outgoing tag, the outgoing interface, and other outgoing link level information are examples of information that is stored in a subentry. Routing is accomplished simply by having the tag switch replace the tag with the outgoing tag (and any outgoing link level information) and send the packet out the outgoing interface.

The tag information in Tag Switching is carried in the packet one of three ways: as a small "shim" between the layer-3 (network) and layer-2 (data link) headers, as part of the data link layer (as with ATM), or as part of the network layer header as with IPv6. Tag Switching may be implemented across any media type on a point-to-point or multipoint basis using one of these encapsulations. Note that adding even a small shim header can make a packet exceed maximum packet size. Thus Tag Switching (or MPLS, for that matter) may introduce the need for packet fragmentation.

Tag allocation within the TIB is flexible. Tags may be allocated by *downstream allocation* (egress control in MPLS terminology), *downstream allocation on demand,* or *upstream allocation* (local control in MPLS terminology). With downstream allocation, tags are created for all incoming traffic and tags are obtained for all outgoing traffic. Tag bindings are advertised to other adjacent tag switches via piggybacking on existing routing protocols or using the tag distribution protocol (TDP). Downstream on demand allocation implies that routes are distributed by the downstream switch only when a request is made by the upstream switch. Upstream allocation means that switches create tag bindings for all outgoing tags and receive bindings for incoming tags. Upstream allocation is the exact opposite of downstream allocation. Table 4.4 summarizes the tag allocation options for Tag Switching.

A S I D E . . .

The terms "downstream" and "upstream" come from describing how a river flows. Think of the Mississippi River that flows north to south through St. Louis and New Orleans. New Orleans is downstream from St. Louis, and St. Louis is upstream from New Orleans.

A N O T H E R   A S I D E . . .

Tag Switching separates interior and exterior routing. This enables border routers to maintain routing information on exterior routing, shorten the time necessary for table convergence, and reduce the size of tables and table exchanges.

It is important to note that Tag Switching attempts to allocate tags for all incoming and outgoing ports so that routing based on tags can be done. *Tag Switching does not, however, preclude conventional routing at any time; it is completely complementary.* Routes that don't have tags are simply routed using the conventional routing protocols. In fact, since the network dynamically configures

Table 4.4 Tag Switching Allocation Options

Tag Allocation Method	MPLS Terminology	Definition
downstream	egress control	Tags are allocated and distributed in the reverse direction of the flow.
downstream on demand	no equivalent	Tags are distributed in the reverse direction of the flow when requested.
upstream	local control	Tags are allocated and distributed in the direction of the flow.

tags (manual configuration is possible just like setting up static routes) after initialization, routing can take place before the tags are initialized and transparently can "switch over" to use tags once tags are in place in both directions.

Like MPLS, Tag Switching is based on the topology of the network, not on individual flows. This enables Tag Switching to take advantage of the knowledge already present in the routing tables, reduce the overall instability with dynamically changing flows, and ultimately enable the solution to scale for large networks.

Tag Switching, complementary to Cisco's NetFlow switching, provides high-performance value-added layer-3 services. QoS, customized routing paradigms based on various packet information, and business-specific policies can be used to control the packet forwarding. NetFlow switching coupled with Tag Switching goes far beyond traditional routing based exclusively on destination address.

A S I D E . . .

One issue with Tag Switching is that it does not address loop prevention. Loop prevention is difficult but very important. As mentioned previously, one can only envision how a loop might exacerbate the volume of traffic with multicast traffic!

4.13 IP Navigator

IP Navigator is technology developed by Cascade Communications, now Ascend Communications, Inc. IP Navigator has features similar to those of MPLS, yet it makes some simplifying assumptions that enable it to utilize existing technologies. Like MPLS, IP Navigator

- relies on IP forwarding at the edge and label forwarding in core.
- utilizes topology-based label assignment.
- allows for multipoint-to-point trees.
- coexists with standard ATM.
- supports multiservice networks.

IP Navigator simplifies its implementation by supporting only the OSPF protocol within interior routing domains and by extending OSPF to add QoS-type information within LSAs. In fact, IP Navigator's own Virtual Network Navigator (VNN) routing protocol is based on OSPF. IP Navigator also supports only explicit routing, making traffic engineering easy (the topology is always available), simplifying label assignments, and eliminating the chance of routing loops.

VNN offers connection-oriented routing with multiservice network integration of ATM, SMDS, and ISDN interfaces. VNN combines built-in intelligence of routing and switching to establish reliable end-to-end connections. Because VNN maintains session context, traffic engineering and customizable QoS are available. VNN corrects for the problem of network outage of any link by using the routing topology to find a detour and establish another VC. Ascend positions VNN as providing a scalable, reliable solution and a seamless integration of IP and switching.

Another important feature of IP Navigator is that it provides a solution for dynamically establishing VCs across a network. This enables IP Navigator to set up a fully connected VC mesh automatically, without tedious, error-prone, manual configuration. Once preestablished virtual paths are set, packets are able to get the benefit of switching without the need to parse through the IP header at each hop.

Ascend indicates the IP Navigator is able to provide end-to-end QoS over its switched VCs. VNN maintains session information about switched paths, enabling intelligent, dynamic load balancing and traffic engineering to meet QoS requirements. IP Navigator provides ATM-quality QoS for IP and takes advantage of existing ATM features such as larger buffers, weighted fair queuing (WFQ), rapid convergence, and rerouting provided by OSPF. In fact, IP Navigator provides the granularity to configure IP QoS on a port, route, or IP address basis. IP Navigator also fully integrates with RSVP.

IP Navigator offers Multipoint-to-point Tunneling to eliminate the need to mesh the network fully. Ascend states that its Multipoint-to-point Tunneling (patented technology) enables each edge node in the network to use a single multicast address to connect to all other switches within the network, greatly reducing the exponential scaling problem of fully meshed networks.

Finally IP Navigator supports a two-level hierarchical labeling scheme. This approach builds on OSPF's two-level area architecture that provides scalability without the added complexity of a multilevel hierarchical approach. Support of a multilevel hierarchy is expected to increase the difficulty of traffic engineering.

4.14 ARIS

Aggregate routed-based IP Switching (ARIS) is IBM Corporation's approach to layer-3 switching. At the time of this writing, the ARIS specification[4] is in IETF draft form. MPLS and ARIS have many similar characteristics, not surprising

---

4. The "ARIS Specification" (an Internet-Draft written in March 1997) is by Nancy Feldman and Arun Viswanathan.

since one of the ARIS authors is one of the authors of the MPLS architecture specification. ARIS has its own unique terminology. Table 4.5 presents the most commonly used terms. The following list is based on factual information from the ARIS draft specification. The ARIS draft specification

- maps network layer routing to link layer switched paths.
- relies on IP forwarding at the edge and label forwarding in the core.
- utilizes topology-based label assignment.
- supports IP and other network protocols.
- is able to coexist with traditional routing and ATM switching.
- provides an explicit loop prevention mechanism that is especially important for operation over ATM.
- ensures that the TTL to egress is known, allowing support of traceroute.
- allows switched paths to be attached directly or to have an endpoint at an egress node with switching occurring between intermediate nodes.
- provides both a tunneling and a hierarchical labeling scheme.
- uses VC Merge to provide multipoint-to-point trees.
- uses Ingress Control for multicast, allowing for policy control.
- provides an explicit routing option.

Once ARIS neighbors are active, they may begin to exchange Switched Path Labels (SPLs) via a simple messaged-based protocol. Table 4.6 summarizes the messages with their meaning.

ARIS allows a significant amount of flexibility with respect to what may be used as an Egress Identifier, clearly leveraging existing network information. The following may be Egress Identifiers under ARIS:

- **IPv4 address:** The standard version 4 IP address.
- **BGP next hop:** The BGP NEXT_HOP attribute may be the IP address of a BGP border router, the address of an external BGP peer.
- **OSPF Router ID:** The router ID obtained via an OSPF LSA.
- **OSPF Area Border Router:** The router ID obtained via an OSPF external link advertisement.
- **Explicit Path:** An explicitly defined source-routed path manually configured or configured based on a Dijkstra calculation with a certain metric like QoS. The explicit path identifier may be egress or ingress based.

Table 4.5 ARIS Terminology

Term	Definition
Aggregate Route-based IP Switching (ARIS)	This IBM-developed technique incorporates labels and routing functionality with switching.
Egress Identifier	This is an identifier for a path through the network.
Forwarding Information Base (FIB)	This database is used to store labels and conventional routing information.
Integrated Switch Router (ISR)	Switch augmented with routing capabilities.
Reverse Path Multicast (RPM)	This multicast set-up technique uses forwarding to upstream neighbors.
Switched Path Labels (SPL)	This label-based path runs through the network.

Table 4.6 ARIS Messaging

Message	Message Meaning
INIT	Periodic (until successful) transmission is used to establish adjacencies.
KEEP ALIVE	This maintains adjacencies by periodically sending a message.
ESTABLISH	A switched path, sent from egress ISR in reverse path multicast (RPM) is created; it is also used to establish an explicit route.
TRIGGER	When routing change has modified the network layer path to an egress, ESTABLISH message is requested.
TEARDOWN	A delete switched path(s) is retransmitted periodically until an ACKNOWLEDGE message is received.
ACKNOWLEDGE	This is a positive or negative acknowledgement to an ARIS message. INIT, TRIGGER, TEARDOWN, and ESTABLISH may receive a negative acknowledge message.

- **CIDR group list:** A manually configured group of CIR prefixes that shares common egress points.

- **Flow-based ID:** An ID based on a constant set of information (port, destination address, and source address). When a flow-based ID is used, no aggregation is possible.

- **Multicast Unique Source Group Multicast Pair:** One switched path tree per multicast pair. This is used by multicast protocols like DVMRP and PIM-DM. We will discuss these protocols further in Chapter 6.

When a node supports ARIS, the Forwarding Information Base (FIB) is extended to associate entries with egress identifiers. ARIS allows egress identifiers to be shared by multiple router entries, greatly reducing the amount of table space required. The savings are especially apparent with explicit routing since even a long string of short labels replicated many times can consume a lot of memory!

Router table lookup is still done by using the longest prefix match, as with conventional routing. If there is a switched path, then the switched path is used; if there is no switched path, the next hop is used. This provides complete transparency and mixing with traditional routing. If a route is associated with both an aggregate switched path and an individual switched path, the longer prefix match is used to make the final routing decision.

An ISR is required to decrement TTL. When the next hop is an ATM switch, the forwarding ISR should account for ATM's lack of TTL knowledge by subtracting an additional one. Unfortunately a series of ATM switches becomes an indistinguishable "cloud" when doing a traceroute across the path. Like conventional routers, ISRs discard packets when the TTL goes to zero.

Loop prevention with ARIS is optional. `ESTABLISH` messages containing the ISR itself are deleted, preventing an obvious loop. The draft ARIS specification states that if an ISR modifies a network layer path, it must not splice the upstream switched paths to the new downstream switched path until it forwards the new ISR list to upstream ISRs via establish messages and it receives `ACKNOWLEDGE` messages confirming the switch. By default, an ISR supports loop prevention.

IP multicast is supported under ARIS by initiating the multicast from the ingress (root) node forming a point-to-multipoint switched path tree. The root of the tree transmits the established Reverse Path Multicast (RPM) to all child links as determined by the multicast FIB. During this process all ISRs verify the message and, if loop prevention is configured, use the router path object to ensure that a loop-free path is created. Both Distance Vector Multicast Routing Protocol (DVMRP) and Dense Mode Protocol-Independent Multicast (PIM-DM) may be used as egress identifiers. In addition, DVMRP tunnels are supported. (See Chapter 6 for more information on multicast protocols.) Once the multicast tree is established, multicast traffic is carried from the ingress ISR to all egress ISRs using multicast switching.

Many routing protocols support load balancing by establishing different paths with different associated metrics. Under ARIS, multiple paths are supported by sending many `ESTABLISH` messages upstream, preserving the switched paths to the egress ISR with different costs. ISRs can also aggregate into one or drop all but one path. If aggregation is chosen, the switching hardware becomes responsible for load balancing.

4.15 Cell Switched Routers (CSR)

The Cell Switch Router (CSR) technology developed by Toshiba Corporation focuses on routing IP over high-speed ATM backbones. This approach has the immediate gain of increased performance and the long-term gain of voice, video, and QoS for IP. CSR technology offers the following:

- **High performance:** ATM switches are able to process millions of packets per second.
- **Cost effectiveness:** Toshiba claims that CSR offers a 20-times-performance gain over legacy routers.
- **Real-time support:** CSRs comply with IETF-based RSVP and IP multicast.
- **Interoperability:** The CSR device interoperates with standard protocols like ATM (UNI 3.0/3.1).
- **Multiple protocol support:** Although CSR is positioned to support IP first, it has been designed to support IPX and other future protocols.

Essentially CSR works by using the "route once, switch many" paradigm. CSR assumes a default path via routers and, based on monitoring individual flows, dynamically creates cut-through switched paths. Instead of using the traditional VPI/VCI pair at each hop, CSR uses a Virtual Circuit ID (VCID) to bind the source and destination address at each hop. The upstream CSR allocates the bindings, and like RSVP, the state of a VC must continually be refreshed as

VCIDs time out. Thus CSR maintains flows in a *soft state*[5] sense and uses Flow Attribute Notification Protocol (FANP) to exchange VCID bindings.

The major criticism of CSR is that dynamically defined fine grain flows (like those in IP Switching) may scale in a LAN but not in the WAN. One can only imagine how many short- and long-term flows are established across the core of the Internet on any given day. How unpredictable the flows are! Is CSR worth the complexity in the core, or should we just stick to topology-driven approaches like Tag Switching in the core? Based on today's data, topology-driven approaches look good. Perhaps though, CSR is a good fit for a corporate LAN.

4.16 IP Switching

IP Switching (a solution developed by Ipsilon Corporation, now Nokia) provides an alternative to routing all multihop packets. IP Switching is similar to Toshiba's Cell Switch Router (CSR) technique. Like CSR, IP Switching converts IP packets into ATM cells and then sends them over an existing ATM virtual channel. At the end of the channel, the cells are reconverted to packets and are locally switched to their final destination, eliminating the intermediate routing decisions necessary at each hop along the way.

IP Switching is intended to take advantage of connection-oriented, high speed, scalable ATM switching. In the future it will provide a means to support many services, such as voice and video. IP Switching does not use end-to-end signaling or resolve IP addresses to ATM addresses; this greatly reduces the overhead of using ATM. Because IP Switching relies on IP routing, packets can be dynamically routed around any network failure without the overhead of reestablishing an ATM connection via a code-intensive signaling operation.

IP Switching uses a simple protocol, General Switch Management Protocol (GSMP), to provide control between an IP switch controller to provide standard IP routing capabilities and the ATM switch core. Because the IP switch control is integrated into the same ATM switch device, the ATM switching core must be modified.

Interdevice communication is provided by Ipsilon's flow management protocol (IFMP) to associate flows with unidirectional virtual circuits. In a sense IFMP is a simple signaling protocol that decides whether a packet should be switched based on the longevity of the communication. Because IP Switching

---

5. "Soft state" refers to a state that must continuously be refreshed, otherwise the state times out and is lost. Resource ReSerVation Protocol (RSVP) discussed in the next chapter is also a soft state protocol.

provides standard routing, many short-lived packets are simply routed in the traditional sense.

A S I D E . . .

Coming up with an algorithm to determine when a flow is short-lived and when to cut over to IP Switching is difficult. A good algorithm invariably requires some recording of the flow state at intermediate hops. Flow state requires memory and initial setup.

IP Switching and MPLS share many of the same concerns such as packet reordering around the ingress and egress of the switched path. However, it does not appear that IP Switching provides a solution for this problem as VC Merge does. TTL is included in the flow identifier and is decremented along the switch path, resulting in a TTL value equal to the value it would have if it were forwarded hop-by-hop. Packets with a TTL of 0 are purged from the network, enabling tools like traceroute to see the full ATM switched path rather than a nebulous cloud.

IP Switching fully supports IP multicast and policy-based and contract-based QoS. IP multicast is supported in IP switching using "off-the-shelf" Internet Group Management Protocol (IGMP). IP Switches can make a policy-based QoS decision based on flow classification that is further based on fields within the packet header. For example, protocol, source address, destination address, source port, destination port, and protocol type may be used to distinguish how a particular flow is managed. This provides a way to customize and prioritize (like layer-4 switching) packet flows. Contract-based QoS uses the standard Resource ReSerVation Protocol (RSVP); a reservation may be accepted or denied by each switch along the path using RSVP *flowspec*.

There are a few drawbacks to IP Switching:

- The solution requires ATM that might not already be deployed in the LAN. Introducing ATM and having the knowledge base to support ATM can be expensive.

- Since this approach sets up fine-grain flows, it may not scale well for the WAN. The initial setup of the virtual channel (unless one exists) can be slow.

- The solution is proprietary, which may make it difficult to use equipment from many different vendors.

- The solution requires change to existing ATM switches and does not provide any traffic management.

An advantage of this approach is that the routing decision is made only once, and a router table lookup is not necessary for every subsequent packet. Since routers control the path instead of the flows, routing loops can be eliminated. IP Switching results in line-speed loop-free switching of IP data. It is questionable, though, with the advent of line-speed layer-3 switches whether these advantages are sufficient to warrant investment into this approach. Refer to RFC 1953 and 1987 for more information on IP Switching.

A S I D E . . .

A Virtual Channel (VC) does not always have to be set up when using IP Switching; it is usually set up only when a "flow" is "long lived."

4.17 Setting Expectations

Line-speed routing (layer-3 switches) and label-based switching are two very powerful technologies that will significantly improve our ability to scale and grow networks. Neither technology is a panacea for network delay, but both clearly raise the bar of what is possible and required to support our networks of tomorrow.

COS and policy-based routing are key benefits of many line-speed routing solutions. Being able to forward traffic based on classification will facilitate better response time for critical applications and data. COS is especially important in connectionless Ethernet environments where bandwidth have been on a first come, first served basis for many years.

Multiservice, flow classification, traffic engineering, explicit routing, service differentiation, and IP QoS (based on ATM) are all key characteristics of MPLS. They address network scaling and the ability to provide network services across the same infrastructure. Virtual Private Networks (VPNs), capable of real-time traffic across a shared Internet, may become a reality largely due to the advent of MPLS.

It is important always to remember that *applications drive networking.* It is our demand for more and more distributed data, voice, and video that drives the need for better, bigger networks that offer more integrated services. Although multilayer switching will not result in instantaneous data acquisition across the network, the switching technologies are expected to facilitate continuous network growth of more and more distributed, diverse information.

4.18 Conclusions

The world is rich with switching solutions:

- Layers 2, 3 and 4 switches provide intelligent line-speed routing and bridging.
- MPOA, IP Switching, and Cell Switched Routers provide ATM-based, flow-driven, cut-through switching.
- Fast IP offers cut-through LAN switching.
- MPLS, ARIS, IP Navigator, and Tag Switching introduce label-based, topology-driven switching.

Initially, switching was exclusively positioned at improving the performance of the network. Layer "x" switching goes beyond performance by adding significant intelligence to how networks function. Both wire-speed route and label switching enable increased control over the forwarding process. Integrated COS, ATM-based QoS, and other ways to provide differential services open many new opportunities for networks. Switching enables us to provide more predictable, reliable, and scalable solutions for the future.

Topology-based label switching solutions scale better and are better suited for the WAN than flow-based solutions; these are well positioned for the LAN. Both, however, reduce the amount of per-packet processing necessary once a route is known.

Multilayer switching is helping to bring together the LAN and the WAN. We are seeing the LAN and WAN boundaries blur as more and more information becomes global, and multilayer switching techniques *combine* the best features of the proven technologies of yesterday to lay down a stronger basis for tomorrow's scalable solutions. It wasn't all that long ago that ATM and IP were discrete solutions; now we are seeing the solutions integrating, allowing both technologies to progress further than the original goals of either technology.

CHAPTER 5

Guaranteed Delivery

5.1 Introduction

When you drop a letter in the mailbox, you expect it eventually to get to its addressed destination. First class service takes two to three days to go between two points in the United States; second and third classes take more time. International mail generally takes even longer. Ordinary mail is economical and rarely gets lost, but it offers no guarantees with respect to delivery. Like e-mail, ordinary mail is a best-effort service.

Services like Federal Express, United Parcel Service, AirBorne, and USPS Express Mail offer guaranteed delivery.[1] Common options of these services are next day delivery, next morning delivery, and Saturday delivery. Federal Express and United Parcel Service even provide a Web-based tracking tool so that you can track your package through one or more intermediate destinations en route to its final destination. These services are instrumental to businesses that must have fast, guaranteed delivery of materials between two geographically distributed sites.

Guaranteed delivery requires a lot of special handling and tracking. Most delivery service vendors use barcodes and automated sorters to route packages quickly; some vendors have a dedicated fleet of planes at major distribution sites waiting to take off as soon as the nightly sorting is complete. Express delivery costs substantially more than ordinary mail in order to cover the cost of the extensive delivery infrastructure and tracking. Guaranteed delivery, therefore, is not for all letters or packages; it simply would not be economical.

---

1. It is important to realize that guarantees are not always based on reservations and circuit setup like ATM. Federal Express, for example, "guarantees" that they have sufficient overcapacity so they can (almost) always meet the demand. In networking we call this "overprovisioning." Read further in the chapter for more detail.

Our current Internet is based on a best-effort packet system, not all that different from any postal service except for package fragmentation. When you send an e-mail or a file, it gets broken up into a series of packets that go from intermediate hop to hop en route to their final destination where the packets are reassembled into the original e-mail or file and delivered to the recipient. Your data transfer can take seconds, minutes, hours, or days, depending on the current traffic traversing the Internet to your data's destination.

Unfortunately today there isn't any alternative to the best-effort model within the Internet. Yes, you could put your data on a tape or on a series of diskettes and use a special delivery service—but what if you need the turn-around to be within an hour or a few minutes? Are you willing to have a voice conversation that is susceptible to intermittent Internet delays caused by congestion? How about an interactive video with sound and picture delays? With only best-effort service, these types of delays are inevitable.

This chapter is about guaranteed delivery—delivery of all forms of data within bounded delays. First we will gain an understanding of delay, resource sharing, and the mechanics of traffic management. We will then look at the solutions provided by the ATM Forum and the IETF. We will explore the ATM's Quality of Service (QoS) model and solutions provided by the IETF to include the Integrated Services Architecture (ISA) and Resource ReSerVation Protocol (RSVP). We will conclude with setting realistic expectations over the next few years for guaranteed delivery.

5.2 Key Solutions Offered

Guaranteed delivery or higher-priority delivery provides a badly needed alternative to the best-effort networks of today. In order for networks to continue to grow, provide new service needs, and expand to service real-time applications, networks must provide mechanisms that ensure delivery within sensible bounds or offer preferential treatment to certain traffic.

Networks must manage their resources in order to provide *differentiated services*. (Differentiated service refers to providing service alternatives, such as first, business, and coach classes in the airline industry.) By managing network resources, the network infrastructure can prioritize some traffic, allocate *dedicated* (not shared) bandwidth to other traffic, and continue to support best-effort traffic with the remaining bandwidth. Supporting best-effort traffic *complements* supporting prioritized traffic as it enables network providers to "fill in" the bandwidth with best-effort traffic when dedicated demands are low.

Both the ATM Forum and the IETF have solutions for providing differentiated traffic services. The ATM Forum's efforts are more mature than the IETF's solutions since ATM was built from the ground up with integrated QoS. Both solution sets share the same conceptual base of traffic management and similar goals of support of multiple types of traffic while maintaining their own unique features. It is expected that the emerging solutions within the next few years will be a combination and integration of the best ideas from both efforts.

There is a lot to guaranteed delivery. It is important to understand where network delays are, what needs to be shared, how sharing is accomplished, and how resources are managed. This chapter covers all of this, giving you the background of QoS and the current working solution sets.

5.3 When Does Delay Matter?

Delay matters only for *interactive* communication. If someone is not waiting for a graphic to download, watching a video clip, or participating in a voice conversation, network delay is not an issue. It is often thought that all video and voice require special network treatment—*not true!* Only real-time video (that which you are sitting in front of) and interactive voice (when you are having a conversation) are delay-sensitive. Non-real-time video and recorded voice can incur network delay.

5.4 What Causes Delay, Anyway?

Before we get too involved in understanding QoS, Class of Service (COS), and service classes, it is important to understand where the network delays are. This quick survey enables us to pinpoint the "delay" areas where we should focus energy. Delay is caused by many factors; we can get a lot more specific than just claiming "The network is so slow!"—not that anyone has ever heard that before. . . .

The total cause of delay is somewhat abstract. In an effort to make delay more visible, we will build upon a simple sample application. This will enable us to understand better the notion of application delay and to provide a framework on which to introduce the language of QoS. Table 5.1 contains definitions of terms that are used when discussing network delay. Take a moment to study the table.

Let's start with a simple application and data source, namely your favorite Web browser running on a common PC. We'll assume that the browser is installed and that it is capable of supporting multiple instantiations at the same

Table 5.1 The Language of Network Delay

Term	Definition
congestion	Heavy traffic volumes result in a backlog of packets at various places in the network. Often places of congestion are referred to as *congestion points*.
contention	Two or more processes (or network sessions) compete for the same shared resource—the more processes competing, the higher the level of contention.
delay	This is the waiting time between transmitting data at one point in the network and receiving the data at its final destination. Sometimes we talk of *round-trip delay*, which refers to sending the data to a node and receiving a response from that node, commonly done when "pinging" a node.
latency	The layman's definition is that latency is an alternative term meaning the same thing as delay. A more exact definition is that "latent" means "hidden." Everyone know that bigger files and packets take longer to transfer, but as you reduce the packet size to zero, the time it takes for transfer does not go to zero. What is left (speed of light, propagation delay, forwarding delay, and so on) is the latency (the hidden component of delay, the delay intrinsic to the network itself, not related to packet size).
response time	This is the total amount of time it takes to send data to a node (for example, a Web server) in the network and receive a response.

time on the same machine. Now pretend to bring up the browser and first view a *local* (not a networked) HTML file that you just happen to have on your hard drive. The performance of viewing the HTML file depends largely on the *operating system* (O/S) you are running, the *processing power* of your machine, the overall amount of system *memory for caching* the file, and any *other applications* concurrently running on the system. The O/S needs to schedule the applications and arbitrate system resources. It is largely bounded by the speed at which it runs (processing power) and the amount of resources (memory, disk speed, and disk space for caching, for example). Thus the first thing to note is that *even without a network* there are a number of local factors that can cause delay. Before we bring the network into the picture, let's focus a bit more on concurrency. Figure 5.1 illustrates the components that must be shared across multiple applications running within a PC.

While you are cruising through your HTML document, play a ".WAV" sound file and a ".AVI" video clip. Pick large sound files and video clips so that you can get the three applications running concurrently. Keep adding instantiations of the ".WAV" and ".AVI" files until you start to see delays. The actual number of concurrent applications that you can run before you see noticeable delays will again depend largely on the processing power of your machine, its O/S, its memory, its caching scheme, and the number and demand of your concurrent applications. All applications must *share* between a finite pool of resources; sharing is the key component of delay, especially as we introduce networking.

Now let's introduce a very simple network, consisting of a Web, a server, and your PC. The two machines will be connected via an Ethernet hub (see Figure 5.2). Now all data (video clips, sound files, and text) will be embedded in Web pages and downloaded from the simple Web server.

The simple network introduces another delay—the network itself. It adds media propagation delay (bits can travel only so fast over a wire[2]) and general

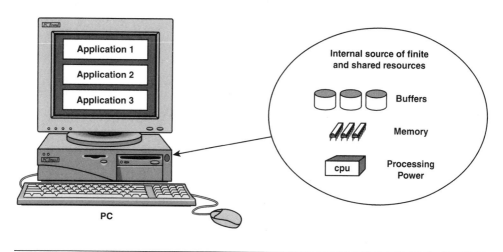

Figure 5.1 Sharing of resources across multiple concurrent applications running within a PC

---

2. As mentioned in Chapter 1, the speed of light in fibre and electrical delay in copper are two delays that we cannot eliminate. For example, the speed of light in fibre is about 2/3 the speed of light in a vacuum, or about 200,000 km/sec. This results in a delay of about 5 ms for each 1000 km traveled.

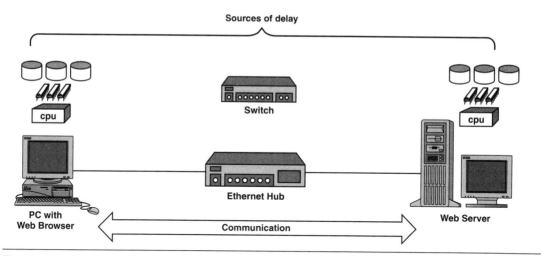

Figure 5.2 Simple network with multiple sources of overall delay

network protocol (in our case, IP) delay. One generic network protocol delay is the general "packetizing" delay caused by breaking data into chunks at one end and reconstructing the data at the other end. The larger the packet, the bigger the theoretical effort to packetize the data. Recall that one of ATM's claimed benefits is that ATM cells are quite small (only 53 bytes), so packetization delay is small.

Data loss and data corruption also cause network delay. What happens when a congested Internet router drops packets due to insufficient buffers for incoming data? What happens when data gets corrupted in the network? Loss and corruption are treated identically by TCP; it "backs off" and packets are resent causing more network traffic and delays.

Remember, too, that the network is not a static entity. Links go up and down causing data to be rerouted and delayed. When a router goes down, the network topology must account for this and attempt to find an alternative path. When a router *suddenly* goes down, all of the traffic it was currently processing often has to be retransmitted via another route.

Network serialization is another delay. Because we are using a simple Ethernet hub in our example, all data transfer is essentially *serialized.* Ethernet is a shared, first-come, first-served technology that can allow only a single instance of communication at any given time. Things aren't so bad in our network because network sharing is limited to two PCs. What happens, though, when we add many users to our hub? We get more contention and longer delays.

Ethernet LAN switches provide an effective means for mitigating the delays by providing separate Ethernet segments for one or more network devices. Still, even with switching the Web server can become a bottleneck since it is taking multiple hits from many users at once. In fact, in some cases performance to the server may be worse with switching since the server can no longer hide behind the serialization of the network; as with the switch, the server is bombarded with many requests in parallel.

A S I D E . . .

LAN switching uses a hierarchy of pipes to address the capacity of the network. Having a 10 Mbps connection to the desktop and a 100 Mbps connection to the server is common today. Gigabit Ethernet (1000 Mbps) adds the next extension to the Ethernet hierarchy.

All right, let's extend our network to the next step—multiple subnets (see Figure 5.3). Our Web server is on the other side of a router, and communication must now traverse multiple network interconnection devices. Our instantiation of applications must contend with delays caused by sharing at the local

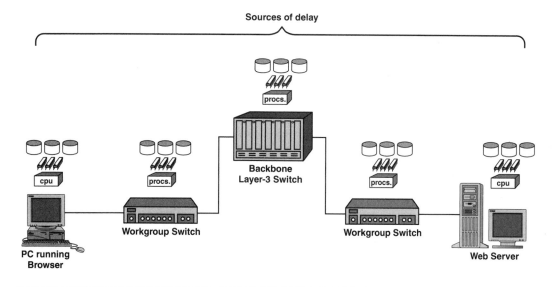

Figure 5.3 Simple subnetted network showing multiple sources of possible delay

system other applications, the local hub or switch to which the system is connected, a router, the local hub or switch servicing the Web server, and the Web server itself. All of these devices have a finite amount of processing power and memory for buffers and caching. In addition the network adds propagation delay and *queuing delay.* Because the network services other network devices and users, requests must be queued when demand exceeds the capacity of the network.

We have one more level of networking to introduce: the WAN (see Figure 5.4). Now our Web server is on the other side of some WAN cloud, and we have

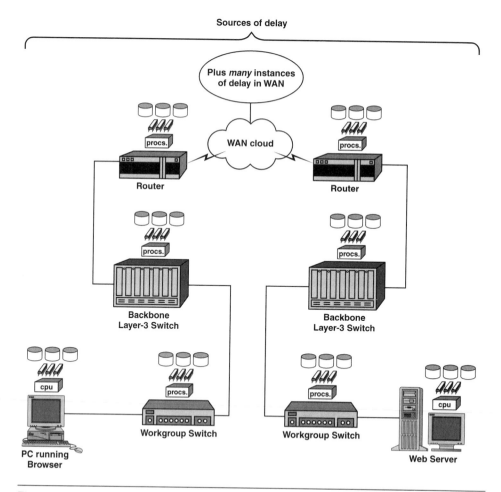

Figure 5.4 Communication going across two LANs and WAN showing some of the many sources of delay

to contend with our extended network, the external router, the WAN cloud itself, and the extended network on the other side of the cloud. All of these devices have their own set of limited resources that must be shared to service your application needs.

The WAN is often the biggest factor of network delay; some of this delay is the inherent propagation delay caused by distance. Locally it is quite simple and relatively inexpensive to fatten the pipes. Usually the local network administrator has control of the local cabling and network configuration. Increasing the capacity of WAN pipes is, however, often prohibitively expensive, and when you are sharing the network with other Internet users, you can expect delays. Less sharing, less network activity, and fatter pipes mean fewer delays; it is as simple as that, and this is about as good as it gets with exclusively best-effort, first-come, first-served networking.

5.5 Resource Sharing

Networking is all about resource sharing. Since resources are finite, resource management is fundamental to providing a predictable service level across a network. The current Internet model that exclusively provides a best-effort, first-come, first-served "free-for-all" is incongruous with providing a predictable service level. This isn't to say that best-effort service and a great infrastructure aren't needed—they are! Performance on the Internet, however, can be wildly unpredictable, and it can be difficult (if not impossible) to make any service-level guarantee with confidence.

There are three questions that come to mind when thinking about resource sharing in a network:

1. What level of resource sharing is important for our networks?
2. What are the applications that require guaranteed service?
3. How do we tune our networks to work well for multiple application requirements?

First, best-effort service is a fundamental requirement of any resource-sharing solution. Best-effort service is responsible for delivering large volumes of data every second on the Internet. Just as it would be prohibitively expensive to send and track all mail using a guaranteed delivery service, it would be astronomically expensive to send and track all data on the Internet. Besides, as previously mentioned, best-effort service can be used to "fill-in" unused bandwidth when there are lulls in guaranteed delivery traffic.

Second, different types of data have different types of service-level requirements. Ordinary data transmission is least sensitive to delay and bandwidth constraints; therefore it works well in a best-effort network. Users have grown accustomed to doing data transmission in the background knowing that the transfer will eventually happen. However, waiting for an HTML page to download *interactively* can indeed be frustrating. Interactive voice and real-time video have tighter constraints, largely because of their real-time nature. Having intermittent pauses in a conversation or real-time video transmission is annoying, if not plain unacceptable. In addition, some noninteractive data transmissions also need to be timely.

Interactive voice doesn't require a lot of bandwidth, but it is particularly sensitive to too much *jitter*, that is, delays in the network that cause a stream of data to arrive at an uneven rate. In the case of voice, a continuous conversation experiencing network jitter will contain instances of voice delay, not allowing for a smooth, real-time conversation.

Real-time video is delay- *and* bandwidth-sensitive. Unlike interactive voice, real-time video requires significant bandwidth and results in poor quality playback when bandwidth is constrained. Compression can help to some degree (used for voice as well), and buffering at end points can be used to "smooth out" transmissions. Nonetheless sending real-time video at peak network usage can be less than desirable over a best-effort infrastructure.

5.6 Overprovision, Precedence, Dedicated Resource

Essentially there are three solutions that can be used to reduce network delay. Each of the three solutions comes with a different probability of delay, and at a different cost. The chance of delay and the overall cost are often location-sensitive; for example solutions in the WAN tend to be far more costly to implement. They can be used in combination with one another.

The first technique is to *overprovision* the network. Simply stated, this means to throw bandwidth at the problem. If the LAN is slow, go from 10 Mbps Ethernet to 100 Mbps Ethernet. The basic idea here is simple: Bigger roads means less congestion and better performance. This is the driveway, country road, divided highway, and superhighway way of thinking: *Find out where your bottlenecks are, get out the bulldozer, and add more lanes.*

Overprovisioning can result in better performing networks: If you have a link that is highly utilized, increasing the size of the link may mitigate your problem (at least temporarily). Creating a hierarchy of bandwidth—using Gigabit

Ethernet at the backbone, Fast Ethernet at servers and workstation switches, and standard Ethernet at the desktop (1000/100/10)—is often used when setting up a LAN.

Overprovisioning can, however, shift the location of the bottleneck. Take the classic example of a simple hub servicing multiple users; install a LAN switch. Now communication between the users is great, but communication to the shared server is worse! By reducing the overall network contention, we have opened the server to being literally bombarded with requests. So in addition to moving to switching, a server upgrade (or perhaps use of multiple servers) is required.

In the LAN environment overprovisioning is widely used; in the WAN environment, where overprovisioning is costly, it is not. Having extra, unused bandwidth between network spikes is all right in the LAN, but not in the WAN where resources are precious and expensive. Overprovisioning is not a cost-effective WAN solution as it might be in the LAN. Even in the LAN, overprovisioning cannot provide an ironclad service-level guarantee, although it can be used to reduce substantially the probability of excessive delay.

The second technique to reduce network delay is the introduction of network *precedence*—the express lanes in the grocery store, the commuter lanes on the highway. By giving certain traffic precedence over other traffic, you can increase the overall response time for higher-priority traffic. Rather than having a single first-in, first-out (FIFO) queue at a network interconnection device, your network device may sort traffic into one of several queues based on some marking within the data. Certain queues have precedence over others so that higher-priority traffic experiences less delay. This powerful technique is appropriate for both the LAN and the WAN.

Note that as with use of overprovisioning, network delay cannot be guaranteed with precedence. It is expected that delay will be less than that of best-effort, but precedence still relies on shared resources. Whenever communication shares resources, it is subject to data spikes and bursts of other users; therefore delay is definitely going to happen. Precedence is appropriate for providing priority (good) service.

Who sets precedence is another consideration. Does the network set the precedence? How does the network know what traffic to prioritize? Do applications set the precedence? If applications set the precedence, will they tend to hog bandwidth, even when idle? Or is it a combination of the network and the application? Is there a central network policy for precedence? These are important considerations of any precedence scheme. Since Chapter 7 discusses network policy, we won't get into it here.

The last technique is to assign a *dedicated resource* for a communication flow. This technique is more expensive than using precedence, because flows must be managed and idle times in a communication flow cannot be used by other traffic. Having a dedicated resource does, however, result in the most predictable performance and therefore is appropriate for guaranteed (premium) service. Providing dedicated resources implies a connection-oriented network infrastructure as provided by ATM and our favorite telephone network. This technique is applicable to the WAN and the LAN.

One important point about service is that *better service costs more to deliver.* Let's go through best-effort service, traffic-precedence service, and dedicated-resource service—from least expensive to most expensive.

1. With best-effort service, all traffic is treated the same. When traffic becomes congested and buffers start to overflow, routers just drop the traffic. TCP detects the data loss and backs off. The user notices the delay when the network is busy.

2. With traffic precedence, applications and/or the network must mark traffic. Network devices must sort traffic based on precedence and be synchronized with respect to how traffic is sorted. Traffic precedence requires more management.

3. Dedicated-resource service requires that communication be prenegotiated prior to happening.

With ATM, signaling is used to set up a connection even before a byte is transmitted. The advantage of having signaling is that it allows ATM to choose a path that satisfies the service level required and to be able to offer a service-level guarantee since the resources are allocated for exclusive use by that communication session. The disadvantages of signaling are that the resources cannot be shared, it takes time to set up the connection, and intermediate switches must maintain state of the connection. It is not surprising then that *the more formal the service level, the more expensive the service.*

5.7 The Guaranteed Reservation Paradox

When you make a reservation at a restaurant, you are allocated a table for a certain period of time commencing at a certain time. This table is for your exclusive use during that time. If someone else comes into the restaurant without a reservation and your reserved table is the only free table, the customer must wait for another table to become available (as your reservation is honored). In essence the customer is denied immediate service.

Reservations in networks work in a similar way. If you reserve bandwidth for one user, you must deny the bandwidth for use by other users. The only way to guarantee that no one is refused service is to create a network that can satisfy the demand at every peak need. And, if you can do this, then why do you need reservations, anyway? As ugly as it may sound, *service guarantees come with service denial—plain and simple.*

5.8 Quality of Service (QoS) Basics

Now that we understand the sources of delay and resource sharing, let's delve into the technologies that provide the solution set for delivering QoS. We will start by going through the vocabulary of QoS and the general requirements of providing a QoS guarantee across a network. This discussion will prepare us for the next section where we'll dig into the fundamentals of traffic management before we examine the two solution sets provided by the ATM Forum and the IETF, respectively. Table 5.2 provides many of the important concepts that serve as our base for QoS. Take time to review these definitions, as they will be used throughout this chapter.

5.8.1 What is QoS, Anyway?

QoS is *an overall measurement of the service quality based on certain key parameters.* When we pick up a telephone and make a call, we expect the conversation to be clear, crisp, and without delay. We also expect the call to connect within a reasonable amount of time (seconds) or to be notified with a tone that the line is in use.

Networking requires a certain QoS to be effective. Error-free transmission and reasonable response time are fundamental service requirements of our best-effort Internet. Use of the Internet for interactive voice and real-time video requires more stringent levels of QoS. As mentioned previously, certain types of transmission, namely interactive voice and real-time video, require minimal delay. Too much jitter with voice transmission or too little bandwidth with real-time video transmission can result in unacceptable communication on the network. Minimizing jitter for interactive voice and ensuring sufficient bandwidth for real-time video are fundamental requirements of providing interactive voice and real-time video services on the network.

Generally speaking, providing any level of QoS better than best-effort requires regulated and managed resource sharing across the network. For example, if you want to connect points A and B and provide guaranteed service between those two points (end-to-end), each of the devices and any interconnection devices between them must initially have the required resources and

Table 5.2 Base QoS Definitions

QoS and Related Terms	Definition
Class of Service (COS)	This priority scheme divides traffic into two or more service classes depending on one or more attributes of each packet. Various queuing techniques are used to ensure that certain classes experience higher priority than other classes.
Coarse-grained QoS	This QoS takes into account only generalized packet or flow characteristics. It requires less state information (smaller tables) and provides less customized services, often with weaker guarantees than a finer-grained QoS.
Call Admission Control (CAC)	This process within each switch determines whether to accept or reject a connection during the initial and any subsequent renegotiation phases of establishing a service-level agreement.
Differentiated Services (DS)	This collection of two or more communication options provides different options and features.
Fine-grained QoS	Fine-grained QoS takes into account very specific packet or flow characteristics. It requires more state information (stored in tables) but provides customized services, often with strong guarantees.
First-In, First-Out (FIFO)	FIFO is a very simple queuing technique where packets are queued based exclusively on time of arrival. When the queue is full, packets at the end experience the maximum delay. FIFO is often used in best-effort networks.
Integrated Services Architecture (ISA)	ISA is a suite of IETF standards that define how QoS will be achieved over IP networks. RFC 1633 provides an overview of this suite.
QoS (Quality of Service)	QoS is an overall measurement of service quality based on certain key parameters. In the ATM world,

continued

Table 5.2 Base QoS Definitions (continued)

QoS and Related Terms	Definition
	Cell Error Ratio (CER), Cell Transfer Delay (CTD), and Mean Cell Transfer Delay (MCTD) are three attributes used to measure QoS.
Random Early Detection (RED)	This TCP/IP technique purposefully drops packets (or takes some other congestion-related action) on a random basis as a link approaches saturation. *No packets are discarded until the link is saturated, and the buffers are close to overflowing.* This technique is used to prevent network congestion.
Service Contract	This prenegotiated agreement defines the communication that a certain flow can be expected to achieve. A service contract may go end-to-end or span a single hop.
Type of Service (TOS)	This IP-specific precedence information field is found within IP packets, although it is not currently used in most networks.
Priority Queuing (PQ)	PQ is a simple, bucket-based queuing technique that categorizes traffic into buckets; it always transmits data from the highest-priority bucket that has data waiting.
Weighted Fair Queuing (WFQ)	This sophisticated, popular queuing technique is designed to minimize delay for priority packets and to keep overall queue sizes low.

reserve the resources for your communication needs (refer to Figure 5.4). We often call this end-to-end agreement a *service contract.* If you want to use precedence, a policy must be in place to administer access to the network and to be distributed across the network.

When we talk about QoS, we often talk about *fine-grained* and *course-grained* QoS. Generally speaking, fine-grained QoS guarantees require more state information across the network and more management to ensure quality; consequently it is more expensive than course-grained QoS.

One type of course-grained QoS that is provided by many switch vendors is Class of Service (COS). It uses priority queuing (PQ) and either implicit or explicit packet marking to give certain traffic precedence over other traffic. Within the network packets may be marked explicitly or implicitly by using attributes such as packet type or well-known port number (for example, HTTP). Although COS cannot provide a service-level guarantee, it can provide a service that probably gives a certain (that is, better) service level most of the time. Often this provides an acceptable solution that is far less expensive than providing a dedicated link.

There are many queuing techniques used to provide COS: Weighted Fair Queuing (WFQ) and Weighted Round-Robin Queuing (WRQ) are commonly used within today's switch hardware. We will talk more about WFQ in a later section since this technique is particularly popular in switching solutions.

Explicit packet marking is somewhat controversial. Even today, the Type of Service (TOS) bits found within every IP packet travel across the network completely unused. Packet marking does raise questions, however:

- Where should packet marking take place? Should network packets be marked by the sender, the network, or both the sender and the network? After packets are marked where should packets be unmarked?

- Does the network really know how to prioritize the traffic coming from the applications?

- Given free rein, wouldn't the applications just choose to send everything with the highest priority, discounting any prioritization scheme?

- Although ATM and frame relay implicitly tag data, where do you tag Ethernet data?

We have already discussed in detail MPLS; later in this chapter we will discuss other packet marking developments that have been proposed. We will also cover WinSock 2, an Application Programming Interface (API) for client/ server communication. WinSock 2 provides optional fields that enable an application to *specify* a required QoS—a first (albeit small) step in the right direction of actually *receiving* a QoS.

Providing a QoS that guarantees a service level requires prenegotiation of the service level and traffic management during the communication to ensure that the service level is maintained. In the case of ATM, a service request is signaled across the network. At each switch in the network the Call Admission Control (CAC) that controls the resources for the switch decides whether to accept or reject the request. Accepted requests are recorded and managed.

Providing guaranteed QoS requires setup, dedicated resources (which go idle when unused by the session), and management. Guaranteed QoS is expensive.

Another technique for achieving a level of QoS is devoting a dedicated infrastructure to higher-priority traffic. Although this is logically equivalent to having different mail services like the U.S. Mail, FedEx, UPS, and AirBorne, it is important to remember one key point already stated: Combining priority service with best-effort service has the advantage of getting better utilization of bandwidth. Idle bandwidth is simply filled in with best-effort traffic.

A S I D E . . .

Compression is a technique that minimizes network use by decreasing the amount of data sent. There are various "lossless" compression algorithms that compress data without losing it. Compression is a valuable tool for achieving acceptable levels of QoS with interactive voice and real-time video.

The best QoS agreement is end-to-end. Since they require coordination across two or more network devices,

QoS must be synchronized across the network from end-to-end. Having four of five network devices set up a certain QoS for a flow does not provide a service-level guarantee. Providing an end-to-end agreement is a big challenge.

Distributed solutions are expensive to build, technically challenging, and difficult to manage. Scaling of distributed solutions is always an issue. Sometimes having an end-to-end agreement is not possible and/or affordable. It may be possible to have a QoS agreement made between only two intermediate points of a communication session. It is expected that we will see *partial link* service agreements (or guarantees between certain destinations only) as QoS agreements become available from service providers.

A N O T H E R   A S I D E . . .

It is important to realize that providing a QoS guarantee across a connection will not make up for inadequate bandwidth. If you establish a marginal connection (for example, 9.6 Mbps) to your ISP, a QoS guarantee will not make your real-time video and interactive voice magically acceptable. QoS guarantees will only be as good as the weakest link between two points, because a QoS guarantee can be made based only on the resources available between the points.

5.9 Traffic Management

Traffic management focuses on regulating and controlling the network resources used to provide communication. Because resources are shared, access and use to the resources must be regulated and managed in order to make any guarantees about network delivery. Without such control and regulation, you essentially have what we have today for the Internet—a best-effort, first-come, first-served type of communication service. With the introduction of traffic management, it is possible to have many service levels including guaranteed priority *and* best-effort.

The first requirement necessary to understand traffic management is clear identification of the critical shared network resources and the key processes that must be in place to control these resources. Network device *buffers* and *bandwidth* are the critical resources; *queuing, communication setup, shaping,* and *policing* are the key processes.

5.9.1 Buffer Management

Buffer management is easy to understand. In a network interconnection device, switches and routers take data coming in from multiple input ports and, based on some level of packet reading, output the data to an output port. If the output port (or, depending on design, the input port) is busy, the data must be temporarily *buffered.*

The number of *buffers* within a network device is always finite. When a network device runs out of buffers, it drops packets (or frames at layer 2). When TCP packets are dropped, TCP backs off because it uses a congestion detection heuristic and responds to congestion. In order to make a QoS guarantee, buffers must be preallocated and reserved for use by a designated communication process.

5.9.2 Bandwidth Management and Queues

Bandwidth is the other critical resource that must be managed. In order to guarantee service, bandwidth must be reserved and tracked in network device tables within interconnection devices (like switches) across the network. Prior to being accepted, new service requests must be evaluated against existing utilization. When bandwidth is exhausted because of existing communication needs, service must be rejected.

Queues can be used to help sort packets and to regulate the use of bandwidth. Several packets or frames destined for the same output port must be queued; often separate queues have separate buffer pools. There are many queuing techniques used to regulate flow, and we will discuss the most popular in order of sophistication to give you an idea of what is possible. Sometimes these techniques are even combined to form hybrid queuing solutions.

The use of sophisticated queuing within switches is the foundation for Class of Service (COS). COS provides differentiated services based on existing attributes within packet headers. For example, separate queues can be set up for HTTP traffic or for FTP traffic and they can be given different priorities with respect to scheduling. They provide ways to classify traffic and to differentiate classes of service.

First-in, first-out (FIFO) is the simplest of all queuing disciplines. Although it is extremely easy to implement, it does result in long delays for packets at the end of the queue. These delays can be particularly lengthy for small packets that are behind many large packets.

Simple priority queuing falls in line as the next technique used by switching hardware. With priority queuing, packets are placed in two or more queues (eight queues is popular), depending on the type of traffic. It is quite common to sort according to well-known port numbers; for example, HTTP traffic and FTP traffic may have their own queues. Simple priority queuing is straightforward to implement, yet it results in a FIFO queuing for any particular service class. Thus if you are doing an FTP transfer and all FTP transfers share the same queue, you may be competing against all other FTP transfers for bandwidth.

Fair queuing is another technique used to solve this problem. Fair queuing allocates multiple queues (one for each flow), servicing each queue in a round-robin fashion. Each queue gets equal treatment, resulting in a disadvantage for short packets since queues are emptied per packet and longer packets take a longer period of time to complete. This technique is analogous to waiting in a grocery store line to purchase only a single item but stuck behind customers with carts heaped to the hilt.

Weighted fair queuing (WFQ) is perhaps the most popular queuing technique featured in advanced switching solutions today. Like fair queuing, WFQ manages queue flows individually. WFQ has a very sophisticated scheduling algorithm that enables certain flows to be scheduled more frequently, implicitly providing these queues with more bandwidth. Frequency-based queuing results in out-of-order scheduling. When a queue is scheduled, it may send exactly one packet, but WFQ provides bounded delays and allows flows to be given a customized amount of bandwidth. WFQ provides very fine control over delay within the network and overall tends to minimize the amount of queuing that is even necessary; in fact, queues are often empty! WFQ is complex and requires the same granular flow management as fair queuing.

A S I D E . . .

Not all WFQ algorithms that are implemented by switches are the same. Some switch vendors advertise WFQ but do not maintain individual flows. It is popular to combine priority queuing with the frequency-based scheduling technique of WFQ.

5.9.3 Traffic Management Control

Traffic management can be broken into three main components:

1. **CAC:** This process manages communication requests.
2. **Traffic Shaping:** This process "smoothes out" data to reduce overall delays.
3. **Policing:** This process monitors communication requests, ensuring that they operate within their agreed-upon bounds.

The next sections discuss the need for each of these components.

5.9.3.1 Communication Admission Control (CAC)

The Communication Admission Control (CAC) process is responsible for managing QoS contracts. This includes accepting or refusing a communication request based on the availability or absence of the required resources, allocating buffers and bandwidth for each accepted communication request, and overseeing the queuing process.

The CAC process owns and dynamically allocates the communication resources of a switch. It provides a central place to "check out" resources and "set up" QoS-based communication requests. The CAC maintains all outstanding requests and reserved resources (bandwidth and buffers) in one or more tables, enabling it to keep careful tabs on its communication resources. Setting up a QoS-based communication request from end-to-end requires getting commitment from each switch's CAC along the way. Sometimes a network device's CAC maintains a certain configurable amount of reserved buffers and bandwidth so that it may continue to service best-effort traffic even when it has exhausted its supply of buffers and bandwidth for guaranteed requests.

CACs typically run through a set of actions during the set-up phase (or set-up renegotiation phase) in order to determine whether to accept or reject a connection. Bandwidth and buffers can be allocated based on a peak bandwidth, an average bandwidth, or a maximum sustained bandwidth. The problem with basing resource allocations on peak values is that the resources tend to be under-utilized. The problem with allocating resources on an average value is that simultaneous bursts may result in significant packet dropping due to lack of buffers and/or bandwidth. Using sustained bandwidth, the most difficult to predict, is probably the best "happy medium" as it provides a constant level of output. Frame relay works quite well by bounding the Committed Information Rate (CIR), the Committed Burst Rate (CBR), and the Excess Burst Size (EBS).

A S I D E . . .

Often overlooked when setting the CAC policy on a switch is ensuring that the CAC policy across your network is consistent. Providing any level of service guarantee across a network with highly divergent CAC policies is challenging, if not impossible. This is even more difficult across many ASs within the Internet.

5.9.3.2 Traffic Shaping

In statistics we often talk about smoothing out the data; traffic shaping follows the same idea. For a guarantee to be made, the traffic of a communication flow must be mapped to exhibit approximately the characteristics of a certain pattern. This enables the network device to make a service-level guarantee as long as the traffic follows a predicted pattern. Sometimes traffic is reshaped (even allowing a link to go idle) to ensure a service-level guarantee downstream.

The most popular model used for traffic shaping is the simple leaky bucket. Essentially the data enters the opening at the top of a bucket and exits via a hole in the bottom. The larger the hole in the bottom (symbolizing bandwidth), the faster the bucket will empty. There are many derivatives of the leaky bucket model (token leaky bucket and dual leaky bucket are two that come to mind) used today to regulate and anticipate traffic flow.

5.9.3.3 Policing

Policing refers to the process of ensuring that flows stay within the bounds of their contractual agreements. It works with shaping to manage overconsuming flows. When a flow has been detected to be in violation, a smoothing algorithm might be used to "smooth out" the overconsumption. Sometimes this results in packet dropping or, in the extreme, complete flow dropping. Without policing, some flows would ultimately take advantage of the lack of monitoring and cause other well-behaved flows not to receive their service-level guarantee.

5.9.4 Random Early Discard (RED)

No discussion on traffic management would be complete without devoting a few paragraphs to Random Early Discard (RED), a very effective technique for providing congestion control. The algorithm proactively discards packets when, based on average queue size, it anticipates pending congestion. When packets are dropped, TCP sessions back off and congestion is avoided.

In addition to preventing congestion, Floyd and Jacobson (see References) point out that by *controlling the average queue size* with RED you are ultimately *controlling the average delay.* This important concept is especially relevant to providing a service-level guarantee. Floyd and Jacobson also indicate that RED eliminates the need to have to synchronize congestion control across many routers since RED prevents the onset of congestion.

A S I D E . . .

It is important to remember that TCP is session-based and has the built-in intelligence to back off; other protocols such as UDP do not. In essence any UDP application has license to flood the network in an uncontrolled manner. Protocols like SNMP (which typically runs over UDP) and IP multicast do not have any notion of session like TCP nor will they be well behaved like TCP. Although SNMP does not tend to flood the network, IP multicast certainly can. As IP multicast becomes more prevalent, other measures will have to be taken.

5.10 The ATM World

From day one, ATM was built with integrated QoS. Since ATM is connection-oriented, initial call setup provides the perfect opportunity to negotiate the required resources for the communication session. And, if resources are unavailable anywhere along the way, the communication session is rejected.

5.10.1 ATM's Built-In QoS

B-ISDN Digital Subscriber Signaling System Number 2 User-Network Interface (UNI) Layer-3 Specification for Basic Call/Connection Control (Q.2931) serves as ATM's signaling standard. Signaling has the complex job of setting up a communication connection across one or more hops; the process *ensures* the availability of resources and *reserves* these dedicated resources for a session of communication. Signaling works with ATM's routing protocol called Private Network-Network Interface (PNNI) and its integrated traffic management. It is complex and can take considerable processing power and time to complete, making signaling impractical for communication sessions that are short in length. E-mail and an SNMP "get" are examples of communication instances that are too short to justify the use of signaling. Many criticize ATM for its slow signaling implementations, although vendors are currently starting to make significant improvements with signaling performance.

ATM sends a *source traffic description* via its signaling protocol to specify the QoS for a communication session. This description includes many parameters including the Peak Cell Rate (PCR), Maximum Burst Size (MBS), Sustained Cell Rate (SCR), end-to-end delay, Cell Delay Variation Tolerance (CDVT), and the Cell Loss Ratio (CLR). (See Table 5.3 for ATM-specific terminology related to QoS.) The source traffic description parameters must be interpreted and agreed upon at each ATM switch hop that is required to set up a communication link. ATM switches have a CAC to manage resources and to make the decision on whether a call is accepted. ATM also incorporates traffic shaping, policing, bandwidth, and buffer management. Both buffering and CAC algorithms within ATM switches are proprietary, as there are no standard algorithms provided by the ATM forum.

A S I D E . . .

The ATM Forum's glossary found at `http://www.atmforum.com` provides a complete list of ATM acronyms and terms.

5.10.2 ATM Service Classes

ATM defines four service classes:

1. The *Available Bit Rate* (ABR) Service Class provides best-effort service with integrated feedback to the source. Source must use feedback

Table 5.3 ATM-Specific Terminology Related to QoS

ATM Terminology	Definition
Cell	The basic 53-byte unit is used to communicate. The first 5 bytes are the header; the remaining 48 bytes are the payload (data).
Cell Delay Variation (CDV)	This is the variance in delay between transmission of any two ATM cells.
Cell Delay Variation Tolerance (CDVT)	This is the maximum allowed CDV between transmission of any two ATM cells.
Cell Error Ratio (CER)	This is the ratio of cells with error to cells without error.
Cell Loss Priority (CLP)	A one-bit field in the ATM header indicates a cell's importance with respect to discard, if the network experiences congestion. A cell with a CLP of 1 is more likely to get discarded than a cell with a CLP of 0.
Cell Loss Ratio (CLR)	This is the ratio of cells lost to total cells transmitted. Note that the CLR is not accumulated; it is simply compared at each hop.
Maximum Burst Size (MBS)	This is the upper bound of the total number of cells that may be transmitted over a VC.
Maximum Cell Rate (MCR)	This is the maximum transmission rate guaranteed with the ABR Service Class.
Peak Cell Rate (PCR)	PCR is the maximum transmission rate within a VC.
Resource Management (RM) Cells	These are the cells that are used to regulate ABR traffic flow.
Sustained Cell Rate (SCR)	SCR is the maximum burst rate that a VC can maintain.
Traffic Management (TM)	TM provides composite control with respect to buffer management, turning up or down transmission rates, and ensuring flows adhere to signaled contracts (policing).

(RM cells) to adjust data rate to what the network can handle. A low CLR is guaranteed if the source is compliant.

2. The *Variable Bit Rate* (VBR) Class includes two subtypes:

- The *non-real-time Variable Bit Rate* (nrt-VBR) Service Class is for non-real-time traffic. Although traffic may contain bursts, it is not real-time sensitive, and provides guarantees with respect to delay, cell loss, and latency. Nrt-VBR is like frame relay service.

- The *real-time Variable Bit Rate* (rt-VBR) Service Class, for real-time traffic, might be used for compressed video that is bursty and delay-sensitive. This class guarantees delay, cell loss, and latency.

3. The *Unspecified Bit Rate* (UBR) Service Class provides service without latency, throughput, or CLR guarantees. It is equivalent to a "best-effort" service where PCR is specified at setup.

4. The *Constant Bit Rate* (CBR) Service Class provides minimal delay and jitter and is for real-time uncompressed voice and video. CBR is like today's telephone network; it guarantees QoS as it allows for specification of PCR, CDV, and CLR.

ATM supports both Permanent Virtual Circuits (PVCs) and Switched Virtual Circuits (SVCs). Permanent Virtual Circuits are manually configured and therefore do not require signaling; SVCs must be signaled. Today's ATM installations are largely PVCs and provide only a UBR service; subsequently they are not taking advantage of ATM's QoS.

A S I D E . . .

If a single cell within the frame is lost, it is often most effective to discard the entire frame during the discard process. Since even one cell invalidates a frame, it is a waste of bandwidth to transport the remaining cells, only to be discarded at the receiving end. Many ATM switches have this "early frame discard" feature.

5.11 The IP World

The IETF has proposed standards that form the Integrated Services Architecture (ISA). The main goal for Integrated Services (IS) is to provide a level of QoS in an IP-based network—in other words to provide the ability to move real-time traffic in addition to non-real-time, best-effort traffic. It follows that this architecture must provide an evolutionary path from the current best-effort Internet; the luxury of a clean slate is not given. See RFC 1633 for the specification of the architecture.

The ISA divides traffic into two categories: *elastic* and *inelastic*. Elastic traffic, flexible to delays, tries to use the maximum bandwidth available but will back off when congestion is apparent. Our current Internet is well suited for elastic traffic since it provides only a best-effort service. File transfer using FTP is a good example of elastic traffic.

A S I D E . . .

It should be noted that deployment of adaptive applications is another alternative to requiring a strong QoS guarantee. Applications that are adaptive (or elastic) dynamically adjust (or scale back) their network usage if resources become unavailable. Elastic applications can make use of the network even if the network is sluggish. Inelastic applications take a "give me a network with a QoS guarantee or give me nothing" approach.

It is expected that creative ways to make applications elastic will become more prevalent. For example, start off with CD-quality stereo. When the network is congested, back off to mono, then to phone quality, and finally to heavily compressed audio. Or perhaps start a video stream with 30 frames per second (FPS) full-screen color, then drop the frame rate, the resolution, the color, and so on to adapt to reduced bandwidth.

Inelastic traffic is delay-sensitive. Interactive voice and real-time video are good examples of inelastic traffic that requires minimal delay, packet loss, and variance between packets (jitter). And we know that our current Internet is not well suited for inelastic traffic, especially when the network becomes congested. The ISA attempts to resolve this deficiency, while simultaneously preserving the best-effort delivery model found within IP-based networks.

As the specification (RFC 1633) indicates, the overall ISA solution is expected to include the general purpose QoS components that we have already discussed:

- A CAC to set up and administer QoS
- Routing with other QoS parameters beyond least cost
- One or more packet-discarding policies like RED
- Sophisticated Queuing Algorithms

- Packet classification and scheduling
- Integrated management for specifying and managing policy across the network

The IS model also uses the term "Service" in the phrase *QoS Control Service*. A QoS Control Service is a named, coordinated set of QoS control capabilities provided by a network element which includes devices that route and end stations. (See Sections 5.12 and 5.14 on RSVP and WinSock 2 to see how an end station can participate in the IS model.) A QoS Control Service includes the

- functions performed by a network element,
- information required by the element to perform services, and
- information made available by the element or other elements of the system.

Although the IS QoS Control Service is *not* end-to-end, it does share a lot of the characteristics of the ATM service categories.

The ISA divides traffic into three categories:

1. *Guaranteed Service* (GS): A service level providing an assured capacity level, an upper bound for queuing delay, and absolutely no queuing loss. GS provides assured bandwidth with a bounded delay with no loss due to congestion. Although it is similar to ATM's CBR Service, there are some differences:

   - Queuing delay is only *somewhat controllable* by adjusting the overall service rate, although there is no way to minimize overall jitter (the variance in queuing delays).
   - GS guarantees *no* data loss, clearly different from ATM's CBR Service.
   - GS is for real-time applications that require packet delivery within a guaranteed delivery time without packet discard due to queue overflow.
   - GS maps approximately to rt-VBR and CBR services provided by ATM.

2. *Controlled Load Service* (CLS): A service level providing an approximate to best-effort service in an uncongested, lightly loaded network. Unlike Guaranteed Service, there is no upper bound for queuing delay or queuing loss guarantee. The service indicates that a high percentage of traffic will successfully be delivered and is suitable for real-time applications that can adapt to changes in network conditions, but cannot change for

nonadaptive real-time applications. CLS should not impact guaranteed service or best-effort. Clearly it would be undesirable to make best-effort service always "sluggish," regardless of network load. CLS maps approximately to nrt-VBR and ABR services provided by ATM.

3. *Best-effort Service* (BES): A service level without any guarantees. This is the service we have today on the Internet. When the network is not congested, you receive better service; when the network is congested, you receive worse service. This is "pot luck" service similar to what you get on any well-traveled highway in the United States. At off-peak times traffic tends to move swiftly; during rush hour it piles up. This service is suitable for non-real-time traffic such as a file transfer or the delivery of mail. BES maps approximately to ABR and UBR services provided by ATM.

A S I D E . . .

In the same way that ATM running over connectionless SONET frames is able to provide QoS guarantees, you can build a QoS absolute guarantee on a connect-less technology like Ethernet by taking advantage of dedicated link technologies like full-duplex Ethernet.

5.11.1 Resource ReSerVation Protocol (RSVP)

RSVP is a protocol aimed at providing a level resource reservation across a desired communication path and is positioned as a QoS solution for native TCP/IP LAN environments. In order to work RSVP requires built-in support from the following network devices across the communication path:

- **End Stations:** must use an RSVP-enabled protocol stack—for example, WinSock 2.
- **Applications:** must employ Real-time Transport Protocol (RTP) (a real-time end-to-end protocol that operates at end stations).
- **Routers or layer-3 Switches:** must support RSVP. Reservations are negotiated at each link—not end-to-end as with ATM.

One big challenge for the network administrator is getting the RSVP solution installed across the LAN and managing mixed environments (non-RSVP-enabled devices coupled with RSVP-enabled network devices). Mixed environments are inevitable whenever several devices along a network path are involved in a solution. Before tackling these problems, though, it is important first to understand fundamentally how the technology works.

5.11.1.1 RSVP Specs

"Specs" are fundamental to learning about RSVP. They are transported by RSVP to set up QoS. As mentioned previously, RSVP doesn't know anything about the QoS, but the QoS parameters are contained within an Integrated Service's "Specs" that RSVP carries across from hop to hop.

There are many Integrated Services Specs used to set up a QoS for a flow:

- Advertisement Specification (AdSpec)
- Flow Specification (FlowSpec)
- Traffic Specification (TSpecs)
- Resource Specification (RSpecs)

They each have discrete roles within the setup of QoS, and it is important to understand their differences.

AdSpecs summarize downstream path characteristics. They propagate *toward* the receiver(s) and are adjusted along the way to record the characteristics of the path. Prior to making a service request, AdSpecs, containing the path MTU, bandwidth, the minimum bandwidth, and a break bit, tell the receiver what level of communication is even possible.

A break bit within the AdSpec indicates that the path goes through one or more systems that do not support RSVP. Since the break bit must be set *after* a router that does not support RSVP is passed, the specification makes clever used of TTL. At every hop an exact copy of TTL is maintained within the AdSpec, except when passing through a router that does not support RSVP; in this case the old TTL remains. When the AdSpec gets to the next hop, the actual TTL and the copy of the TTL within the AdSpec no longer match, indicating there is a break in RSVP support across the connection. Subsequently, the break bit is set.

A *FlowSpec* propagates upstream and sets up the actual QoS. It contains both a Traffic Specification (TSpec) and a Resource Specification (RSpec).

An *RSpec* signals the QoS that is desired across the network. It is specific to a particular service and contains such attributes as maximum delay and packet loss rates.

The *TSpec* describes the traffic pattern for which a service is requested; it is therefore part of the contract between data flow and the service. TSpecs specify the flow allowed, not necessarily the actual traffic pattern.

5.11.1.2 RSVP Messaging

RSVP has seven message formats that are used to facilitate communication across the network. Table 5.4 summarizes these message types.

RSVP uses two of the message formats to set up and maintain a flow between two devices wishing to communicate. It is best explained by an example in Figure 5.5.

Device A wants to communicate with Device B. The data flow is critical and time-sensitive so the application on Device A decides to use RSVP. The

Table 5.4 RSVP Message Formats

Message	Meaning
Path	This message, used to record path information from sender to destination, flows via the best-effort route using standard IP routing and advertises a sender's capabilities. It contains both a TSpec and an AdSpec.
Resv	This message, used to request a reservation along the path, contains a FlowSpec that includes both a TSpec and an RSpec. It is used to refresh a flow's QoS periodically.
PathTear	This message, used to remove a reservation, can originate from a host or router.
ResvTear	This message, used to remove a reservation, can originate from host or router.
PathErr	This message is used to send a path error message.
ResvErr	This message is used to send a reservation error message.
ResvConf	This message is used to confirm a reservation.

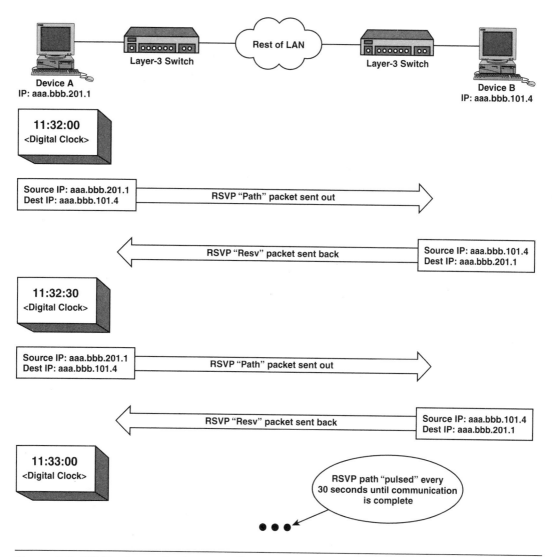

Figure 5.5 RSVP setup and subsequent flow "pulsing"

interface to RSVP for Device A is found in extensions to WinSock 2—the application's interface to the network. Using WinSock 2, the application on Device A sends out a "Path" message to Device B. This protocol message goes through each router (for simplicity we will assume that all routers along the way support RSVP, although tunneling through non-RSVP routers is possible). At each router, the state of the RSVP "flow" is saved in a special table. Once the RSVP Path message reaches Device B (assuming that Device B is willing to accept the flow), it sends back a "Resv" to the application on Device A. The "Resv" message goes back through the network using the same path that the "Path" message set up. Along the way each router activates the reservation, possibly debiting some resource counter for RSVP bandwidth. Once the "Resv" makes it back to the sending application, the setup is complete. Note, though, that the application must periodically pulse (refresh) the reservation using the "Path"/"Resv" protocol. Without these refreshes, the reservation would "time out" and disappear.

5.11.1.3 RSVP Key Facts

The IETF RSVP draft specification summarizes some key points about RSVP. The following are some of the key points from the draft specification:

- RSVP is the signaling protocol for IPv4 and IPv6. It does not provide QoS or even know about QoS, but it is the vehicle for sending QoS requests across a network. QoS is carried by RSVP in the form of a FlowSpec.

- RSVP facilitates resource reservations for both unicast and multicast applications. In fact, RSVP was designed to scale with one form of IP multicast, a one-to-many IP multicast. Although RSVP is designed to support many receivers, it supports only one or a few sender(s). With many senders RSVP tends to break down.

- RSVP leverages subsequent reservation refresh pulsing dynamically to make adjustments for changing group membership and routes.

- RSVP messages are sent on top of unreliable IP, indicating that they may or may not arrive when sent. This is mitigated to some degree since messages are periodically refreshed. It may be important, though, to give RSVP messages preferential network treatment so that they do not get "lost" at congestion points within the network.

- RSVP depends upon present and future routing protocols; it is not in itself a routing protocol. RSVP uses local routing databases to obtain routes.

- RSVP supports transparent operation through routers that do not support it. Note that breaks in RSVP support severely discount the reservation. A `NonRsvp` flag bit is used to signal that the reservation is passing through one or more routers that do not support RSVP.

- RSVP provides QoS for layer 3 (routing) only. It has nothing to do with tagging or prioritizing at layer 2 (bridging/switching).

- RSVP supports merging of flow specifications. Thus an application can "attach" to an existing flow, allowing RSVP to scale for very large multicast groups. Refresh messages may also be consolidated, although there is no penalty (albeit extra router processing time) for sending out too many refresh messages for a flow.

- RSVP is not bidirectional. If a QoS is required in both directions, it must be set up and managed independently.

- RSVP does not require any new headers to be added to IP packets; it uses the same IP header and signals via the data portion of the packet.

- `ResrErr` and `PathErr` are messages used to propagate errors; RSVP "teardown" messages are used to remove path and reservation information immediately.

There are many differences between ATM signaling and RSVP. The following are some of the key distinguishing attributes:

- RSVP is receiver-oriented not sender-oriented. The receiver of a data flow initiates and maintains the resource reservation used for that flow.

- RSVP relies on the sender to advertise paths and on the receiver(s) to request resource allocations.

- RSVP provides a mechanism to signal a soft-state QoS where periodic refreshes are required. This is much different than ATM which provides hard-state QoS.

- RSVP allows the QoS to be renegotiated after it is originally set up; current ATM does not allow renegotiations.

- RSVP is not integrated in any way with routing protocols. Subsequently RSVP always uses the current routed path. This is much different from ATM's signaling which is integrated with how traffic is routed.

5.11.1.4 RSVP and the Real-Time Transport Protocol

It is expected that RSVP will be used in conjunction with Real-time Transport Protocol (RFC 1889) instead of TCP. Note that RTP

- allows for multicast traffic (not just point-to-point unicast traffic like TCP).

- provides a way to limit the delay variation of packets.

- includes timing information (unlike TCP and UDP) in each packet.

- provides a way to mix streams from multiple sources into a single packet stream.

- runs over UDP.

- provides identification of data source *with* type of data.

- provides real-time monitoring useful for diagnostics and application feedback.

- provides a way to mix multiple traffic types into one flow.

RTP has a separate control protocol, Real-Time Transport Control Protocol (RTCP). RFC 1889 indicates that RTCP will provide feedback on congestion and performance reports containing error rates (for example, jitter, lost packets) for both senders and receivers. This will provide network managers a window into how well the RSVP system is working.

5.11.1.5 Issues with Deploying RSVP

RSVP is currently being tested in some networks. Widespread deployment is still at least one to two years away, although we will see pockets of use sooner. There are many questions concerning RSVP, and some of the more common questions include the following:

- How many flows can routers manage across a network? In other words, how well can RSVP scale?

- How secure is RSVP?

- When is it appropriate to use RSVP, and when is it inappropriate?

Scalability is the biggest concern and rightly so. The IETF never intended RSVP to be used for short communication sessions of a few packets, nor to scale in order to manage thousands of flows. RSVP is tuned to work for IP multicast with a single sender to many receivers, and it is designed for small Intranets. The IETF makes it very clear that RSVP is only one piece of the Integrated Services Architecture and not the entire solution.

Security is another concern that RSVP does not currently address. In its current form it would be relatively easy to tie up lots of bandwidth if used in a public network. It is expected that RSVP will be made more secure as it matures during implementation testing.

5.12 Integrating ATM with RSVP

An obvious concern when attempting to provide end-to-end QoS solutions is how RSVP integrates with ATM. The following questions exist:

- How are service levels mapped?
- How are signaling protocols mapped, that is, RSVP to ATM signaling?
- How are flows to virtual circuits mapped?
- How does multicast work across mixed technologies?
- What happens when you add in NHRP and IPv6?

Unfortunately there are more questions than answers. ATM services are more granular than the IETF's, making it difficult to end up with anything other than a least common denominator (LCD) fit. The fact that RSVP works as an upstream reservation system and ATM works as a downstream system makes mapping difficult. The granularity between flows and VCs is problematic, as is the capability of RSVP to adjust a reservation dynamically. Multicast means the solutions must scale and exacerbate only the problems of integration. Finally, when you add mixed addressing and "shortcutting" as done in some switching solutions, the problems become more complex.

It is expected that over the next few years our ATM solutions and IETF solutions will need to become a lot more integrated. This will involve considerable work and will require compromises on both sides. Without convergence, it is unlikely that end-to-end QoS will ever be a reality; this fact strengthens the push to integrate the two diverse solutions.

A S I D E . . .

RSVP is good for maintaining state and exchanging QoS requirements, but it is important to realize that this is only one small component of making QoS happen. As discussed earlier in the chapter, operating systems and interconnection devices between endpoints must all participate in making QoS happen.

5.13 Type of Service (TOS), OSPF, QOSPF, and QoS

Within every IP packet there are option bits that allow the specification of five different Type(s) of Service (TOS). These bits include

- normal,
- least monetary cost,
- maximum reliability,
- maximum throughput, and
- minimal delay.

Currently these bits go across the network in billions of packets, totally unused!

In the early specification of OSPF, the routing protocol was designed to route based on these TOS bits. Because these bits have not been used to date, the OSPF specification recently removed the ability to route based on TOS. This is unfortunate because it is the routing protocol that exchanges topology information across the network on a regular basis. Consequently it is also well suited to exchange information regarding traffic congestion so that packets can be intelligently routed around problem areas. The knowledge of topology coupled with TOS yields a very powerful story. MPLS is expected to rejuvenate the power of combining policy exchange with topology exchange.

Another draft Internet proposal titled Quality of Service Extensions to OSPF or Quality of Service Path First Routing (QOSPF)[3] explores extending OSPF to consider network resource information during route calculation. With the proposed QOSPF, network resources are advertised in addition to topology information in the form of Link Resource Advertisements (RES-LSA). Then the RES-LSAs are incorporated into the Dijkstra link-state algorithm used to calculate routes. The specification points out that when RES-LSAs are incorporated into the calculations, links with insufficient resources are ignored. This adds a level of traffic engineering intelligence to ordinary link-state routing.

A S I D E . . .

There has been a resurgence of activity revisiting the use of TOS bits within packets. As of November 1997 there have been several Internet drafts positioning TOS as an alternative to RSVP and ATM to fulfill QoS needs. See `http://diffserv.lcs.mit.edu` for more information.

---

3. Quality of Service Extension to OSPF or Quality of Service Path First Routing (QOSPF) was written by Zhang, Sanchez, Salkewicz, Crawley, Nortel Networks, Avici Systems, Redback Networks, and Gigapacket Networks (September 1997).

5.14 WinSock 2

WinSock 2 is a new 32-bit standard Application Programming Interface (API) developed by a group of companies across the industry. WinSock 2 uses WinSock 1.1 as its base, although it extends WinSock 1.1 considerably. Nonetheless it is backward compatible with WinSock 1.1; in fact, backward compatibility was a fundamental requirement. WinSock 2 is based on the material in RFC 1363 that defines the concept of flow specifications.

WinSock 1.1 provides a TCP/IP-only standard interface to the network, enabling an application to open, close, and read and write data across a network connection. The functionality of WinSock 1.1 is based on Berkeley Software Distribution (BSD) UNIX sockets that were developed many years ago. The BSD Socket APIs found on UNIX systems are quite powerful; for example, they enable client/server applications to run over IPX, DECnet, and AppleTalk, and they can do DNS-based name to address resolution.

WinSock 2 was designed to "open up" QoS, allowing applications to negotiate and renegotiate network service in real-time. WinSock 2 includes integrated optional QoS support for both IP (RSVP) and ATM, although ATM support is significantly more integrated. WinSock 2 uses two flow specifications for each socket, one for each direction; these flow specifications include parameters like a source traffic descriptor, latency, level of service guarantee, and type of service.

A S I D E . . .

In many ways RSVP support in WinSock 2 appears to be an "add on." Perhaps this is because of RSVP's model that relies on the receiver to negotiate QoS and use of periodic QoS refreshing. The ATM model, which sets QoS up at service initiation, provides a greater natural fit with how the socket API works with its open, send, close paradigm.

Winsock 2 includes a notification mechanism that enables the network to tell the application that because of network conditions, the original QoS can no longer be honored. This gives the application the opportunity to abort out of the communication session (close the socket) or renegotiate the QoS with the network provider.

Winsock 2's algorithm for guaranteeing bandwidth is a credit-based scheme that uses token buckets. Bandwidth is specified in terms of maximum volume in bytes and rates in bytes per second. Applications treat the bucket much like a checking account: They can write checks (send data) when a balance exists and must wait until payday (suppress sending or discarding traffic) if there isn't enough credit balance. No check bouncing (sending data without the proper credit) is allowed!

Winsock 2 has a future "cost parameter" to be used to identify cost of service. It is expected that network QoS will be available at a premium price and this cost "hook" provides a way to let the application know what the charge for a transaction will be. In addition to API features for applications to exchange QoS requirements with the system, WinSock 2 provides a lot of new functionality including

- multiprotocol support including IPX, DECnet, and AppleTalk.
- multipoint communications using IP multicast.
- Protocol-Independent name service resolution—Domain Name Service (DNS), Network Information Service (NIS), and X.500.
- security support.

It is unclear as to whether the API exposes too much lower-level functionality. One must ask the following questions:

- Should my application really need to know whether it runs across an IP or an ATM network?
- What if the network is a combination of ATM and IP?
- What is a good default for real-time traffic, priority traffic, and best-effort traffic?

It is expected that as the API penetrates the industry, more effort will be placed on resolving these types of questions and providing a simpler way to specify the correct QoS for an application.

As mentioned in a recent Aside, it is important remember that having an API to specify QoS is only one part of provisioning a QoS across a network. Operating Systems such as Windows/NT and UNIX need to incorporate QoS in their scheduling capabilities. In addition, each interconnection device between two end points must participate in the QoS negotiation. This may seem relatively straightforward in a LAN, but once we enter the WAN across many ASs, it becomes very difficult to achieve.

5.15 IPv6

IPv6 resolves many problems of the current IP version (IPv4). Extending IPv4 addressing is the most important problem that IPv6 tackles. From a QoS point-of-view, IPv6 offers a priority field that is simpler than the type-of-service (TOS) field within IPv4.

Recall the unused TOS bits within IPv4. There is one bit to minimize delay, maximize throughput, maximize reliability, and minimize monetary cost, respectively. Only one bit may be set at any one time. If all four bits are zero (as they are today), normal best-effort service is utilized. Perhaps it is the difficulty of knowing what bit to set that has contributed to the lack of deployment.

Within the IPv6 header is a 24-bit flow label field and a 4-bit priority field. These fields are used to help optimize the Internetworking of packets across multiple hops. The idea is simple: Switches can route and forward packets by reading only the flow label, greatly reducing the time to make routing decisions. Likewise, the 4-bit priority field can be used to influence the queuing priority of packets; an example of use might be to give delay-sensitive audio a higher priority. Use of the flow field comes with the typical problems of

- maintaining state information across several devices in the network.
- aging out stale flow labels from a table.
- storing many labels.
- not having a flow label in the table.
- using some protocol to refresh labels periodically.
- interoperating with empty labels.

The priority field is considerably simpler as it does not require state storage. It is sufficient to maintain a simple agreement that the bigger the value, the higher the packet priority. This field helps prioritize packets in the state of congestion, where values of 0 to 7 indicate that the packet is resilient to congestion (can be dropped), and values of 8 to 15 would indicate that it is not (perhaps delay-sensitive data or a bank debit from your checking account).

A S I D E . . .

"Flow" is a confusing term used in many contexts. In the Integrated Services Architecture (ISA), a "flow" is a set of packets that are traversing the network, all of which are covered under the same QoS request. Packets may be from one session or from an aggregation of traffic from many sessions. In IPv4, a "flow" is defined by a sequence of packets with the same source address, path, and so on. In IPv6, flows are identified by a flow ID.

5.16 Setting Expectations

We are a long way from providing an Internet with different levels of QoS. In some cases it appears that we are not progressing at all but rather regressing. Having inactive TOS bits in the IP header seems somewhat unusual; removing TOS routing from OSPF is a setback. We must remember, though, that solutions that span multiple network devices penetrate a large distributed infrastructure like the Internet very slowly, if at all. Perhaps the renewed interest demonstrated by the flurry of activity around TOS-type Internet drafts will give TOS-based QoS a place in our future.

Clearly we have outgrown the current single service Internet. The WWW has raised the awareness of how bad delay-sensitive data transmission across a best-effort network can be. Increased business dependency on the network is pushing for differentiated services. In most industries time is money, and sluggish, unpredictable performance for some delay-sensitive data applications is unacceptable.

We are seeing areas of activity helping with the QoS problem particularly in the LAN. New and faster switching technologies are helping to provide bigger networks. Overprovisioning is becoming easier and less expensive, and overprovisioning where bandwidth is inexpensive is a reasonable solution to providing better QoS. It doesn't guarantee delivery, but it certainly can minimize the probability of delay. More sophisticated queuing techniques are being implemented in LAN switches, and layer-3 switching is moving packets at line speed. Recent LAN progress is encouraging.

In the WAN we are seeing more and more activity around making ATM and IP work together. In WANs, bandwidth costs significantly more, making WAN-based overprovisioning solutions less practical. ATM has always had a rich QoS story, although deployment of anything but PVCs has not been common. In most cases we are not taking advantage of ATM's QoS, IP is enjoying its widespread success of best-effort traffic in the Internet, and more attention is being placed on QoS by the IETF, although the ISA appears to be years away. RSVP lacks penetration and does not appear to scale for large applications. MPLS, as discussed in Chapter 4, appears to be another way to distribute policy and route traffic based on differentiation. QoS-aware routing is again beginning to be revisited. In short there is a lot going on, although progress is slow with respect to providing QoS in the WAN.

At the same time we must remember that WAN service providers (for example, ISPs) want more than one product. Margins on providing unlimited monthly service for $19.99 (US dollars) are slim. Service differentiation provides additional products in the same way FedEx, AirBorne, UPS, and USPS

Express Mail provide us with different alternatives to ordinary mail. Service differentiation will give service providers an opportunity to make the margins they need to supplement the best-effort service. We will begin to see VPN services, usage-based billing, voice over IP (VoIP), and other premium services. (Note that we will discuss some of these services in Chapter 7.) Differentiated services will help drive QoS within our WAN network; this is no surprise since *applications drive networks and faster networks provide opportunities for new network uses.* Slow applications push vendors to increase bandwidth, and increased bandwidth opens the door to more applications, placing greater dependencies on the network. This is analogous to the evolution of PCs—more sophisticated applications place higher demands on PCs, and more powerful PCs provide a foundation for new, more feature-rich applications. Ultimately this "push and tug" phenomenon results in more dependency on networking and computers, respectively.

Many believe that end-to-end QoS is a long way off. This isn't to say that we can't make substantial progress and have partial QoS at critical places in the network. We can overprovision and add priority queues (COS) in our LANs. In the WAN service providers can make progress within their autonomous systems (ASs) by using the same techniques. Use of ATM SVCs for certain traffic will become more prevalent, and it is expected that some form of label-based routing will take off across portions of the WAN and ISPs will provide different levels of service. QoS needs to *evolve* over many years as it is a difficult, distributed problem with a solution set that is ever changing for a network that is growing at astronomical rates.

5.17 Conclusions

It is difficult to provide service-level guarantees across a network largely because networks by definition are shared and distributed. Typically there are many network devices involved in the communication of even a simple e-mail. Each network device has a finite number of buffers and outgoing bandwidth. Coordinating the use of these resources across many network devices is a big challenge.

Delays come from many areas across the network in addition to the delays introduced by network device scheduling and resource (buffers and bandwidth) contention. The network adds "packetizing," transmission, propagation, and queuing delays. When the network is congested, packet loss exacerbates the overall delay, and data loss and errors add delay. Delays are difficult to predict especially at peak times of network utilization or when intermittent bursts of traffic clog the network.

Overprovisioning, use of precedence, and dedicated resources are three ways to reduce delays and provide some level of QoS. Only dedicated resources can provide service-level guarantees, although overprovisioning and use of precedence can significantly improve the QoS, especially within the LAN. It is expected that use of precedence will become the preferred solution in the WAN since use of overprovisioning and dedicated resources can be prohibitively expensive. Nonetheless, certain applications warrant the expense, so don't rule out the use of dedicated resources in the WAN.

We will see more and more energy placed on the QoS solution set in the next few years. Providing better than best-effort service is paramount, and both the ATM Forum and the IETF are actively addressing the problem. ATM service classes, ISA, RSVP, IPv6, WinSock 2, and QoS-based routing are some of the partial solutions that are being offered. More and more energy is being placed on ensuring that our QoS solution sets converge and work together across ATM and IP. This convergence is fundamentally important to the breath of QoS and ultimately to addressing the network needs for delay-sensitive transmission and minimal propagation delay.

CHAPTER 6

Multicast in the Network

6.1 Introduction

At most companies if you put a network scope on a well-traveled network link, you will see a proliferation of the same data passing by at virtually the same time. Take the connection to the Internet, for example, and you are likely to see the same stock quotes, Web-based weather/traffic, and the URLs being hit over and over. But then again, these are typically small requests resolved in only a few packets. What happens, however, when duplicate video streams that contain a presentation on corporate quarterly updates start passing? There is likely to be substantial jitter across video players even though the same data is being displayed.

This chapter is about multicasting in the network. Primarily our discussion is focused on IP multicast, although we touch upon developments in ATM multicast. IP multicast is a methodology used to route a single IP packet to multiple destinations. The technology is based on the work of Steve Deering (see Bibliography). It makes more efficient use of network bandwidth by routing a single packet through the network and then, right before the final destinations, creating a copy of the packet for each recipient. IP multicast is good for real-time applications such as video or audio broadcasting as well as transferring a single file to many locations at once. IP multicast may also be used to update many PCs simultaneously, reducing the total cost of maintaining a large number of PCs common in many businesses.

6.2 Key Solutions Offered

Multicast is positioned to save bandwidth by reducing redundant data and getting the same information to many locations nearly at the same time. Although these goals may sound simple and achievable, they are actually quite difficult to realize.

Multicast involves both the maintenance of multicast groups in the LAN and the building and maintaining of trees across LAN subnets and the WAN. Trees are constructed, maintained, and periodically refreshed using multicast protocols. They are stored in routers capable of multicast and can be quite large and memory-intensive. Some multicast protocols use periodic broadcasting to keep trees up-to-date; this practice does not scale well, particularly in the WAN. Change to trees is based on routing table changes and members coming and going from groups. In the network tunnels are used to go across places that do not support multicast; even setting up and maintaining these tunnels can be troublesome at times since both ends must by properly synchronized.

Despite all the current problems with multicast, conserving bandwidth will continue to be increasingly important in our networks. Even with the possibility of practically limitless bandwidth (LAN and perhaps the WAN) the rationale of eliminating redundant transmissions remains. This is especially true with respect to redundant transfer of bandwidth-intensive video across a WAN. As networks become more intelligent and service-rich with QoS guarantees and business levels of COS, it is expected that we will see an increased interest not only in saving bandwidth, but also in sharing expensive data transmissions that use differentiated services. Clearly it is less expensive to send one express-delivery piece of mail with the exact same content from the United States to Austria to fan out to many residents in Tulln, Austria, than to send many separate pieces of express-delivery mail across the Atlantic Ocean.

6.3 IP Multicast in a Nutshell

There is a lot to IP multicast. The following list attempts to walk you sequentially through the high points of IP multicast in an efficient manner. After this discussion, we zoom in on specific areas that require more attention and on the various multicast protocols. And no, you do not need to be an arborist to understand IP multicast, although you would expect the designers of the protocols to be avid landscapers with their use of trees, pruning, and grafts.

- IP multicast uses the Class D IP address range (224.0.0.0 to 239.255.255.255). This range makes for over 268 million addresses; address ranges 224.0.0.x and 224.0.1.x are reserved for administrative use, and 239.0.0.0 to 239.255.255.255 are reserved for private networks. Although initially this may seem like a lot of addresses, take a moment to consider the voluminous number of securities traded across the many stock markets of the world and the need for each to have its own multicast address. You quickly realize that a flat address space of just over a quarter of a billion is less than ideal—perhaps a hierarchical space is in order.

- IP multicast distribution is based on multicast *groups.* A group is a collection of one or more senders and receivers, addressed as an entity with a single multicast IP address. This concept enables members to come and go dynamically without the need for senders to adjust the destination address of packets sent. Senders do not have to be members of a group: A group "subscription" indicates that the host is interested in receiving an application's transmissions. Routers keep track of these groups in the form of source/group (where "source" is the source of multicast transmission) pairs and dynamically build distribution "trees" to chart paths from each sender to all receivers. Note that IP multicast facilitates dynamically attaching to a data stream in progress; there is no need to synchronize subscription based on the start or stop of a data stream. Use of groups provides a very powerful abstraction and flexibility for IP multicast.

- *IGMP* is the LAN-based signaling protocol used to manage group membership. One designated multicast router per LAN queries all hosts periodically to refresh group membership and to enable new memberships. End stations belonging to a group respond with a report for each group to which they want to belong. A TTL of 1 is set in both queries and reports to limit the scope of the exchange to the local subnet. There are three versions of IGMP (discussed later); each version extends the protocol's capabilities.

- *IGMP Snooping* is a technique used within switched LAN environments to mitigate the effect of multicast flooding. Essentially IGMP snooping turns off the flooding of switch ports (at layer 2) based on promiscuously monitoring different ports for IGMP messages. On the ports where IGMP traffic is found, IP multicast traffic is forwarded; on the ports without IGMP messages, IP multicast traffic is filtered, greatly reducing the impact of flooding at layer 2 and the potential for congestion that leads to frame dropping.

- *Expanding-ring search* is a technique that leverages the TTL concept in IP packets to find the closest, well-known, registered, multicast resource. A sender starts by sending a query with a TTL of 1 to find the closest multicast group of a resource. If no reply is received, the sender keeps incrementing the TTL and making queries until the sender receives the closest reply.

■   When extending IP multicast into the WAN and across large campus networks, multicast *trees* are formed. Trees are built using a multicast routing protocol—such as Distant Vector Multicast Routing Protocol (DVMRP)—to link a subnet to all other subnets with members in the same multicast group. There are two types of multicast trees—*source-based* trees and *shared* trees—and various multicast algorithms associated with each type.

■   Source-based trees rely on periodic broadcasting and pruning to build and maintain the multicast tree. Multicast packets are periodically broadcast across the network to advertise multicast data. In order to limit broadcasting and reduce duplicate packets, multicast broadcasting is done only for packets that arrive on ports that the router considers the shortest path back to the source of the packet. Edge (or sometimes called leaf) routers use a technique called *reverse-path forwarding* (RPF) to reduce needless forwarding of multicast packets. If an edge router does not have any subscribers to a multicast stream, it sends a "prune" message back *to cut itself off* from further messages. The upstream router maintains the "prune state," and after some designated time period, a subsequent broadcast to the edge router is made, enabling the router to graft itself back onto the tree if it obtains an interested subscriber in the meantime. Source-based trees do not scale well in the WAN (broadcast tends to be a bad word when used in the same sentence as WAN), yet they are resilient to network failure since separate trees are maintained for each multicast recipient. Source-based trees are efficient since they follow the shortest path, yet they have the drawback of requiring the maintenance of a lot of individual trees and prune states which use a lot of routing table space that could be used for other purposes like routing tables, and so on.

■   Shared trees (sometimes called core-based trees) establish in the network a rendezvous point that becomes the center of a multicast group. End stations that want to receive multicasts explicitly for a certain group send a "join" request to the rendezvous point. Core-based trees reduce broadcasting, flooding, and pruning, thus enabling better scale. Core-based trees do, however, result in less efficient paths and are more vulnerable to network failure if linkage to or near the core is severed.

■   *Tunneling* is used to get across regions of a network where there are routers that do not support IP multicast traffic. Essentially, a tunnel encapsulates an IP multicast packet into a unicast packet and then "unencapsulates" it at the other end of the tunnel.

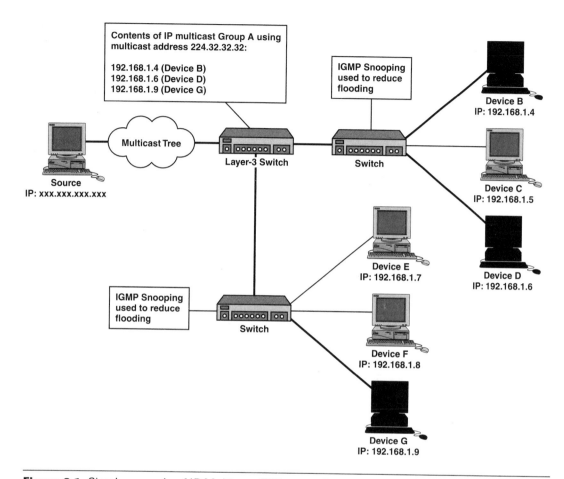

Figure 6.1 Simple example of IP Multicast. "Silhouetted" network devices receive flow based on IGMP subscription; others do not. Data is routed across a multicast tree that may span the WAN, go through tunnels, and use one of the various source-based or shared tree multicast protocols.

- The Multicast Backbone (MBone) is an experimental collection of multicast router islands that are interconnected by tunneling on top of sections of the Internet. DVMRP, MOSPF, and PIM are all used to build the MBone which is designed to test multicast applications before the widespread deployment of multicast routers.

Figure 6.1 illustrates many of the concepts of IP multicast in a switched environment.

A S I D E . . .

Shared trees use the term "upstream" to mean in the direction toward the center of the tree. Source-based trees use "upstream" to mean in the direction toward the source.

A N O T H E R   A S I D E . . .

Traceroute does not work for multicast packets. The ICMP error message, "TTL Exceeded," is not sent in response to multicast packets.

6.4 Internet Group Management Protocol (IGMP)

Operating at the LAN dispersion points of a multicast group is IGMP—without it nothing works. IGMP is used both by end stations (for example, PCs and UNIX workstations) and by routers to manage group membership. End stations use IGMP to join and maintain membership, and routers use the protocol to determine group membership. Thus IGMP is the common language used to manage IP multicast groups; the actual multicast groups are stored in tables on routers.

One router on each LAN periodically sends a *Host Membership Query* to all hosts; end stations (PCs and workstations) respond with a *Host Membership Response* message for each group to which it wants to belong. End stations use a randomly chosen report delay timer for each group membership in order to reduce the overall impact on the network by spreading out reports. In addition, each end station listens for reports for the same group and cancels its report if it hears one. This Query/Response protocol keeps group memberships up-to-date and allows members to be deleted (or "aged out") when several successive queries are made without a corresponding response.

Version 2 of IGMP (IGMPv2) extends IGMP version 1 (IGMPv1, RFC 1112). It has two new messages and a documented way to elect the designated router that performs periodic maintenance queries when multiple routers exist on the same LAN. The two new messages are a *Leave Group Message* and a *Group Specific Query*. End stations use the Leave Group Message explicitly to leave a group; it has the positive effect of reducing the number of repeated queries that must be made by the router in order to age out a membership. The Group Specific Query is used by the designated router in response to a Leave Group Message to direct a query to the particular group that received the Leave Group Message.

This message is used to synchronize the router with group change without having to wait for the normal query message or to query all membership lists. The query election process is based on all routers assuming that they are *the* designated router. Using the protocol message, the routers quickly determine the router with the lowest IP address to be the designated router.

Version 3 of IGMP (IGMPv3) is currently in draft form. This version will add *Group Source Report* and *Group Source Leave* messages to enable an end station to elect to listen only to multicasts from a specific source in a group. Again, like IGMPv2, this feature reduces unnecessary traffic so that the protocol can scale better.

6.5 Distance-Vector Multicast Routing Protocol (DVMRP)

DVMRP (RFC 1075) is a distance-vector protocol that uses reverse path forwarding to define the scope of its multicasting. Essentially reverse path forwarding *floods* (or more correctly *broadcasts*) the first datagram containing the source/ group pair to all leaf routers in the network. If the routers do not have any subscriptions, they return *prune* messages, which reduce the scope of the multicasting required. After a designated time, pruned branches "grow back," giving routers the chance to add subscribers. This prune/"grow back" practice continues as long as the multicast flow continues. In addition to the grow back mechanism, a graft message may be sent by a leaf router if a leaf host indicates interest in an application's multicast flow. In order to maintain this state, DVMRP implements its own routing table which is similar in structure to a RIP routing table. One management problem with DVMRP is that it does not scale well because of excessive use of broadcasting. Table 6.1 summarizes the key information about DVMRP.

6.6 Multicast Open Shortest Path First (MOSPF)

MOSPF (RFC 1584) builds off the base of the link-state protocol, OSPF. With the addition of the source/group pair necessary for multicast traffic, MOSPF uses the same algorithm as OSPF to determine the shortest reverse path. It requires lots of processing power like OSPF and is well suited for environments in which only a few source/group pairs are active. This protocol is particularly poor in environments with unstable links. MOSPF maintains a local group database of group memberships based on IGMP monitoring. One MOSPF router on each subnet becomes the designed router; this router is solely responsible for

Table 6.1 DVMRP-Specific Information

Characteristic	Value
Designed for	Small Network (LAN)
Type	Source-based tree
State	Used in MBone, private LANs
Key Advantages	• Distant-vector algorithms are straightforward to implement. • Using DVMRP is a relatively simple way to attach the edge of Intranet to the MBone, where the protocol is widely used. • Tunneling may be used to connect across routers that do not implement multicast.
Key Disadvantages	• The same limitations as distant-vector algorithms apply, like RIP with respect to scaling; for example, trees are slow to converge and are limited to the same 15-hop diameter as RIP. • It relies on periodic broadcasting to maintain tables. • It requires lots of routing table memory to store prune state records on each router.

listening for IGMP subscriptions and sending host membership reports to all other MOSPF routers. A backup designated router is also configured in the event the designated router goes down. Unlike DVMRP, MOSPF does not support tunneling.

There are two key characteristics of MOSPF that provide multicast scalability:

1. MOSPF allows for the same two-level hierarchy as OSPF. This provides an effective way to isolate local multicast traffic to an OSPF area and to advertise only summary Link State Advertisement (LSA) across area boundaries. Hierarchy is fundamental to scalability as it provides an effective way to isolate local information, reducing the amount of globally advertised information to a small set.

2. MOSPF spreads out multicast route calculations by doing them on demand when a router sees the first multicast packet. This eliminates the need to calculate and store paths for which there are no receivers, as well as spread out the calculations over time.

Table 6.2 summarizes key MOSPF information.

Table 6.2 MOSPF-Specific Information

Characteristic	Value
Designed for	LANs, Autonomous Systems, Intranets
Type	Source-based tree with on-demand, explicit joins
State	Deployed primarily in private Intranets
Key Advantages	• It leverages existing topology and link-state information. • It builds upon OSPF's two-level hierarchy, providing scalability. • There is no need to broadcast to build initial tree; it spreads out route calculations by doing them on-demand. • Expanding ring search is optimized by not forwarding datagrams when routers know that the TTL is too small to reach any group members. • It integrates with DVMRP, using a special DVMRP multicast tunnel that provides a way to integrate MOSPF into the MBone. This capability allows MOSPF to be used internally within a domain, utilizing DVMRP as a gateway protocol between domains.
Key Disadvantages	• It requires OSPF to run on every router participating in multicasting. • It does not support tunneling across routers not running OSPF.

6.7 Core-Based Trees (CBT)

When you hear the term "broadcast" packets over a WAN, you should probably shudder. CBT (RFC 2189) is one of two shared-tree multicast protocols that does *not* rely on periodic broadcasts of "got some multicast information, are you interested?" messages, as employed in source-based tree algorithms to keep the tree up-to-date. As mentioned previously, shared-tree algorithms require an explicit downstream join to a *common* rendezvous point. They are designed to scale for larger scale deployment by reducing the amount of information that must be propagated and maintained to keep the protocol state current. Table 6.3 summarizes the key characteristics of CBT, and Table 6.4 summarizes the messages used to manage its trees.

Table 6.3 CBT-Specific Information

Characteristic	Value
Designed for	WAN and larger scale deployment, although can be used in LAN
Type	Shared Tree
State	Experimental
Key Advantages	• It has protocol independence (that is, it uses existing routing information to build a tree). • It scales better than some other protocols and results in a reduced amount of information that needs to be stored in routing tables.
Key Disadvantages	• It results in less efficient paths. • It is more vulnerable to link failure and traffic congestion.

Table 6.4 CBT Messages

Message	Meaning
JOIN_REQUEST	This message is sent by a designated router to join a group.
JOIN_ACK	This message is returned to a designated router confirming membership.
ECHO_REQUEST	This request message is sent between CBT routers to refresh membership.
ECHO_REPLY	This reply message is sent between CBT routers to refresh membership.
FLUSH_TREE	This message is sent to remove downstream branches.
QUIT_NOTIFICATION	This message is sent by a designated router to leave a group.

6.8 Protocol Independent Multicast

PIM is a scalable, multienterprise protocol that integrates with Interior Gateway Routing (IGP), Intermediate System to Intermediate System (IS-IS), OSPF, and RIP. PIM has two modes, dense mode and sparse mode. Dense mode is designed primarily for LANs where multicast groups are in close proximity, and sparse mode is used in WANs where groups are widely distributed.

6.8.1 Dense Mode (PIM-DM)

PIM-DM has a lot of similarities to DVMRP. PIM-DM is

- an approach to multicasting designed for a small LAN environment.
- a source-based tree protocol, that is, it relies on broadcasting and pruning to maintain multicast membership.

PIM-DM differs from DVMRP in that

- it is protocol independent.
- it uses more broadcasting and explicit pruning to simplify its implementation.

Table 6.5 summarizes the key characteristics of PIM-DM, and Table 6.6 summarizes the messages used to manage its trees.

Table 6.5 PIM-DM-Specific Information

Characteristic	Value
Designed for	LAN
Type	Source-based tree
State	Experimental
Key Advantages	• As the name, protocol-independent, implies, it uses existing routing information to build trees. • It uses the best, most efficient path.
Key Disadvantages	• It doesn't scale well as it requires periodic broadcasting and pruning to maintain tree state.

Table 6.6 PIM-DM Messages

Message	Meaning
PIM_HELLO	This message is sent to detect neighboring PIM routers.
PIM_PRUNE	This message is sent to sever attachment to a multicast tree.
PIM_JOIN	This message is sent to attach to a multicast tree.
PIM_GRAFT	This message is sent to reattach a branch of a multicast tree.
PIM_GRAFT_ACK	This message is sent to acknowledge reattachment.

Table 6.7 PIM-SM-Specific Information

Characteristic	Value
Designed for	WAN, although can be used in LAN
Type	Shared tree (extension of CBT) and selective use of source-based tree
State	Deployed experimentally
Key Advantages	• As the name, protocol-independent, implies, it uses existing routing information to build a tree. • It allows for use of a source-based tree at places where traffic levels are high. • It scales better than some other protocols as it results in a reduced amount of information that needs to be stored in tables at routers. • It requires downstream routers explicitly to join trees rather than broadcasting to routers and making them do the filtering.
Key Disadvantages	• It results in less efficient paths. • It is vulnerable to link failure and traffic congestion.

6.8.2 Sparse Mode (PIM-SM)

PIM-SM (RFC 2117) can be thought of as an extension to core-based trees (CBT). It is also designed for WAN use but recognizes in certain cases that use of a source-based tree may be warranted. Therefore although PIM-SM is a shared-tree protocol, it includes a series of messages that allow it to implement a source-based tree at places in the network where the traffic volume is high and a shorter path is available. Nothing precludes PIM-SM from maintaining both a source-based and a shared tree since source-based trees are set up on a per source basis and there many be many routers downstream. Table 6.7 summarizes the key characteristics of PIM-SM, and Table 6.8 summarizes the messages used to manage its trees.

Table 6.8 PIM-SM Messages

Message	Meaning
PIM_HELLO	This message is sent to detect PIM routers.
PIM_PRUNE	This message is sent to unsubscribe to multicast traffic-shared tree.
PIM_JOIN	This message is sent to subscribe to multicast traffic-shared tree.
PIM_ASSERT	This message is used to validate tree branches.
PIM_REGISTER	This message is sent to transition to a source-based tree.
PIM_REGISTER_STOP	This message is sent to "unregister" as a source-based tree.
PIM_BOOTSTRAP	This message is used to determine the bootstrap router (BSR), another name for the designated router as described previously.
CANDIDATE_RP_ADVERTISEMENT	This message is used to determine the rendezvous point.

A S I D E . . .

Despite the use of the same prefix, PIM-SM and PIM-DM do not have a lot in common. In fact, care must be taken not to overlap PIM-SM and PIM-DM multicast routing regions. Failure to separate the two will cause multicast hysteria since the two protocols do share some messaging.

6.9 Multicast over ATM (MARS)

As discussed earlier, ATM has its own addressing scheme and is unaware of IP addresses and therefore IP multicast addresses. A multicast address resolution server (MARS) is used as the central location for storing and mapping IP multicast groups to ATM addresses. MARS provides four messages to manage ATM multicast groups: `MARS_JOIN` and `MARS_LEAVE` are used to attach and detach an end station to a multicast group, and `MARS_REQUEST` and `MARS_ MULTI` are used to get and receive the host map (there may be several addresses at once) for an IP group address, respectively.

6.10 IETF Developments

In order to make further progress on multicasting technology standards, the IETF Inter-Domain Multicast Routing (IDMR) working group was formed. The purpose of the IDMR working group is to create a multicast routing solution that scales across the Internet—clearly not a simple task! The IDMR is responsible for the delivery of both PIM protocols and CBT. It is expected that the Internet solution will be a combination of both shared tree and source-based tree, leveraging the abstraction of hierarchical routing across Autonomous System (AS) boundaries. This emerging hybrid solution will build upon the experience and knowledge gained from the MBone and from the many multicast protocols and routing solutions.

6.10.1 Multicast-Border Gateway Protocol (M-BGP)

One of the principal problems of all multicast protocols today is their inability to scale, and scaling is an absolute necessity for widespread deployment of multicast technology. Building and maintaining a flat multicast tree across many hops requires significant processing power and large routing tables to store source/destination pairs. Keeping a large tree intact across a large network would flood the network with updates and require astronomically large routing table caches. For these reasons, network developers are looking beyond the largely DVMRP-based MBone to extend the interior/exterior routing model used in today's Internet. Even though the Internet has scaling problems of its own, today's current size is possible only because of the explicit use of hierarchical routing implicit within the interior/exterior routing model.

There are two approaches to hierarchical multicast that are currently in the early stages of investigation: M-BGP and Border Gateway Multicast Protocol (BGMP). M-BGP extends BGP by adding multicast capabilities. Since BGP is used to interconnect the Internet's ASs, extending BGP provides an attractive (presumed minimally disruptive) way to leverage the hierarchical routing model and interconnection policy already in place. The idea behind M-BGP is to allow any tree-building protocol to use the current routing policy already in place to exchange multicast information.

BGMP, also known as Global Unified Multicast (GUM), extends from the concepts introduced in shared-tree protocols (CBT and PIM-SM). With BGMP, two tree structures are in place: regular shared trees and interdomain source-specific trees. Trees contain domain entries not router entries, and routes are bidirectional. Interdomain trees provide a standards-based (currently emerging), nonproprietary way to communicate multicast information across ASs, whereas regular shared trees are used within an AS. This two-level hierarchy provides an effective way to minimize table sizes and tree calculations, cleverly leveraging what we have learned from hierarchical routing.

6.10.2 Multicast Reliability

When we use a Web browser to access a Web page, we use HTTP that runs over TCP to create a reliable end-to-end connection with the Web server. Although TCP provides assurance that we actually do or do not get the data, *TCP cannot multicast*. Hence IP multicast in its current form (over UDP) does not provide any assurance. In fact, IP multicast thrives on the fact that both senders and receivers can join the same group and are not even aware of each other's membership!

Reliable Multicast Protocol (RMP), Reliable Multicast Transfer Protocol (RMTP), and Multicast File Transfer Protocol (MFTP) are very recent proposals that explore providing some level of assurance that data is actually received. It is expected that adding assurance to the implicit data reduction of multicast will provide a needed base for a whole new slew of applications. Pay-per-memberships and global *confirmed* communications via push technologies are a couple of examples that use reliable multicasting.

6.11 Setting Expectations

Networking solutions that span many devices are inevitably slower to deploy and penetrate than solutions that can be built into a single box. Multicast is a great example of a distributed technology that has been over ten years in the works. What will "push" multicast into widespread deployment? Applications will because *applications drive networking.*

Take a moment to think of the one-to-many forms of communication that we have relied upon for years: television, radio, and print (newspapers, magazines, advertisements, books). Now put an electronic spin on these basic concepts: Videoconferencing, teleconferencing, stock quoting, news feeds, and electronic magazines are some of the obvious uses. Finally add a creative electronic focus and add distributed "chalktalk" (or "whiteboarding"), virtual presence, software distribution, and replication of databases. All of these forms of communication could leverage multicast.

It is somewhat ironic that multicast is intended to save network bandwidth when thinking about new applications. Facilitating multicast traffic has the potential to open up so many bandwidth-intensive applications (not to mention the additional traffic that is generated by the multicast protocol itself to maintain state) that it might result in bringing a network to its knees! There are already many LANs and private Intranets that use the technology on a limited basis for real-time applications and group-based information distribution. Nonetheless, we will see *gradual* penetration of multicast. It is prudent to introduce any distributed technology gradually so that you can learn, enhance, and gain confidence along the way. It is expected that it will take a long time for us to see widespread Internet multicast deployment as the Internet crosses so many network boundaries while making widespread coordination and agreement difficult.

If you manage an Intranet and your company expects to make use of large quantities of real-time video or interactive voice traffic in the imminent future (or is already doing so), you should start (or continue) experimenting with IP multicast. Try attaching some videos to the MBone and running them across a small portion of your network. Always remember: *Start small, introduce in an isolated environment, and give yourself plenty of lead time* before the massive wave of a technology lands on your beach.

6.12 Conclusions

There are many different multicast routing protocols available, each with its own strengths and weaknesses. The biggest concern of multicast is scalability.

Broadcasting across WAN links and storing voluminous amounts of data in routing tables does not scale well. We must look to hierarchical routing techniques as being key to multicast since this is how the Internet has scaled to service so many users and why corporations often deploy OSPF and OSPF areas across their Intranets.

Networks are built on shared resources. As our demands for networking increase, there are three complementary options available to us: We can add, better manage, and/or conserve resources. Switching has enabled us to *add* bandwidth and significantly speed up networks. Emerging technologies like multilayer switching, provisioning of QoS guarantees, and COS solutions provide ways for us to *better manage* our networking resources. Multicast provides a way to *conserve resources,* completing our available options.

Like other distributed solutions (multilayer switching, provisioning of QoS guarantees, and COS solutions), we will see multicast roll out in network pockets, not in widespread deployment. This provides a way to test solutions and get feedback that can be used to enhance and improve technologies, clearly addressing our ever-increasing demands for networking.

CHAPTER 7

Network Policy and Services

7.1 Introduction

The explosive growth of switching solutions has resulted in a networking infrastructure that incorporates many technologies, many networking protocols, and a variety of network switches. This networking infrastructure is used in many ways to satisfy the diverse needs of users. Our networks are becoming increasingly spread out and complex—a necessary evolution to satisfy the suite of rich, emerging networked applications.

Control and customization are fundamental requirements of our networking infrastructure. Without control, our networks become unreliable and unpredictable. Customization provides the means to adapt our networks for use in a variety of ways by many different networked applications. Network customization needs to facilitate dynamic change and diverse, simultaneous use of distributed resources. It incorporates more intelligence into the network, providing a base for new, "not-yet-invented" network use.

We are beginning to see new, creative ways in which our networks are used. These applications are placing more demands on networks such as overall speed, integrated Class of Service (COS), and distributed security. Applications drive network requirements and the overall need for more network control and network customization.

Built-in network intelligence and rich new applications go hand-in-hand. Increased network intelligence allows for new applications to demand smarter network infrastructures. This chapter provides a survey of new technologies that facilitate distributed network intelligence and a few examples of emerging applications positioned to utilize "smarter" networks. Our switched networks are moving quickly beyond basic information transportation systems into intelligent, multipurpose information fabrics.

7.2 Key Solutions Offered

As the network becomes the backbone of businesses, there is more and more emphasis on creating a more robust, faster network to support a suite of more sophisticated network services. Stronger networks require distributed regulation and intelligence so that the network can dynamically adapt to needs that change throughout the day.

In previous chapters we discussed three important emerging technologies: multilayer switching, delivery guarantees, and multicast. This chapter focuses on network policy and two key emerging services: Virtual Private Networks (VPNs) and Voice over IP (VoIP). Network policy can be thought of as the distributed intelligent glue that provides the necessary foundation for next-generation technologies and network services. VPNs and VoIP are two new, powerful network services that demonstrate the need for next-generation switched networks.

7.3 Network Policy

Policy is one of the most elusive concepts in networking. We will give "policy" a very simple definition: *Policy is the set of distributed rules that control how the network is shared.* Let's break this definition apart and demonstrate the important role of policy in our next-generation networks. For starters we know that networks are

- composed of an integrated mesh of many network interconnection devices (for example, many different types of switches).

- distributed and span geographies.

- a shared resource used by many users.

Fundamental to network operation is correct device configuration. Understandably many devices depend on the *proper configuration* of other network devices within the same network for their operation. Routing protocols, such as OSPF, exchange information across routers to keep the network topology up-to-date; likewise MPLS swaps labels with adjacent LRs so that packets are properly routed. COS requires distribution of the rules that govern classification and queuing algorithms used. IP multicast is based on distribution and synchronization of multicast groups to which hosts subscribe via IGMP. To operate properly, networks rely on the distribution of knowledge that defines just how the network is shared. It is this distributed knowledge that is *policy.*

Network managers manually syncing interconnection devices on an individual basis across the network is common today. This method does not scale and is error-prone, slow (especially when devices span ownership and geographies), and not dynamic. Emerging network services require dynamic, distributed change in order to work optimally and, in some cases, properly. For example, in order to set up a video stream for 9 A.M.–10 A.M. on a Monday from London to New York City, you would like to guarantee that you will have the proper bandwidth ahead of time. You don't want any jitter because you are showing the video to an audience that will determine your network funding, based largely on the quality that you provide. Wouldn't it be nice to provision this service for the hour that it is needed and then "unprovision" it after 10 A.M.? In other words, to pay for the preferential treatment only when you absolutely need it?

A S I D E . . .

Policy standardization across geographically spread organizations will be difficult. Various organizations maintain different management styles, goals, and objectives. Policies that consistently interoperate will result in the biggest networking gain. The Common Open Policy Service (COPS) Protocol Internet Draft[1] provides a client/ server protocol for exchanging policy information. This may be one of the most important components of propagating and later negotiating consistent policy across networks.

7.3.1 Service Level Agreements (SLAs)

With the advent of the WWW, there are now many businesses that base their entire livelihood on having network connectivity. When the network is down, their business is down; when the network is slow, online shoppers go elsewhere. Financial organizations lose millions of dollars when their network goes down; fault tolerant networks with consistent network performance are a fundamental requirement.

As the overall business cost of network failure or poor performance increases, the need for formal network service agreements has emerged. These

---

1. The COPS (Common Open Policy Service) Protocol Internet Draft (updated March 1998) by Jim Boyle of MCI, Ron Cohen of Class Data Systems, David Durham of Intel, Shai Herzog of IPHighway, Raju Rajan of IBM, and Arun Sastry of Cisco.

are commonly called SLAs and are most prevalent in the WAN service market provided by service carriers. SLAs *formalize service characteristics and the associated set of metrics used to ensure that the service characteristics are met.* They provide a service-level contract and a set of measurable criteria used to validate services.

SLAs provided by carriers across the globe do not guarantee that the network will be operational 100 percent of the time; nor do they guarantee performance will be unvaried 100 percent of the time. However, carriers do guarantee network availability 99.*x* percent of the time where *x* varies; 99.6 percent overall, though, is fairly common. When you do the math, this means that the network will be down on the average no more than approximately 5.76 minutes (roughly 5 minutes, 45 seconds) per day. When the down time exceeds this guarantee, the customer is usually compensated with free or reduced network service costs.

The granularity and level of agreement specified in SLAs become an important service differentiation between service providers. Provision of customer measurement and validation of level of service are also important. Customers are willing to pay for better (substantiated) guaranteed service in proportion to the criticality of service failure.

7.4 Policy—The Distributed Glue That Ties Everything Together

We have defined policy as the set of distributed rules that control how the network is shared. Now let's dig a bit deeper and identify what defines a network's distributed rules. When building or extending a network, you place an order for hubs, routers, and switches to create or extend your network. Typically when the network interconnection devices arrive at the installation location, they are configured with factory defaults. Your first jobs are to customize the interconnection devices for your environment, test them out in an isolated way, and then incorporate them onto your production network.

Policy data is all about network configuration. Configuration data defines the rules of how networks ultimately operate and includes device-specific configuration, address and name management configuration, and attributes that control security, accounting, and performance configuration. Configuration also includes the definition of automatic network recovery based on fault monitoring.

Throughout this text we allude to the need to manage interactive voice and real-time video quality by using dedicated resources or bumping up the data's priority to ensure that jitter remains under control. We know that security is a fundamental requirement of networks as it ensures that sensitive data running over shared media stays within the hands of its owner. We know that network users must (or perhaps should) pay for their network usage (and, soon, their level of service)—accounting. Finally networks need to adjust dynamically in the cause of network outage based on a set of rules governing fault. Distributed network policy is a fundamental requirement of our next generation networks—it is the glue that ties everything together.

A S I D E . . .

You probably recognize that in the previous few paragraphs we enumerated all five partitions defined by the International Organization for Standardization (ISO) for network management:

- Fault management
- Configuration management
- Accounting management
- Performance management
- Security management

We will revisit this important management list in Chapter 8.

7.5 Network Configuration Repositories

Early in the book we introduced DHCP as a protocol for distributed address management. We also mentioned that many DHCP servers integrate with a Domain Name Service (DNS) to provide name-based address management. Remote Authentication Dial-In User Service (RADIUS) is another widely deployed configuration repository used to authenticate dial-in users in both enterprise and carrier networks.

This section looks at both RADIUS and the next steps for DHCP—two very important network configuration repositories. Integrating these solutions into a distributed policy solution is fundamental, since both RADIUS and DHCP are widespread, and together they define a significant portion of network policy in place today.

7.5.1 Next Steps for DHCP

From Chapter 2 we learned that DHCP provides a general-purpose client/server approach to IP address distribution. Via address leasing DHCP provides a global address management system that improves the overall client mobility and reduces errors inherent in static IP address distribution. DHCP is particularly useful in ISP environments that service the many dial-in users that come and go throughout the course of a day. Generally speaking, the larger the organization, the greater the utility of implementing a DHCP solution.

There are many commercial DHCP solutions currently available. They feature such things as fault tolerance, DNS integration, bulk management of common addresses, and Web browser access. The focus of fault tolerance is to ensure that a user is never without a network connection because the DHCP server is down. Server redundancy with address mirroring between the servers is the common solution for ensuring fault tolerance. Servers should also be connected to an Uninterruptable Power Supply (UPS) in the event of power failure. DNS integration removes the need to synchronize name changes manually with the name server. This option coupled with bulk management of common addresses is extremely valuable in large environments that must manage many addresses. Finally Web browser access provides an O/S platform and geographically portable way to view and manage addresses across an organization. This feature is very useful in environments that span large distances. From a next generation standpoint, DHCP is well positioned to service users with information other than a network address, particularly policy information.

DHCP is already widely deployed across organizations and integrated into O/S platforms like Windows/NT. As mentioned in RFC 2131, the DHCP message has a variable length options field that could be used to distribute user-specific policy information to DHCP clients. After all, the standard explicitly states that DHCP is a framework for passing configuration information to hosts on a TCP/IP network—not an address management system, as many people believe. It is expected that DHCP will play an important role in policy distribution and policy-enabled networks of the future.

7.5.2 Remote Authentication Dial-In User Service (RADIUS)

RADIUS (RFC 2138) is a widely deployed standard used to authenticate dial-in users. It is used to manage pools of modems that service many users simultaneously by providing security, authorization, and account administration.

RADIUS follows a client/server model using a single server to manage the repository of authentication data for many clients. Unlike many client/server solutions, RADIUS protocol runs over UDP.

As the standard states, UDP was chosen over connection-oriented TCP to simplify server implementation, to facilitate better an environment where users come and go frequently, and to provide flexibility with respect to timeout. Maintaining client/server sessions as required by connection-oriented sessions adds complexity and overhead to a server implementation. In dial-in environments users come and go; thus a connectionless service like UDP is a natural fit.

RADIUS Accounting (RFC 2139) extends the RADIUS protocol to provide a programmatic interface to store accounting data collected during a dial-in session. RADIUS accounting again follows a client/server model where the client is the Network Access Server (NAS) (the RADIUS server that authenticates a dial-in session) and the server is the process that accepts and stores accounting data from one or more NASs. The protocol uses a simple *Account-Request* packet to communicate data from the client to the server and an *Account-Response* packet to acknowledge that the response has been received successfully. The Account-Response packet contains an identifier obtained from the Account-Request packet used by the client to "match up" the completion of a transaction. The Account-Response packet includes data that can be used for account billing purposes by an ISP—data like input octets/packets, output octets/packets, and session time.

The RADIUS accounting protocol transmits accounting data in an extensible code/length/value format. This enables the protocol to add new attributes simply by giving them a new code. There are several designated implementation-specific codes and experimental codes that may be used to log other types of data. It is expected that service-specific types of data like data sent using a certain COS, data sent within a certain response time, and other policy information will be added to certain vendor implementations and will perhaps be designated as standard codes over time.

7.5.3 An Example of RADIUS in Use

The following provides an example of RADIUS in use:

1. A user dials in from home to his ISP account providing a user name and password previously given to or agreed upon by the ISP.

2. As part of the login process, the ISP's Remote Access Server (RAS), a RADIUS client, authenticates the dial-in user by sending an Access-Request message with the name, password, and port number to a

RADIUS server to which the user is attempting to connect. The RADIUS server is sometimes called a network access server (NAS). Passwords are encrypted using the Message-Digest Algorithm 5 (MD5) (RFC 3121). A timer is maintained by the RAS since a response is not guaranteed and the request may need to be retransmitted.

3. Upon first receipt of the request, the RADIUS server validates the authenticity of the client—in this case the RAS. The RADIUS server will respond only to requests from known clients; requests from unknown clients will be dropped. Valid RADIUS clients share a secret with their RADIUS server, and the specification points out that the secret between client and RADIUS server should be at least 16 octets and "unguessable."

4. After validating the client, the RADIUS server uses the information in the Access-Request to validate the user. In this example if the name, password, and port number form a valid combination, an Access-Accept is returned to the client; if any attribute is invalid, an Access-Reject is returned.

5. Even in the event that all conditions are met, the RADIUS server might still issue an Access-Challenge response to ask the client for more information. In this way the server has some knowledge of context when it receives a subsequent response. An Access-Request returns the additional information. There is no limit to the number of challenge cycles that may occur.

ASIDE...

The officially defined port number for RADIUS is 1812 *not* 1645 as used in many early erroneous implementations. In addition, the officially defined port number for RADIUS accounting is 1813 *not* 1646.

ANOTHER ASIDE...

When talking about Remote Access Concentrators (RACs), you often hear of RADIUS AAA support. The three A's stand for Authentication, Authorization, and Accounting. A fourth "A" has been added in some discussions to represent "Auditing."

7.6 Introducing Distributed Policy Is a Large Challenge

Networks are anything but static: Devices come and go; IP addresses are assigned and reassigned via DHCP; new applications get added to the network, constantly changing traffic patterns; a layer-3 switch goes down causing traffic to be rerouted; employees dial in to corporate networks, remotely check their mail, and log off. The dynamic nature of networks requires network policy to adjust to change constantly.

In addition, networks are broadly distributed. It's not uncommon for a corporation to span two or three continents and to have widely dispersed data. Some businesses have several sites within the same city or across a large corporate campus. Retail stores have presence in many different cities and use the network to distribute data. Network policy must be distributed and must be dynamic due to the inherent requirements of networking.

Networks are constructed of devices from many vendors, and although standards enable interoperability, there is still a need to keep track of data that is device-specific. Vendors often use proprietary features to differentiate themselves; these features must be managed. Policy must provide a way to generalize common device attributes and yet allow for vendor-specific features. Policy must facilitate the heterogeneous nature of networks.

Finally, networks are large and growing. ISPs cannot add modem pools fast enough to keep up with the demands of remote access. A network manager may be able to get by with manual configuration and periodic maintenance of ten switches, but having one hundred switches (often geographically dispersed) to configure and maintain is more problematic. Network policy must scale.

In order for network policy to facilitate dynamic, distributed, heterogeneous networks and simultaneously scale, networks must evolve to formal distribution and administration of policy. This section discusses some important standards and emerging efforts that are positioned to solve some of the inherent problems of network policy.

7.6.1 Lightweight Directory Access Protocol (LDAP)

LDAP is an IETF standard pioneered by the University of Michigan in 1991. It provides a common way to store and access network data in a hierarchical format. LDAP builds upon the Consultative Committee on International Telegraphy and Telephony (CCITT) X.500 standard, an International Telecommunications

Union-Telecommunication (ITU-T) standard that provides a central or distributed way to store and retrieve directory information throughout a network. X.500 is used today to consolidate directory information in e-mail, making the information accessible via an agent from any workstation or PC.

So you ask, what is a directory service, and why is it important to networking? Directory services provide an efficient mechanism to reference and access a *single, consistent* collection of related information about a network entity across an enterprise. This collection of related information is called a *namespace.* For example, X.500 provides access to a namespace about an individual network user such as the user's e-mail address, country name, organization name, and name. Key to X.500 is that it provides the actual hierarchical structure of how the information is stored, identifying a common way to reference and access a given namespace.

This hierarchical structure is represented in a tree format and provides a uniform, extensible way to identify and access a given namespace. In our previous example, the X.500 hierarchy would be country, organization within the country, and individual name within the organization. Once you traverse to the individual, a *single* collection of attributes about that individual can be stored, as in our case, in an e-mail address.

Note the use of the word "single" is important as duplicate, disparate information can be eliminated as a single hierarchy services all network clients. This namespace is the perfect place to put other attributes about an individual, such as the preferred printer, network priority, and any other network customization. Having a directory service provides an extensible, consistent mechanism to represent the hierarchical structure of a network and its associated configuration data.

Key to LDAP's recent popularity is that it provides a *lightweight* hierarchical directory service. X.500 is not lightweight, and accessing information through X.500 via its access protocol—Directory Access Protocol (DAP)—from a common PC can be slow. Sluggishness is precisely the reason that X.500 never caught on as a widespread service despite its introduction many years ago. X.500, however, provides an excellent, well-seasoned distributed directory service. Used in conjunction with LDAP, X.500 provides a viable solution to storing, referencing, and accessing distributed configuration network data.

In short, LDAP provides the following:

- Vendor *interoperability* via a *common* client/server interface for setting up and maintaining network devices across a heterogeneous network environment. Since network information is stored in an LDAP database that is accessible via a common API, applications can access and manage devices in a common way. This is analogous to the support of Management Information Base-2 (MIB-2) via the Simple Network Management Protocol (SNMP).[2]

- *Centralization* and *distribution* of security, policy, and network configuration across a network. Since both applications and users can "float," network information needs to be assessabled from anywhere on the network. A network application needs to be run anywhere on the network with the same "view" of the network. Likewise a mobile user requires access to customized network account data regardless of where the network connection is made.

- Network *scalability* by reducing redundant information. Since information about a network device is stored only in one place in the network hierarchy, duplication of information is greatly reduced. In addition, many network devices can be set up to inherit information higher in a hierarchy, allowing network change for thousands of network devices via a single attribute change. And, since LDAP provides a logical view of network devices, the actual physical device can change without affecting the binding to a user or application; this is important to providing network evolution without major network disruption.

These components are all essential to policy-based networking as they provide the essential glue (or binding) for many disparate pieces of network information across a widely distributed set of network devices.

7.6.1.1 How LDAP Works

There are four RFCs that define LDAP:

1. RFC 1487 defines LDAP version 1 (LDAPv1).
2. RFC 1777 defines LDAP version 2 (LDAPv2) and obsolesces RFC 1487.
3. RFC 1823 defines the LDAP Application Program Interface (API).
4. RFC 2251 defines LDAP version 3 (LDAPv3) expected to be standardized in 1998.

Where LDAPv2 replaces LDAPv1 and provides the base functionally set deployed today, LDAPv3 extends LDAPv2 by

---

2. MIB-2 is a common MIB used to manage *like* attributes across network devices. SNMP is the protocol used to set and retrieve MIB-2 attributes.

- supporting a variety of authentication schemes,
- supporting a referral service,
- providing dynamically extensible schema capabilities, and
- providing support for international character sets.

Authentication in version 2 is limited to Kerberos and use of a simple text password; version 3 adds strong authentication via the X.509 standard. The referral service provides a way for an LDAP server to redirect a client to another server to satisfy a client's query. This referral capability is modeled after one found in the Directory Access Protocol (DAP) that serves an X.500 directory. The dynamically extensible schema capability enables applications to write private data, such as configuration or user preference data, in the directory. LDAP localization provides support for international character sets.

Like X.500, LDAP is a directory service that maintains a namespace that contains collections of related information organized in a hierarchical fashion based on a directory model. With the directory there are entries; each entry is associated with a distinguished name. Applications and users retrieve and define information in the namespace by using the LDAP API, which is connection-oriented and works over the TCP/IP stack by connecting to an *LDAP* server. Although an application or user typically connects to only one LDAP server, one or more LDAP servers may synchronize data with each other providing a distributed LDAP repository (by replicating information) that spans an enterprise.

The LDAP "C-based" (using the C programming language) API, as defined in RFC 1823, outlines the typical four steps that an application performs to retrieve or modify information in an LDAP repository. Please refer to RFC 1823 for exact parameters and sample code; the following text provides only the high-level flow designed to show how straightforward the API is—not to duplicate the API specification.

1. **Open** the connection to the LDAP server using an `ldap_open()` call. The open returns a connection handle used by all subsequent requests to the LDAP server as a reference to the LDAP session. The LDAP server may service many clients at once.

2. **Authenticate** the connection using an `ldap_bind()` call. There are many bind calls. Kerberos authentication (version 4.1 and 4.2) and simple authentication using text password routines are provided.

3. **Perform** one or more LDAP operations using a set of straightforward routines. `ldap_search()` is used to find an entry within the LDAP directory; `ldap_first_attribute()` and `ldap_next_attribute()` are used to step through attributes associated with an

entry; `ldap_get_values()` is used to retrieve the values of an attribute; `ldap_modify()` is used to modify an entry; `ldap_add()` is used to add an entry; and `ldap_delete()` is used to delete an entry.

4. **Close** the connection to the LDAP server using an `ldap_unbind()` call. This completes the session and enables the server to free resources.

7.6.2 Directory Enabled Networking (DEN)

DEN[3] began as a join initiative by Cisco and Microsoft to define a network directory architecture. The emerging standard has since been transitioned to the Desktop Management Task Force (DMTF) in an effort to make the standard more widely accepted across the industry. DEN builds and extends LDAPv3 by standardizing the directory information itself, ensuring that all directory information follows the same format. In database terminology we often refer to data's format as a "schema." One current limitation of LDAP's use and deployment is that it does not define a consistent directory structure and naming convention to be used across all vendors. This lack of standard results in inconsistent naming and structure, making it difficult (if not impossible) for an application to work across multiple vendors' LDAP server implementations. Since networks are made up of equipment from many vendors, having standard naming conventions and a standard directory structure are very important requirements of maintaining a repository of networking data.

DEN is expected to enable applications and network managers to utilize the hierarchical network data repository of network policy and configuration information in many different ways. For example, since the hierarchical network data can contain network device and user information that is assessable via an API using a *consistent data schema,* a network manager can customize a user's configuration across a network by associating a user with specific network properties. Customization might include priority levels, which printer to use, or which file server to access. Customization might span multiple devices enabling configuration of many types of switches across the network. A simple, powerful search within the database is done to locate where the resources are and how they are deployed in the context of the network. One example of how this networkwide data might be used is to set up and tear down a certain level of QoS at a given time for a specified user across many network resources. One can only speculate how this might be integrated with label swapping of policy data in MPLS.

---

3. "Directory-enabled Networks Specification" (Version 2.0.1-3). The editors are Steve Judd and John Strassner, February 17, 1998.

The power that DEN provides is *uniformity* of the structure of the network data that brings together multiple vendors' network devices into a single consistent model. This consistent model coupled with the LDAP API and support of a distributed database creates a complete, very powerful solution for managing a network manually by a network administrator or automatically with the use of an application. Management of network devices becomes vendor-neutral as vendors provide support to manage their devices using the uniform model. This uniformity creates a very powerful infrastructure for network customization.

The DEN draft specification clearly points out that there are already in existence many schemata to support device-level management. There are both common and proprietary Simple Network Management Protocol (SNMP) Management Information Bases (MIBs) for most devices, as well as the Common Information Model (CIM) defined by the DMTF that provides an object-oriented conceptual model used to manage a complex system. In addition to DNS, DHCP and RADIUS provide consolidation services for management of dispersed information. DEN is not intended to replace these existing structures or services. These data schemata and services can and will continue to exist—the penetration at this point is clearly too great. DEN incorporates this network data into a hierarchical common structure representative of the network itself, providing the added value of consistent access within a defined network context.

Although the class hierarchy proposed for DEN is clearly in the early stages of definition, it makes sense to take a quick look at the parts of DEN that are specific to network devices, policy, and service. For continuity we will start with the top-level class hierarchy. This survey will reinforce the power of DEN and will support the need for such an infrastructure for our next generation networks. These class hierarchies come from the DEN draft specification as referenced previously.

Figures 7.1, 7.2, 7.3 and 7.4 present the class hierarchies from the DEN draft specifications that are directly relevant to this book. Figure 7.1 is the top-level DEN hierarchy with the three classes represented in the subsequent figures.

The *Managed-System Element* provides a base class for all physical devices that can be modeled. Although it includes software components, its main emphasis is to encapsulate aspects of a device that can be physically seen like cards, slots, ports, port connectors, and device connections to the network. See Figure 7.2 for the expanded Managed-System hierarchy.

The *Policy Element* provides a base class for administering policy across the network. This hierarchy includes configuration and security, as well as separate elements to manage, distribute, and control routing and switching. See Figure 7.3 for the expanded Policy hierarchy.

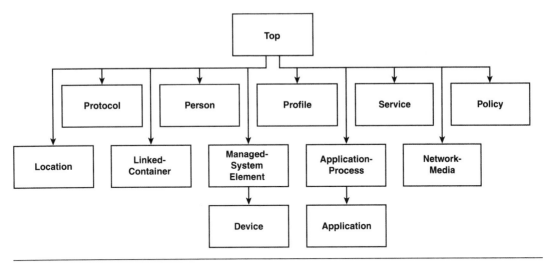

Figure 7.1 The class hierarchy from DEN specification

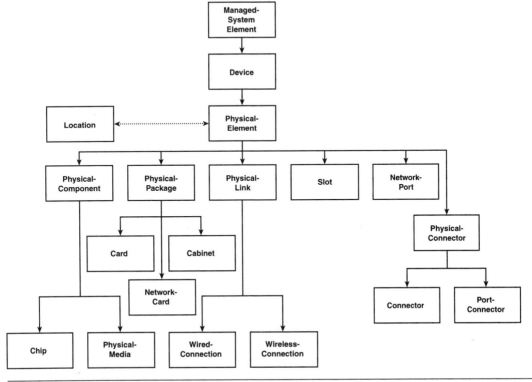

Figure 7.2 The Managed-System Element class hierarchy from DEN specification

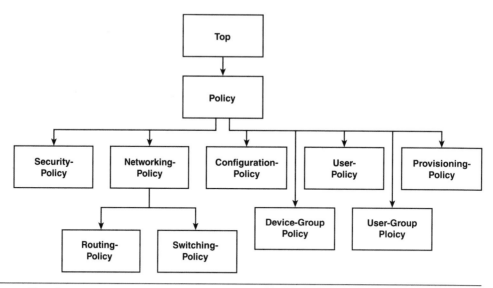

Figure 7.3 The class hierarchy for Policy from DEN specification

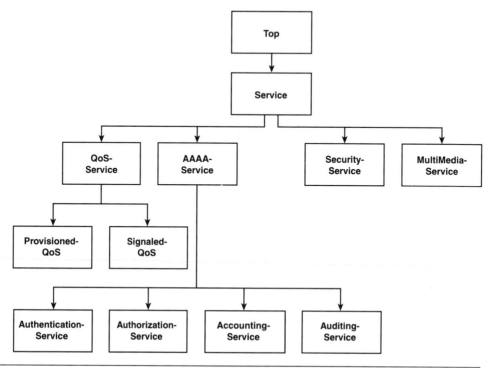

Figure 7.4 The class hierarchy for Services from DEN specification

The *Service Element* provides a base class for services available on the network. QoS (both provisioned and signaled) is one service component. Note that provisioned QoS refers to setting up a service by configuring all the devices required ahead of time. Signaled refers to setting up QoS dynamically when a connection is made (as with ATM). Authentication, authorization, accounting, and auditing are also included as the 4 A's required to manage carrier-provided services and accounts. See Figure 7.4 for the Service Class Hierarchy.

7.7 Network Services

In order to demonstrate the need for distributed network policy with concrete examples, this section provides a concise discussion of VPNs and VoIP, followed by a short section on video. In this book we have discussed the many different types and uses of switches throughout the network. Network services work across many different switch solutions to provide a useful saleable product to customers. Network services benefit from existing switch infrastructures across LANs and the WAN, the introduction of new switches (in the case of VPNs, the Extranet switch), and the augmentation of switches to support VoIP. In addition, network services are expected to benefit from advancements in MPLS, delivery guarantees, IP multicast, and distributed network policy. Sophisticated network services require the switched infrastructure of today and the emerging sophisticated solutions of tomorrow. VPNs and VoIP are only two of the exciting emerging services; as our switched infrastructure gains the intelligence of QoS and distributed policy, we will find that the possibilities for services are nearly endless.

7.7.1 Virtual Private Networks (VPNs)

One of the emerging services that switches are providing the infrastructure for is VPNs. They enable the connection of geographically diverse corporate sites over the Internet—connections that normally would require point-to-point connections, *extended Intranets,* or use of cloud technologies like frame relay or X.25. VPNs also provide dial-in access, called *remote access* VPNs, for remote use. Finally VPNs can be used to provide access to customer-applicable portions of a corporation's network, called *Extranets.* Electronic commerce (e-commerce) is expected to become a popular use of Extranets. Figure 7.5 illustrates the three types of use for VPNs.

What is the motivation? VPNs provide considerable cost savings and allow for flexible, dynamic, "anywhere to somewhere" connections. Corporations can

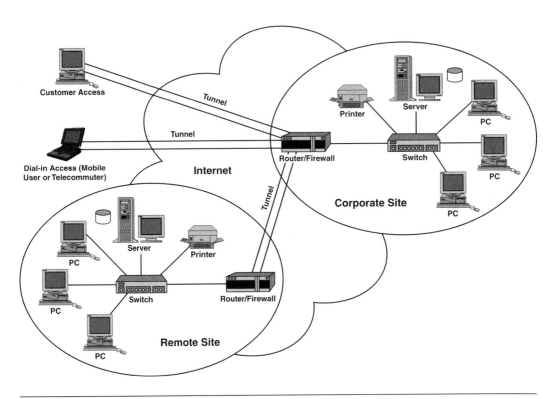

Figure 7.5 Three types of use for VPNs

use "free" Internet-based connections rather than a costly 800 number to provide remote access. Likewise the number of modem pools and access lines can be reduced. Connection between two sites no longer requires the large cost (management and monthly maintenance) of setting up a frame relay connection, and corporate interconnections can be more dynamic as the typical lengthy installation delay of a leased service goes away.

What are the concerns? The biggest concern is security followed by the difficulty to predict reliably the overall end-to-end latency. In order to gain an appreciation for security, just think about your bank account number or your credit card number going across the Internet without encryption, vulnerable to interception and unauthorized use. Use of the best-effort Internet provides a big delay variable as we have already discussed. In addition the tunneling and encryption techniques used to maintain security could significantly impact the overall performance. VPNs require security, some level of performance predictability, and manageability, including easy install, configuration, monitoring, and troubleshooting.

7.7.1.1 How Are VPNs Made Secure?

Data encryption, used to secure data, involves the use of several mathematical transformations to the data using an encryption key. Once data is encrypted, it is no longer readable as plain text and may traverse public networks with limited concern of being altered, read, or spoofed (intercepted, altered, and retransmitted). Once the data arrives at its desired destination, it is decrypted using the same key that was used to encrypt it.

The two major issues associated with data encryption are key distribution and performance. Secure key distribution is critical to ensure that security is not compromised. Data transformation can be very computationally intensive, creating additional load on network devices to encrypt and decrypt data. After all, encryption requires that an extra set of steps be done to every packet that crosses the network!

VPNs use *tunneling* to transmit different protocols and encrypted data across an IP network. The idea is simple and visual: Data goes through tunnels unexposed to the public daylight. Rather than sending plain, ordinary packets exposed across public networks for anyone to read, packets are encrypted at one end, sent (or burrowed in the tunnel sense) across the public portion of the network, and decrypted at the other end. In other words, tunneling provides a methodology for encapsulating optionally encrypted data (putting the data into an envelope), sending it out over an IP network, and "unencapsulating" the optionally encrypted data at the receiving end (removing the data from the envelope).

There are four protocols used to secure data across the Internet:

- Point-to-Point Tunneling Protocol (PPTP)
- Layer-2 Forwarding (L2F)
- Layer-2 Tunneling Protocol (L2TP)
- Secure Internet Protocol (IPSec)

PPTP is a protocol-independent (supports IP, IPX, AppleTalk) point-to-point layer-2 tunneling protocol standard that is widely used for dial-in access to corporate networks. PPTP follows a client/server implementation paradigm. Point-to-point tunneling standards cannot simultaneously maintain a VPN connection and Internet access using the same tunnel. Layer-2 tunneling requires explicit termination at the end of the tunnel by a PPTP-aware remote node or another piece of customer equipment. (Layer-3 tunneling requires no special vendor-specific code on either side of the tunnel.) PPTP might be considered lightweight with respect to security since it does not provide packet authentication, adhere to an encryption standard,[4] or utilize any standard key management such as Internet Security Association Key Management Protocol (ISAKMP)/Oakley or SKIP. In PPTP environments there is no specified user authentication protocol; environments often use Challenge Handshake Authentication Protocol (CHAP), Password Authentication Protocol (PAP), Kerberos, or Token ID. PPTP is widely used since Microsoft provides it in its NT 4.0 server software, which may function as a Remote Access Server (RAS), and offers it as a service pack to Windows 95. Microsoft is currently intending to bundle it with Windows 98.

A S I D E . . .

Point-to-Point Protocol (PPP) is a communication standard for transmitting multiple protocols (IP is popular) across a dial-up or leased line. Point-to-Point Tunneling Protocol (PPTP) (RFC 1171) is an extension to PPP that provides a mechanism to transfer data safely from a remote client to an enterprise server using a VPN. PAP and CHAP are protocols to authenticate a PPP connection. PAP uses plain-text password, and CHAP encrypts the password.

L2F, introduced by Cisco, is a protocol-independent (it supports IP, IPX, AppleTalk) point-to-point dial-in alternative to PPTP. As the name implies, L2F is a layer-2 solution with the same explicit termination drawback as PPTP. Although many vendors support it, it does not have encryption or tunnel flow control and has only the same weak user authentication options as PPTP.

L2TP, a hybrid of L2F and PPTP, is an emerging standard. Like L2F and PPTP, L2TP will provide layer-2 client/server remote access. It will, however, have the added security of IPSec for packet authentication, encryption, and key management.

As the name implies, *IPSec* is a secure version of IP that incorporates packet-level optional authentication and encryption. Like IP, it will be host-to-host and will not follow a client/server model like the other VPN technologies. IPSec is currently an IETF standard that was originally proposed by Cisco and Microsoft. It is required by IPv6 and will be optional for IPv4, the IP in use today. IPSec will use 56-bit Data Encryption Standard (DES) and 112-bit Triple DES, Message Digest 5 (MD5) packet authentication encryption, and

---

4. If a Windows NT server is used, Rivest, Shamir, and Adleman Cellular Digital Packet Data Algorithm RC-4 (RSA RC-4) is used for encryption and decryption. Consult a book on security for more information on security protocols.

key management via SKIP and ISAKMP/Oakley,[5] although it is designed to be flexible with respect to authentication and encryption algorithms.

IPSec packets include two headers that are used for authentication and encryption—the IP Authentication Header (AH) and the Encapsulation Security Payload (ESP). The emerging IPSec standard provides two options regarding the amount of the packet that is encrypted and authenticated. Tunneling (as in VPNs) can encrypt and authenticate the entire packet. When using IPSec as a secure IP transport without tunneling, only the transport-layer segment of the packet needs to be encrypted or authenticated.

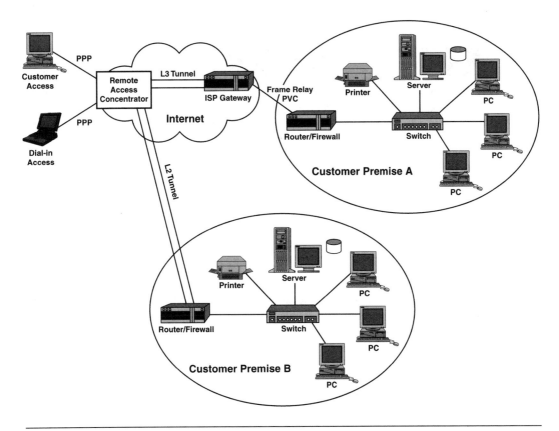

Figure 7.6 Customer access via an L3 tunnel and dial-in access via an L2 tunnel

---

5. For more information about this and other security standards, please consult a book on security.

IPSec is expected to emerge as the preferred protocol for VPNs largely because it has a complete security solution—not just user authentication—including packet authentication, encryption, and key management. IPSec is also a layer-3 solution that will simply plug in to existing environments that currently support IP and PPP stacks providing support for multipoint-to-multipoint connections.

Figure 7.6 depicts both layer-2 and layer-3 tunnel implementations, clearly showing the termination responsibility (and additional security requirement) on the customer premises. The customer premises must be protected against unauthorized users; it must expose its Internet addresses and synchronize with the ISP or carrier on its tunneling protocol. This is a heavy cost and an obvious reason why layer-3 tunneling via IPSec will be the VPN protocol of the future.

A S I D E . . .

Since protocol encapsulation in tunnels makes packets invisible to firewalls, tunnels must be terminated before firewalls. Note that this is in addition to host-to-host security.

7.7.1.2 How Does a VPN Work?

Perhaps the best way to understand how a VPN works is with an example. The following text walks through what happens when an employee logs into the company's network using a previously set-up VPN infrastructure. Although this is only one use for VPNs, other uses would follow similar steps, perhaps with additional authentication. VPNs that facilitate the creation of Intranets using the public Internet would require movement of the authentication and tunnel management processes into the distributed sites, or leverage the capabilities of a network carrier to provide the networking infrastructure at both ends. Another distinction would be that VPN-based Intranets often have less transient tunnels. Let's now go through the step-by-step process of using dial VPN.

1. Remote employee x needs to dial in to the company's network. The employee boots up his PC and dials the local number for the VPN carrier provider that supports the company's extranet connection. A PPP connection is made, and the RAS in the carrier's local Point of Presence (POP) accepts the call.

2. The RAS authenticates the user using the password and the user ID (often including the company name since the carrier may service many

companies) using PPP Packet Authentication via PAP or alternatively CHAP, which is more secure.

3. During this authentication process, the tunnel creation process commences. It is necessary to set up the tunnel before authentication completes to prevent the Network Control Protocols (NCP) from starting before a tunnel to the starter company's network is set up.

4. In order to set up a tunnel, the user must be authenticated with the tunnel management system (TMS) within the carrier's network. TMSs typically provide a server with a defined interface that can validate user authenticity for many dial-in clients at once. In addition to authenticating the user, the TMS determines if a tunnel must be created. Remember, a RAS provides other services besides dial-in access to company networks. If the user ID is validated and a tunnel needs to be set up, the TMS returns to the RAS the information on how to create a tunnel.

5. Minimally the information from the TMS includes the IP address of the gateway, authentication server, and authentication server protocol (very often RADIUS). The tunneling protocol, necessary tunneling key, frame relay DLCI, and other information may be returned, depending on how many optional configurations the carrier provides. For example, if the carrier provides both layer-2 and layer-3 tunnels to connect directly and indirectly via a gateway, respectively, this information must be provided. Remember that the tunnel may be a layer-2 tunnel directly to the corporate network or a layer 3-tunnel to a service provider gateway in the same area as the corporate network, depending on how the corporate network was set up. In this example we will assume that a service provider gateway is used. See Figure 7.6; it illustrates the two alternatives.

6. The RAS then sends an authentication request to the gateway, which then uses the authentication protocol (often RADIUS) to talk to the authentication server and to validate access. As part of the validation process, the IP, IPX, or AppleTalk address for the remote node is determined and assigned. Finally (assuming the user is authenticated), the tunnel is established and the gateway returns to the RAS the address and perhaps the actual frame relay DLCI to the company for optimization.

7. At this point, the RAS and the remote node complete the PPP authentication phase. The user is online to his company's network.

8. A subsequent termination request brings the connection down and closes the tunnel.

A S I D E . . .

The Mobile IP communication protocol (RFC 2002) may be used during the process of setting up layer-3 tunnels. Although beyond the scope of this book, it is worth looking at the RFC and understanding how this rich protocol works.

7.7.1.3 Next Steps for VPNs

There are two components of VPNs (Extranets, Intranets, and Dial VPN) that are critical to their widespread deployment. First and foremost is the confidence that data will remain secure going across public portions of the network. In the same way that the telephone network must ensure security, data networks must provide secure solutions. Second is that performance will be acceptable and predictable.

The final ratification and adoption of the IPSec standard is positioned to provide the necessary security for VPNs. The layer-2 tunneling protocols are expected to adopt the encryption standards provided by IPSec. In addition, significant pressure will be placed on the developers of encryption algorithms to ensure that data can be quickly secured and unsecured. It is expected that moving encryption into hardware (as with switching) will be a common solution to make for well-performing encryption. Predictability places pressure on providing QoS and SLAs. It will be a combination of overprovisioning in LANs and the use of precedence/dedicated resources in the WANs that will provide the solution set for predictable VPN performance.

Policy and policy distribution will also fill an important role in our future VPN solutions. Security key distributions, distribution of authorization of resource usage, and user authentication are all necessary prerequisites for VPNs. It is conceivable that MPLS labels might be used to associate the policy and QoS for a VPN that spans the WAN. Certainly we can live without DEN to a point—automatic distributed policy will, however, be the key to enabling networks to scale to meet the pervasive penetration of VPNs.

One key point you should take from this discussion is that network needs, particularly network services, drive the advancement of networking. Each of tomorrow's networking technologies such as MPLS, QoS, COS, IP Multicast, LDAP, and DEN could be developed based on the technical challenge and excitement of the technology as a research project. It is, however, the financial reward of providing advanced network services that motivates and fuels network advancement. Network services drive network development—network services that advance our lives and reduce the apparent distance of information.

7.8 Interactive Voice over Data Networks

As with VPNs, there is currently a plethora of interest and emerging products aimed at using data networks for interactive voice traffic. The theory is simple: By using existing data networks for voice traffic, considerable money can be saved and carriers can have an additional service to sell. This is analogous to the VPN scenario of having employees dial in to a local carrier POP rather than a company-sponsored 800 number and saving long distance toll charges. In practice, though, Voice over IP (VoIP) presents a number of different challenges than VPNs.

The biggest challenge of VoIP is delay—especially inconsistent delay. Many of us know how painful satellite-based phone calls are with an overall latency of 250 ms to 500 ms during a call. Although estimates of the maximum target goal for delay range from 100 ms to 250 ms, let's assume that 100 ms is the upper limit. Now let's itemize what causes delay drawing from information in the chapter on guaranteed delivery and augment that list with delays specific to voice.

1. The first built-in delay is end-to-end network latency. This delay is attributed to resource sharing within data networks and the "packetizing" and "depacketizing" of data done at either end. At the time of this writing we can use the rule of thumb that there is 10 ms delay for each 1000 miles[6] that data is networked. This means that using New York City as the center point and having a 3000-mile radius, we can get to most of Europe and North America with an approximate 30 ms delay.

From Chapter 5 we know the solutions to reducing and providing consistent delay: overprovisioning, use of precedence, and dedicated resources. Since long distance data communications tend to involve switching across many carriers and several switches, it will be difficult to impact this delay greatly. Certain connections, perhaps between major cities like London, New York City, and Los Angeles, may be optimized much in the same way the airline system has created direct routes. Traffic prioritization, particularly using the TOS bits in the IP packet, perhaps offers the least disruptive, best way to reduce and, more important, to make latency consistent.

2. The second and biggest cause of delay is compression/decompression (codec) algorithms used to reduce bit rate while maintaining voice

---

6. The pure speed of light delay alone (in fibre) is 8 ms per 1000 miles. Einstein indicated that we would never do better than that.

quality. Both 64 Kbps and 8 Kbps voice compression use International Telecommunications Union-Telecommunications (ITU-T) standards G.711 and G.729, respectively. G.729 is part of the ITU H.323 standard that specifies how to transmit real-time voice and video over packet networks or other networks that don't provide any QoS guarantee. H.323 is a de facto standard since several Internet phone products endorse the standard. The call set-up and encoding/decoding processing done under the H.323 standard is estimated to cause a 25 ms one-way delay.

A S I D E . . .

The H.323 standard consists of seven other standards: H.225, H.245, G.711, G.722, G.723.1, G.728, and G.729. The H.xxx standards specify call setup, and the G.xxx standards provide various encoding/decoding specifications. G.723.1 is the default encoder and is required for H.323 compliance. G.723.1 provides compressed voice and is designed to produce high-quality output at low-bit rates.

A N O T H E R   A S I D E . . .

Frame relay has a standard for voice called FRF.11. This standard includes how voice is carried and how compression algorithms ensure voice interoperability among frame relay providers. FRF.11 has two classes of compliance for voice encoding/decoding algorithms: Class 1 uses G.727 for high-bit rate voice, and Class 2 uses G.728 for low-bit rate, lower-quality voice.

Moving "codec" algorithms from software into hardware (a technique widely used in switching) and the use of jitter buffers are two ways to mitigate codec delays. Jitter buffers are buffers of memory that store 50 to 100 ms of voice/video data at either end of the communication session. They facilitate packet resequencing (remember that in a packet network packets may take different routes and come out of order) and provide a way to smooth out the packet flow.

A S I D E . . .

Care must be taken in compression not to overcompress data. Cut-through touch-tone dialing—that is, cut-through dual-tone multifrequency (DTMF)—is widely used by voice response systems to route calls without user intervention. Too much compression can reduce the tonal quality enough to cause these systems not to work. This is a good example as to why establishment of and adherence to standards is so important.

7.8.1 Voice over Data Challenges

Our current voice network provides mature, feature rich, reliable service. Data solutions must first focus on reliability and basic quality before adding (and perhaps extending) the feature set. This makes voice over data networks unattractive for some, at least in its current state. However, the cost savings of providing an internal voice infrastructure for a geographically distributed company is noteworthy and attractive to many. Some quality can be forgone internally if care to ensure communication to external customers (perhaps via the conventional telephone network) is maintained.

The voice network scales very well and has the capacity to service all but the busiest holidays. Achieving the same or similar scalability is a big challenge for data networks. "Making it work" with thousands of users isn't good enough; the solution must scale with quality connections.

Our voice network is set up for emergency service and is fault tolerant. As many are aware, there is a low-voltage current that the system uses for dial tone. Since this is independent of the electrical network, dial tone is present even when power lines are down. Most data networks are not necessarily so fault tolerant. Are we prepared to have phone lines go up and down when a switch is rebooted?

Unlike data, interactive voice traffic that arrives late is of little value. In fact, the whole notion of timing out and resending old interactive voice is pointless. Old interactive voice traffic and late traffic need to be dropped as early as possible since there is no sense transporting packets that will be dropped at their destination. Note that dropping voice packets is with penalty; many dropped packets in a row will result in an audible clipped speech. Treating interactive voice packets differently might be handled using the TOS in IP packets or the ATM rt-VBR Service Class across ATM links.

Other challenges of supporting interactive voice over data networks include the following:

- How much silence compression should be done? (Silence compression technique is used to save bandwidth by background-noise elimination, many people talking simultaneously, and conversation pausing.)

- How is billing done and managed? Are there different rates for domestic and international usage? How closely does charging map to what is currently in place for the telephone network?

- How are telephone numbers mapped to IP addresses? Are they dynamically or statically defined? If they are statically defined, will we quickly run out?

Although there are many more questions, the point here is simple: The telephone network is a very mature technology developed over many decades. Extreme care was taken to provide a reliable, fault-tolerant, quality service. The telephone network was customized and optimized for voice and works very well. We cannot expect data networks to match this level of service instantly, especially over our existing best-effort networks.

A S I D E . . .

As mentioned in an earlier chapter, the Signaling System 7 (SS7) protocol is used to route telephone calls. One voice and data network integration will be to integrate SS7 technology into data switches and Remote Access Concentrators (RACs). This will give data switches access to call routing as well as to the advanced services of caller ID, call forwarding, call waiting, and so on.

7.8.2 Deploying Interactive Voice over an Intranet

Deploying interactive voice over an existing Intranet is being implemented with some success. By rerouting internal corporate traffic over the existing corporate Intranet, toll charges can be saved. In addition, external calls within the same remote site locations can be rerouted over the Intranet and made as a local call. For example, if a corporation is located in both New York City and California, it is possible to reroute calls from NYC through the existing corporate Intranet. Once the call is at the other side of the Intranet, it can be placed as a local call. Figure 7.7 illustrates the use of a corporate Intranet for internal and limited external voice and fax use.

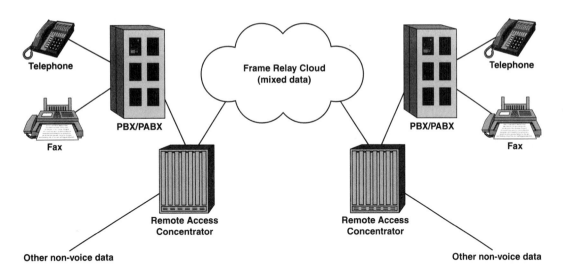

Figure 7.7 Telephone and fax over an Intranet

7.8.3 Network Services Depend on Network Policy

Fundamental to the widespread deployment of new, innovative services such as VPNs and VoIP is a distributed network policy infrastructure. We will see pockets of isolated success without a distributed policy infrastructure; clearly there are corporations already using both VPN and VoIP technology without a full-blown distributed network policy solution. *In order to make sophisticated services scale and become ubiquitous, we need to "tune up" our networking base with the addition of a distributed network policy solution.* Distributed policy will provide the necessary infrastructure for services that span over many switched interconnection devices.

7.9 Real-Time Video over Data Networks

In a sense, voice is a precursor to the needs of video. If we can satisfy the delay-sensitive nature of interactive voice in our networks, then we are well along to satisfying the needs of real-time video. There is one exception, however—real-time video requires significant amounts of end-to-end bandwidth! Satisfying real-time video within our switched networks will minimally require packet precedence and will ideally require bandwidth reservation. It is expected that

IP multicast can be used to reduce the strain of duplicate video streams consuming the network and providing the same real-time video nearly simultaneously across many diverse locations. Clearly both interactive voice and real-time video will benefit from switched network advancements around QoS guarantees, IP multicast, and faster, more intelligent forwarding techniques.

7.10 Setting Expectations

We will see the introduction of more and more services over the next few years. These services will be aimed at providing end-to-end solutions that place increasing demands on our networks. VPNs and VoIP are two such services that show great promise but also present great challenges to our switched networks. Clearly security and QoS guarantees are at the top of the list for these two services, respectively. It is expected that aspects of IPv6 (security and flow labeling), RSVP, RTP, and IP switching would facilitate the real-time and security needs of VoIP, whereas IPSec and aspects of IPv6 will be important to the future of VPNs.

It is important to note that end-to-end anything in networking can take a long time; as a simple rule of thumb, the time may be directly proportional to the number of players between ends and the size of the each player's infrastructure. In the case of a LAN or an individual ISP's network, you may have only one player but a very large infrastructure, making change difficult. For these reasons we will see partial solutions first—solutions that provide QoS guarantees across a LAN or ISP infrastructure, rather than end-to-end solutions. Security is expected to follow a similar path; we will see secure VPNs across private carrier infrastructures similar to what is currently done with frame relay networks long before we secure Internet VPNs. End-to-end is the dream, and partial solutions are prudent steps toward achieving the dream.

Distributed, synchronized network policy with consistent access methods and directory structure will become increasingly important to the success and viability of providing these end-to-end solutions. We will see policy solutions going directly into switches with Dynamic Domain Name Service (DDNS), LDAPv3, and DHCP providing policy access. Consistent policy across a network provides a necessary formal communication language—a protocol for abstracting away the local details into an "English" that all network subsystems understand. DEN is an important initiative in networking and has the potential to provide a significant piece of the solution for providing consistent policy and end-to-end networking.

7.11 Conclusions

As our demands of networking become increasingly sophisticated, varied, and widespread, the need, granularity, and distribution of network customization become more evident. Network services are demanding that our networks react dynamically to meet transient needs such as provisioning a dedicated pipe with a QoS guarantee for two hours between points A and B. Creative solutions such as VPNs are taxing network security and pushing us toward distributed security models. VoIP is challenging our best-effort Internet service, pushing us toward providing QoS guarantees using dedicated resources, or implementing a class of service model across the WAN. VoIP and real-time video underscore the fact that real-time data requires traffic management, plain and simple. Even though most networks are not ready for the complex issues and quality level of interactive voice that we are used to, it is expected that the economic savings of voice over packets will continue to push progress at a solution. It is no longer adequate for networks to maintain their status of loosely connected islands with disparate repositories of configuration data; this data needs to be integrated in some way to meet the end-to-end demands of our networks.

This is not to say that we want to change the model that we already have for the Internet of many autonomous systems that are loosely connected using the BGP protocol. This model works and scales quite well; it abstracts the intimate local details that are not relevant on a global base. The use of distributed hierarchy with well-defined formal interfaces (such as BGP) is one of the fundamental powerful techniques for building systems that scale.

Perhaps we need to exchange more than routing data across these network systems—certainly we are seeing this with MPLS. Perhaps we need to maintain policy in a more global way to define better who has access to what, to gain end-to-end security, and to provide QoS guarantees. It is possible that we need to look at modular extensions to our routing protocols, as with MOSPF to manage multicast data. After all, dealing with the dynamic nature of network devices going up and down and changing configurations is what our routing protocols have done so well. OSPF with its hierarchical, scalable solution and BGP used to integrate autonomous systems begin to look very attractive as possible ways to distribute policy information.

The need for consistent structure is coupled with distribution. The DEN proposal formalizes the structure of network data and provides a consistent interface to the data by leveraging LDAPv3. DEN provides the necessary "glue" to integrate user, application, and network device profiles with network policy. It shows great promise for providing this network of network policy data, particularly since it takes the evolutionary approach of integrating existing data repositories and access methods such as DNS, DHCP, RADIUS, and SNMP.

There is no doubt that innovative, new networking services are pushing our networking infrastructure—this is a normal, healthy phenomenon. The primary purpose of networks is to service applications and to reduce the "apparent" distance between users and remote users or users and remote data. Distributed network policy is key to the evolution of our networks as they provide the foundation for end-to-end services. As policy matures, so will the ability to provide better SLAs that may be used to guarantee (and measure) the QoS provided.

CHAPTER 8

Managing Our Demands for Networking

8.1 Introduction

Clearly, switching solutions have taken center stage in networking. Nearly every new network interconnection device is called a *switch:* We have various flavors of LAN switches, ATM switches for the LAN and WAN, frame relay switches, and Extranet switches. There are switching solutions at layers 2, 3, and 4 of the ISO Reference Model, and we are seeing a surge of development aimed at providing QoS guarantees and special switch processing around COS. MPLS is an emerging standard providing label-based switching across WANs. Switches that are capable of multicast routing are available, and some switches use LDAP for accessing distributed configuration information. The promise of DEN and policy-based networking is emerging, so solutions based on switching technology are important offerings satiating our thirst for networking.

This chapter concludes our study of switched networks with a focus on a critical component that makes and assures that everything works: network management. As our solutions become more sophisticated, distributed, and dynamic, the need for strong management becomes increasingly important. *Businesses are built around networks.* Because network sluggishness, unpredictability, and downtime can cost business a significant loss of revenue and customers, having a comprehensive network management solution is critical.

8.2 Key Problems Addressed

As networks continue to grow in size and complexity and support more and more mission-critical needs, the cost of network failure, performance glitches, and security holes becomes increasingly higher. Network management is all about supervising and maintaining network control, ensuring that the network is reliable, predictable, and secure. Network management is used to provide

- underlying metrics necessary to validate SLAs and QoS guarantees.

- monitoring of devices and the filtering of traffic for security purposes.

- validation that the network is properly configured and secure.

- performance tracking/tuning and fault management to keep networks running smoothly.

- network usage data for network billing purposes.

Networks must incorporate the correct level of network management to ensure that we satisfy our network demands: networks that are capable of real-time transmission, plug-and-play portability, minimal propagation delay, and 99.9 percent availability. Network management is necessary to complete our networking solutions by overseeing and controlling the network, ensuring that it runs as a unified system that satisfies our demands for networking. Strong network management is key to the switching solutions of today and to those emerging tomorrow.

8.3 The Basics of Management

As mentioned in Chapter 7, the International Organization for Standardization (ISO) has partitioned network management into five functional areas:

- **F**ault management
- **C**onfiguration management
- **A**ccounting management
- **P**erformance management
- **S**ecurity management

Even as networks become increasingly more complex as new services are added, we can fundamentally go back to the five functional areas known as the *FCAPS* (Fault, Configuration, Accounting, Performance, and Security) as our base for management.

Fault management includes discovery, isolation, and resolution of network problems. It is used to alert the network administrator that something is wrong in the network. Fault management is both device-based (monitoring one device in the network) and system-based (monitoring the interaction of two or more devices in the network). Periodic polling and "direct your attention over here" events (or traps) are used to detect and alert the network manager of potential problems.

Configuration management is the process of initially setting up the network and maintaining an up-to-date blueprint of how the network is constructed. This blueprint includes complete device configuration and user profiles containing personal customization and authorization. Configuration management is an important part of network management because if the network is not properly configured, it may not work at all, it may fail unexpectedly, or it may not be giving optimal performance.

Accounting management records network usage, ensuring that usage is accurately logged and optionally billed. Accounting management requires tracking of usage logs (RADIUS is popular) and network flows. Often accounting works with security management to notify when network policy is violated.

Performance management tunes the network and determines ahead of time when to make network and design changes. Performance is measured via periodic polling and trap-directed polling. Trap-directed polling is used to associate an event sent by a network device like "performance looks real bad over here" with the immediate need to check performance by polling for the attributes that are used to measure performance.

Security management refers to keeping network data in the correct hands and out of the wrong hands. It includes the monitoring and administration of user, network device, and network authorization. Trap-directed polling, periodic polling, and password management are used to monitor security.

8.3.1 The Sources of Network Management Data

Fundamentally there are only three ways to pass data to and get data from devices that make up a network. A network administrator or network management application can

- Set attributes (or device objects) that customize a device to perform in a certain way.

- Get or Poll for (request once or repeatedly) attributes from a network device that give you the device's current state. Polling is used to determine both device and network health.

- Trap an event from a network device telling you that something about the device might require attention. As discussed, sometimes traps are used to initiate subsequent polling of attributes; we call this *trap-directed polling*.

Network management is built around three simple techniques: sets, gets, and traps. Configuring devices (setting attributes), periodically polling for attribute values, and responding to asynchronous events can be used to manage devices effectively. Moreover, network management can use its global view of many network devices taken together to determine the relationships between devices, the proper attribute settings across devices, and the correct amount of polling and event processing to assume.

8.4 Engineering Problem Solving Applied to Network Management

The distributed and dynamic nature of tomorrow's switched networks clearly presents a big challenge for network management—not to mention sophisticated and distributed features found in QoS, MPLS, and IP multicast. This section provides some problem-solving techniques that have been used in the past to converge on management solutions. These techniques are commonly used within software engineering to solve complex problems. It is expected that these same techniques will be used to step up to the challenge of tomorrow's switched networks.

1. Encapsulate, layer software, hide information, and create formal interfaces: Object-oriented programming is built around the principle of hiding unnecessary information. By modeling objects as discrete entities within a program and formalizing the interfaces between objects, programs can be "built up" and extended to solve more and more complex problems. Encapsulation and layering is also fundamental to networking, as we have seen with the ISO 7-layer reference model.

Network management benefits by breaking management problems into discrete pieces, formalizing the interfaces between the components, and putting the solutions together to form an integrated management system. We will see later in the chapter how layering is used to provide device-, network-, and service-level management, where service management builds on top of network management and network management builds on top of device management. Layering and encapsulation provide an effective way to reduce the complexity of difficult problems, solve them independently, and put them together in flexible ways to provide powerful solutions.

2. Reduce and eliminate redundant data: Redundant data becomes inconsistent over time; it's as simple as that. Having to maintain the same data in different repositories can be a nightmare. Good software engineering practice teaches the centralization of program data and the use of a formal interface to access the data in one way—and one way only. "Formal interface" means having discrete methods to read and write data so that the same interface is used to change the data. This practice eliminates "behind the back" change.

Network management must also seek to reduce (and if possible eliminate) redundant data. Not only is collecting and storing extra data a burden on the network and data repositories, but it can be downright bad as well. Consider this: three distinct images of configuration information for a single device, each image managed by a separate management tool. What is the correct, current configuration? Nearly redundant configuration data can result in uncertainty as to the "correct" configuration.

3. Optimize areas of repetition: Doing the same task hundreds or thousands of times is what computers are all about and what humans are not all about. Computer programs can be optimized to do the same task quickly and efficiently—without error. Humans lose interest in repetitive tasks; the more repetition, the slower we go and the more errors we make.

In the same way that switching has optimized the repetitive tasks of frame forwarding and IP packet routing, network management must optimize the repetitive task of managing hundreds of the same switches and end stations across the network. Bulk network management can provide an efficient means to manage the many components of a network and the many discrete ports of switched devices, with far less error than a human will make. And, as our networking needs become increasingly dynamic, programmatic interfaces become a requirement—manual change across lots of devices is downright slow (not to mention error-prone)!

4. Divide-and-conquer: Divide-and-conquer refers to problem isolation. When debugging a software problem, often the best way is to narrow the scope of the problem by eliminating portions of the software that are possible problem areas.

Divide-and-conquer is a very powerful management technique used to solve networking problems. By methodically reducing the problem space with various assumptions and tests, you can disprove certain possibilities. *It is as important to determine what the problem isn't as it is to determine what the problem is.* Often by going through the process of elimination of what the problem isn't, you will discover what the problem is, even if you have never encountered the problem before.

5. Dedicate resources to and/or prioritize critical processes: Some processes are more critical than others and require preferential treatment. Computer operating systems typically allow for priority scheduling of critical, time-sensitive processing. In the same way, reporting a critical security violation or network failure would take precedence over running a routine report. It is expected that the dynamic and real-time aspect of tomorrow's switched networks will result in the management of more "critical" processes.

6. Use distributed processing to scale solutions and to process data more efficiently: Often by having multiple computers crunch on aspects of the same problem, a result can be attained sooner. Parallel processing is often employed in engineering solutions to provide better response time and to leverage idle processing power across a network.

Network management can use distribution to perform data processing and data reduction closer to its source and to reduce the amount of network management traffic that is rolled up to a central site. Distribution can also be used to keep up with voluminous amounts of network management data processing required in large installations by having multiple management stations working in parallel.

7. Test early and often: The best way to build reliable software is to validate the software during the process of building it. By testing small software components prior to integrating them into a larger system, problems can often be identified and dealt with sooner, making integration go more smoothly.

Network management systems should also be tested on a reduced scale, enabling them to be perfected prior to large-scale introduction. Sometimes small, isolated test networks are used to validate management solutions prior to incorporating them into a large production network. Network management solutions should be introduced gradually so that they can be validated to work properly before widespread deployment.

8. Use top-down and bottom-up design: Software is built with both top-down and bottom-up designing. Top-down designing is starting from the big picture and gradually working on smaller and smaller details. Bottom-up designing starts with the details and gradually works up to the complete system. Software solutions often have a formal architecture, or they should at least have a well-thought-out design. By using both top-down and bottom-up designing together, engineers can converge on the best solution to satisfy user requirements while simultaneously creating a well-structured, extensible design.

Network management solutions should be designed by using both top-down and bottom-up methodologies. A top-down design view can ensure that the network management solution satisfies the functional requirements while a bottom-up view can validate the robustness and extensibility of the solution.

When building network management solutions, it is important to take the time to analyze normal administration workflows. By thoroughly understanding the steps that management follows to manage a network, a management solution that provides a natural fit and complements existing processes can be created.

Another way to validate management solutions is to define a matrix of network problems and play the matrix against the management solution. Scenario-driven validation can be used to ensure that common workflows are optimized and that the management solution solves the correct set of "real" network problems. All too often network management applications look good and seem to work well, but they solve network problems only in a convoluted, inefficient, nonintuitive way.

8.5 Switched Networks Challenge Network Management

Early in this book we defined switching as the burning of software into hardware that results in adding significant performance improvements. These performance improvements ultimately address the biggest challenge of networking—*scaling* to meet exponentially growing needs. Networks are growing swiftly in size and complexity; network applications are becoming more distributed, data-intensive, and real-time; the volume of users, their expectations, and their network dependency are also expanding astronomically. Burning software into hardware (switching) is facilitating rapid network growth and introducing new network management needs.

The solutions that switching provides become the challenges of network management. Networks are perpetually growing with increased expectations from both applications and network users. Network management must scale, provide robustness, and allow for user and application customizations. Users are demanding fault tolerance and delivery guarantees; applications require traffic prioritization and optimization; and network management must protect data and ensure that network security is not compromised. Network management has all these responsibilities—in an environment where businesses want to manage their business, *not their network!* With the increased dependency on networks, perhaps the network is the business?

So, how do you solve the switched network management problem of scalability? Three words:

Distributed Hierarchical Layering (DHL)

Clearly DHL is a mouthful and requires a fair amount of explanation. It's also noteworthy that networks are distributed, hierarchical, and layered. It is not at all unusual for solutions to mirror one another or to share characteristics with the problem that they are solving, particularly in networking. Let's dig in and build a distributed, hierarchical, layered network from the bottom up.

Let's start by dissecting a switch. Take a LAN or WAN switch—your pick. As we discussed earlier, all switches have inputs and outputs. Some vendors call these ports; others call them interfaces—we'll go with ports. Switches typically have many ports. From each port you can observe traffic flows and customize how the port is configured. *Each port, however, must be managed.*

Now let's take the switch itself as a network entity. A switch is made up of a bunch of ports, perhaps a power supply, a fan, a chassis, and some LEDs showing the status of each port. Today's switches run agent software, do intelligent data filtering, offer COS, and perform bridging and routing. Tomorrow's switches will perhaps implement MPLS, integrate with distributed policy, and provide QoS. *Each switch (and other interconnection devices) must be managed as an entity.*

MPLS, distributed policy, QoS guarantees, and routing are good examples of protocols and data that span multiple switches (and other interconnection devices). Networks are composed of network devices that work together as a system. In the Internet we have many ASs that can be managed individually. Likewise Intranets involve putting together multiple LANs across WAN links; each LAN is typically managed individually. *Networks, consisting of multiple devices working together, must be managed as a system.*

Services involve a new area in networking. We discussed VoIP and VPNs briefly in Chapter 7 as two examples of services. Services are built by combining multiple networks with "end-to-end" QoS guarantees, SLAs, and distributed policy. *Network services must be managed.*

Last we have advanced planning and analysis necessary for deploying emerging services. In essence this layer of management is about proactively assessing the overall impact of introducing a new network service prior to introducing it into the network. *Network management must be an integral part of a service and available at service inception.*

8.5.1 Layered Management

The International Telecommunications Union-Telecommunications (ITU-T) Telecommunications Management Network (TMN) M.3100 architecture model provides a guideline of how to break down the complexity of management into five layers. Figure 8.1 presents a conceptual representation of the various TMN layers showing their various functions that we have just defined. We will go from the bottom up describing each layer and giving examples of management solutions at each layer.

Network devices reside at the Network Element Layer. These devices provide the interconnections necessary to build networks. Integrated into each device are management capabilities with access provided to users and network management stations using HTML, Telnet, SNMP, Common Management Information Protocol (CMIP), and text files.

At the Network Element Management Layer is element management, providing the network manager with the ability to manage devices individually.

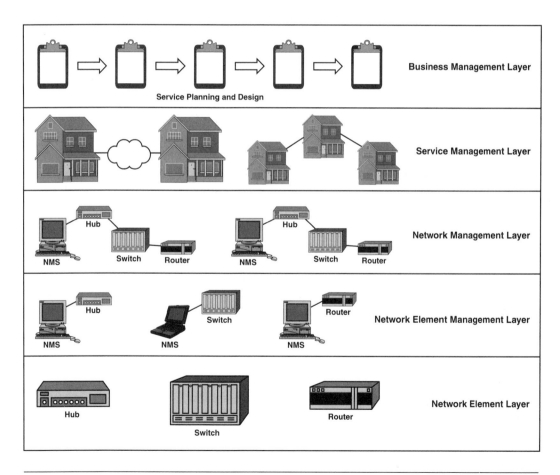

Figure 8.1 A pictorial representation of the TMN layered management model

Typically element management includes a front panel view of a device that provides a visual representation of the device. In addition to showing the board installed, port connectivity, connector types, and device state, these tools provide a convenient context-sensitive way to view port statistics, board attributes such as revision level, and device attributes such as fan status.

Moving up the hierarchy, is the Network Management Layer. Sometimes referred to as a *system* view of the network, this layer provides management of network devices working together across a network. Bulk configuration, Remote Network Monitoring Versions 1 and 2 (RMON, RMON2), probes, and analysis tools all operate on a network system level. Bulk configuration involves managing several ports or network devices as one entity.

Bulk management is particularly important in switched networks where there may be several thousands of ports and hundreds of network devices (switches, hubs, and routers) in a single managed network. Examples of bulk management are backing up all the configurations of all your switches and setting attributes of a certain group of ports to a particular value. Often bulk management includes consistency checking and verification and validation of widespread changes that ensure operations are safe.

RMON and RMON2 provide a set of composite metrics useful for determining the overall health of your network as an entity. Network utilization and matrices of types of traffic flowing are two examples of RMON data. In a switched environment, using RMON is particularly challenging since data must be collected from so many discrete points in the network to get a complete network view. To address this challenge, many vendors provide embedded RMON/RMON2 solutions; unfortunately these solutions usually cover only a subset of the RMON/RMON2 groups. In traditional shared networks, an RMON probe could "see" all the data for the network from only a few points, making it easy to get the entire pulse of the network.

The Service Management Layer is responsible for providing tools that facilitate management of network services typically spanning many enterprises and/or carrier networks. Examples of services include VPNs (dial VPN, Extranets, and Intranets) and Voice over IP (VoIP).

The focus of the Business Management Layer is to provide advanced planning and design consultation for determining customized business-level decisions. In essence the business management layer involves the proactive management of network service deployment before a service is offered in the network. Planning and design include doing a feasibility study of adding a new service (clearly assessing the impact on the existing network infrastructure), determining network enhancements required to support the service, doing "what-if" scenarios against the network, and predicting service growth. This process often involves market research, testing services in a limited (yet real network) setting, use of network simulation, and documenting and verifying deployment rollout.

8.5.2 Hierarchical Management

Hierarchical organization facilitates management scalability and flexibility. The use of ASs within the Internet or OSPF areas across an Intranet are good examples of the power of hierarchical structure. Just as having all your files on your workstation or PC at the top-most (or root) directory would be unmanageable, having to manage a large network without some level of hierarchical grouping is unwieldy. By establishing a hierarchy, the details below a level can be abstracted away providing natural boundaries of management responsibility. Only certain designated information needs to propagate up and down; the rest of the information is managed locally. Hierarchical organization reduces the amount of information that must be known at higher layers, directly impacting the amount of information that must be stored and processed.

A S I D E . . .

One important caveat with the creation of management hierarchies is to not go excessively deep! Traversing down many levels of a hierarchy can become as awkward as having a flat space. Often it makes sense to mirror the network structure (subnets, buildings, campuses, and so on). Always have a good reason for every level in a hierarchy.

8.5.3 Distributed Management

In the same way that we use hierarchies to divide management responsibility and facilitate scaling, we use distribution to facilitate management across geographies and to make local management solutions scale better. Can you imagine sending *all* your management data for a large distributed Intranet across expensive WAN connections so that *all* management could be done centrally? Likewise, having certain management locally (particularly when a physical intervention is required) just makes good sense. Even in a LAN setting, flooding a network with lots of management traffic is often less preferable to a distributed "roll-up-only-what-makes-sense" approach. Finally, distribution facilitates scalability (and robustness) by spreading the management load across several management stations.

8.5.4 DHL Management

Now that we have zoomed in on each necessary component of our switched management solution, it is time to put them together and show how they provide the powerful, scalable solution that we need to satisfy our demands for networking, today and tomorrow.

As we mentioned very early in the book, the world is seeking networks that are secure, capable of real-time transmission, compatible with any end-user piece of equipment, and not controlled by any one organization. Networks must offer minimal propagation delay; and they must be plug-and-play, customizable, always available. Networks must have all these characteristics—and at a reasonable price.

We spent several chapters discussing key emerging technologies:

- Multilayer switching (MPLS)
- Quality of service (QoS)
- Class of service (COS)
- Resource ReSerVation Protocol (RSVP)
- IP Multicast
- Network Policy
- Service Level Agreements (SLAs)
- Directory-enabled Networking (DEN)

DHL management is the last essential component that completes our networking solution by providing FCAPS management for a very complex DHL network. We know how quickly networks evolve and how scalability is fundamental to networking.

- Two PCs connected by a hub sharing a printer becomes
- several PCs and workstations connected by a switch sharing many printers/databases becomes
- two geographically distributed LANs, each containing several PCs and workstations connected by a switch sharing many databases becomes
- several geographically distributed LANs, each containing several PCs and workstations connected by a switch sharing hundreds of databases becomes
- An Intranet of LANs using VPNs, VoIP, and distributed network policy.

DHL management uses

1. Distribution

   ■ to mirror the structure of a distributed network, doing local management and data reduction locally, rolling up only certain critical data to a central management site.

   ■ to scale and provide fault tolerance by using multiple management stations to process data simultaneously.

2. Hierarchical network organization

   ■ again to mirror the structure of the network making it easy to navigate through the network and to designate management responsibility.

   ■ for scalability, by limiting the amount of data that must be known and processed at higher layers.

3. Layering

   ■ to build a management solution from base management components, providing management solution consistency and uniformity in management.

   ■ to provide scalability, customer choice, and better integration with existing and new systems.

It is the combination of distributed, hierarchical layering that enables management to solve complex management problems such as security, traffic prioritization, delivery guarantees, and traffic optimization. DHL management can provide end-to-end management of policy by leveraging DEN as an infrastructure. DEN provides consistency and distribution and builds on a hierarchical database model; these characteristics are much of what DHL is all about. DHL management utilizes the network to manage the network and enables us to satisfy our demands for networking, now and in the future.

8.6 Network Management Needs of Switched Networks

In Chapter 1 we identified a set of network management needs that are fundamental to tomorrow's switching solutions. This section introduces the concepts of proactive and reactive network management. Following this introduction, network management needs are presented in context with the solutions discussed in earlier chapters.

8.6.1 Proactive versus Reactive Management

Reactive management is really a euphemism for fire fighting. The network is down; a user cannot get to a server; the president of the company cannot read e-mail—you get the idea. There's no time for delay; the management team needs to jump on the problem immediately.

Proactive management refers to monitoring your network to predict and prevent/preclude problems *before* they happen. This is ideally where the management team wants to spend the majority of its time. Proactive management prepares the team well for problem prevention and frees up time for advanced planning and network design. Proactive management involves

- monitoring the state of the network.
- keeping statistics over time and generating reports that give an idea as to how the network is doing and when it is time to upgrade or add new network devices.
- maintaining configuration records and scripts that make it easy to recover when problems arise, enabling rollback to a known state, or setting up a replacement switch quickly and accurately.

Note that some fire fighting is inevitable; the goal, however, is to eliminate the flames quickly, keeping more time for planning and ensuring consistent quality for network subscribers.

8.6.2 Robustness

Proactive management minimizes downtime and maximizes availability. By keeping careful tabs on security, configuration, performance, and faults, small problems can be identified or preferably *anticipated* and fixed before they become major problems. Network management can identify places in the network that are most vulnerable to network failure providing a focus of where to add redundancy. Management solutions can be employed redundantly to ensure management robustness.

8.6.3 Scalability

With the multiplier effect of both users and network resources, scalability will always be high on the list for management needs. Network management solutions must evolve and grow with the fast pace with networks; management, too, must continuously scale. These solutions require a significant learning investment, and they must evolve rather than require wholesale replacement. Network management scalability is achieved by DHL as already discussed.

8.6.4 Security

The need for network security will continue to intensify as more and more network services become available across shared infrastructures. Network data is often a business differentiator, and sometimes it is *the* business. Network management must provide proactive management of security and integrate it with protocols such as IPSec and services like VPNs. Security within the LAN must be taken equally seriously to include both external firewall protection and internal data protection.

8.6.5 Traffic Management

In order to meet the demands for networking, traffic flows must be monitored and managed. RMON, RMON2, and other flow probe technologies provide traffic analysis data, although often only at pockets of the network such as within a campus LAN. The challenge of management is to put all this traffic data together in real-time and to associate it with a dynamically changing topology providing a helicopter-like view of the network. Again the distributed nature of MPLS with integrated policy shows strong potential for helping to manage traffic dynamically across WANs. The DEN initiative is also expected to help provide uniform network access to this distributed end-to-end network view.

8.6.6 Delivery Guarantees and Traffic Prioritization

Sometimes 99.9 percent availability is not enough! Data must be delivered in a prespecified window of time or with a higher certainty of timely delivery. QoS guarantees and COS policies require extensive management. Network management is required to verify SLAs, to monitor resource usage, and to determine where bandwidth is needed. Although end-to-end QoS and COS across WANs are desired, they will be difficult to achieve. Management will need to provide QoS guarantees for a specified leg of a journey as well as "direct flights." COS may also vary along the way depending on the data destination and available network infrastructure. Ideally network management will be able to offer some end-to-end prediction of QoS based on resources available and time of travel. It is expected that MPLS and DEN will provide a distributed way to monitor and manage resources from afar—eventually providing a way to provision a service across a connection.

8.6.7 Traffic Optimization

Multicast is a powerful way to optimize the use of networks. Although we are a long way from having a scalable IP multicast across the Internet, we will see Intranets deploying the technology in order to support real-time networking infrastructures. Multicast management will need to ensure the obvious—that bandwidth is indeed being conserved. Network management will need to keep measurements of potentially detrimental side effects like excessive packet looping, broadcasting, and traffic due to multicast management. Success and study of multicast in the Intranet may help us converge toward a solution that will scale to meet the needs of the Internet.

8.7 Twelve Cardinal Rules of Creating Management Solutions

The following dozen rules of thumb are useful to remember when establishing a management solution.

1. Manage proactively, reducing the need and amount of reactive management. Use network monitoring to find and fix minor problems before they become major problems. Observe network trends (like consistently high utilization) and act on trends before they even become minor problems. Stay ahead of the problems, and the network will run more smoothly and better satisfy its users.

2. Minimize polling; use trap-directed polling if possible. Remember that the network is for user data, not just for management traffic. Polling incessantly for the same information is often not a good use of bandwidth. Trap-directed polling can be used to trigger polling when needed. To protect yourself from not receiving a trap (traps are unreliable), you should do infrequent, periodic polling.

3. Manage from the center of the network out to the edge. A good management strategy is to focus more management energy on the center of the network and less at the edges. The theory here is that a problem in the backbone affects many more users than one at the edges; hence more attention is required. Sometimes it makes sense to establish a few zones (rings of management attention) from the center out to the edges.

4. Always know what you have—maintain a network inventory (including device configurations) and both a physical and logical view of your network. Keeping an accurate, up-to-date inventory of equipment, con-

nections, and back-up device configurations is critical to keeping a network healthy. Device configuration should include network device model names/numbers, network device custom configurations, vendor/support contact procedures, serial/asset numbers, date of purchase, and software version numbers. Device configuration information should be centrally maintained and backed up with a periodic backup taken offsite in the event of network fire. Having a spare component for every network device in a network is also prudent. By having a backup of configurations and spare devices you will quickly be able to go back to a known configuration or replace a failed device. As mentioned in Chapter 3, networks have both a physical and a logical structure. Keep an accurate record of both.

5. Ensure that the correct level of fault tolerance and redundancy is built in to the network. Play defensively and assume that every component in the network will break; understand the result of failure on the network. In many cases device redundancy, purchase of an uninterruptible power supply (UPS), or procurement of a dual power supply may be warranted.

6. Test new solutions in a limited network before going to a large production network. As mentioned earlier, test early and often. Don't bring down an instrumental production network by introducing a new switch before properly testing it out in context.

7. Use utilization as a strong metric of network health. If you have to pick just one thing to manage on a switched network, pick utilization. Keeping tabs on utilization is indicative of the network health of your network. For example, take a switched LAN. If utilization is 0 percent and normal utilization for that same time period is 10 percent, there is a good chance the network defined by that switched port is down. If utilization is too high on an Ethernet segment, chances are good that you have too many users on a single switched port and you need to distribute the users to other ports or upgrade the connection to Fast Ethernet. Utilization is a metric that spans performance, configuration, and fault management—it is an important indicator of network service to the user(s) at the other end of each switched port.

8. Manage bandwidth based on cost; for example, manage your WAN bandwidth! As a rule of thumb, the more expensive the bandwidth, the more carefully it should be managed. A good example is a WAN connection. WAN connections are more expensive than a local LAN connection. Although a backbone LAN connection should be managed

with as much fervor as a WAN connection, it is wise not to neglect precious expensive bandwidth. Kind of like the diamond and the cubic zirconium argument—which should you spend more time keeping track of?

9. Be defensive—assume everything needs to be managed and have a management plan for every network device that is added to the network. Consider every network component as something with the potential to break. That goes for switches, hubs, network interface cards (NICs), cables, and so on. Know what the result of breakage is for every component and identify how every component will be managed.

10. Keep solutions as simple as possible. Perhaps a corollary to rule 9 is that by having fewer parts there is less to break. Simplicity wins over complexity, every day, hands down. Introduce complexity based exclusively on need—do not introduce complexity based on the novelty of some new technology.

11. Automate the common, repetitious processes. Computers are built to perform common, repetitious processes efficiently and without error; humans tire of redundancy quickly and introduce errors out of boredom. As a switched network grows with ports and switches, take time to automate the common redundant management processes such as switch software and configuration backups.

12. Leverage GUI and command line and management interfaces. GUIs are often great and quite powerful, but never underestimate the power of a strong command line interface. Often not as intuitive and definitely not as colorful, command line can be used to create powerful custom scripts and automate network management.

8.8 Policy-Based Network Management

What is policy-based network management? Let's start with the definition that we gave for policy in Chapter 7:

Policy is the set of distributed rules that control how the network is shared.

It is important to realize that this same set of distributed rules defines how the network should be managed. Management is used to enforce policy and to provide a *feedback loop* on how policy is working so that policy can be refined and tuned to better meet our demands for networking. Policy is, in essence, the network configuration. It contains device configuration, system-level configuration, and user profiles. Network usage data is associated with policy at any given time; it records who uses what, for how long, and with what QoS guarantee, COS, and SLA.

Network management uses policy to define how the network is configured and to determine what faults, performance, and security to monitor. Network management provides the input to policy on network tuning based on observed performance and faults. It uses policy to determine user profiles and tracks network usage and associates use with network policy at a given time. FCAPS network management is what keeps policy "in check" and the network running smoothly. Ultimately policy is the DHL data repository of network management.

8.9 A Conceptual View of Managing Tomorrow's Switching Solutions

So let's expatiate a bit with regard to network management and networks of tomorrow by building on DHL and the rest of the material presented in this book. Figure 8.2 provides a conceptual way to look at how our management and our switched solutions might "fit" together in the future. PC-based, UNIX-based, and portable management stations use a distributed hierarchical database and layered applications to provide FCAPS for our switched environment. Network users might access the same database using the LDAP API used by DEN. Meanwhile switches across the network use the database to log network information and to retrieve element and network configuration data such as MPLS label information and network policy data specifying QoS and COS. The distributed hierarchical database with its DEN-schema becomes the glue, the central policy that holds the network together providing centralization for devices and management data necessary to manage the devices. And, if you "snapshot" the database at a point and time, you have a working model of a real network that you can perhaps take into a lab and test new switching solutions and management—pretty powerful indeed.

A S I D E . . .

Although conceptually all data becomes one big repository, there will be many repositories required. Real-time data, such as data used to calculate utilization on switched LAN ports, or RMON/RMON2 data collected over time will require a real-time storage repository.

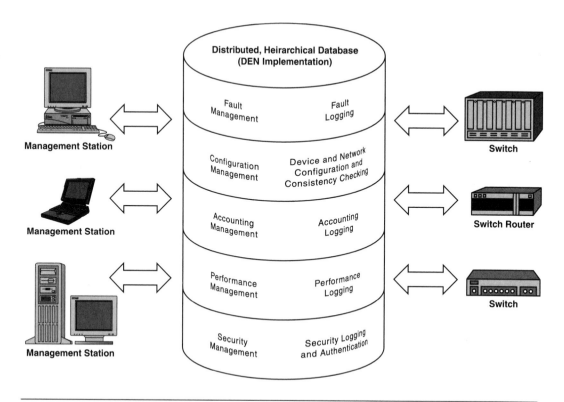

Figure 8.2 How management and switched solutions might "fit" together in the future

8.10 Management Strives to Be End-to-End

With the desire to have end-to-end QoS guarantees and SLAs, it is no surprise that management too strives to be end-to-end. In certain controlled cases (like a local LAN), this will be possible. As end-to-end spans the WAN across many networks (for example, Internet ASs), network management will be as difficult as providing an end-to-end QoS guarantee or SLA. As indicated in Chapter 5, we will see partial QoS guarantees and SLAs for quite some time. This is due to the fact that network policy (the set of distributed rules that control how the network is shared) is owned and managed by a network.

Management will work in parallel with these partial end-to-end solutions. It will take considerable application push and the span of time to result in networks that can negotiate policy across network boundaries and result in end-to-end managed solutions.

A S I D E . . .

The notion of regional policy many be a difficult concept to grasp. Perhaps the easiest way is to think of the ASs that compose the Internet. An end-to-end connection might need to cross many ASs; and since each ASs is individually owned and operated, each AS has its own policy. Thus to make an end-to-end connection, you might need to "tunnel" through network regions that are "foreign" and through which no guarantees can be made.

8.11　Preparing for New Switching Solutions

If you are a network manager, you most likely are under constant pressure to provide more

- Bandwidth
- Database farms and disks for existing farms
- Networked PCs, workstations, and printers
- Ports for new and existing users
- Support personnel for faster turnaround
- Network services
- Network customization

So how do you manage the constant need for *more* of everything while maintaining *fewer* problems? Some keys to satisfying the insatiable appetite for more networking are to

- **Maintain currency:** Keep yourself and your staff current with the latest technologies. Understand how they work, how they work together with other technologies, and which ones your network might benefit from. It is hoped that this book provided you with a good dose of switching solution currency and an understanding of how all the many technologies fit together.

- **Maintain a test network:** If possible you should always attempt new solutions on a test network that is discrete from your production network. Test networks give you a place to try things out without risking possible disruption of your production network. They allow you to gain confidence and technology understanding and can be used for training or to simulate problems.

- **Build a good suite of tools that are tuned for switched networks:** Tools capable of managing many switched ports and aggregating results are particularly useful. Tools that can do operations in bulk (across many ports or devices) are also helpful in switched networks. Traditional network management tools that expect to see most of the network from one place on the network do not work well in a switched environment. Often by observing utilization across each of your network ports you can detect trends and know when to position hardware upgrades far in advance of network trouble.

- **Keep your network solutions as simple as possible:** Remember that everything you introduce is another thing that can break. This includes software, hardware, cabling, and so on.

- **Automate routine bulk tasks:** If you establish a policy to change SNMP read-and-write community strings and other passwords weekly, write a script or get a tool to do this task automatically. Manually doing this type of task is error-prone and not a good use of a manager's time.

- **Proactively manage your network:** Observe trends and fix problems before they happen. Track, isolate, and resolve problems before your users discover them. Maintain an inventory of spare parts, one part for every component of your network, just in case the component breaks. When you purchase a new device, designate how the device may be reused when a newer, faster, better device becomes available. Keep an accurate inventory of your network including all devices and all device configurations. If possible always think about the next enhancements that you will make to your network one to two years out—always know the next solution before you need it.

8.12 Setting Expectations

During the creation of this book there were many suggestions from reviewers to give more insight about tomorrow's networks. You know, get out the crystal ball and look two to three years out. Without a doubt it is somewhat presumptuous for anyone to predict the future—particularly in the dynamic field of networking. As a compromise, though, this short section covers eight trends that hold some promise. These trends are based on historical data, which offers a widely used technique for making educated guesses.

1. It is no accident that for the book we chose four main areas of focus for switched networks: multilayer switching, QoS guarantees, IP multicast,

and policy-based networking. These are the areas that we believe need to converge in order to satisfy our future demands on networking. Does each area need to mature and be deployed in its entirety as documented? This, of course, is a rhetorical question with a simple answer—absolutely not! These technologies will go through many refinements and partial deployments before they meet our needs. Some ideas will work; others will not. As a general rule of thumb, the speed of network evolution is in proportion to the amount of change required to introduce a new technology and the overall benefit.

2. Ethernet will continue to dominate in the LAN over ATM. Why? Ethernet is simpler and less expensive to deploy, not because it is necessarily better. ATM is a solid technology—particularly when you look at its promise of QoS and its ability to scale. But, as networks become more and more pervasive, there is an increasing number of less technical users and network managers who need to use and deploy networks. While you are reading and rereading the information on setting up ATM LANE, you can set up a simple Ethernet network. In addition ATM NICs and switches are considerably more expensive to buy. Simple, fast, and inexpensive solutions catch on the best.

3. IP will (perhaps has) become the English of the world, and foreign languages (for example, IPX, AT, SNA) will be regional and LAN-specific. Yes, there are a lot of NetWare[1] file servers in production today, and there are many AT networks still working just fine. But, if you want to speak outside across the big, bad WWW, you speak IP; it's as simple as that. IP is pervasive and will continue to be.

4. Although it is evident that voice and data networks are converging and it is conceivable that all data may some day travel as IP packets, we will see a merging of the telephone network with the data network—not a replacement of one with the other, but a *merging*. This will provide fault tolerance, leverage of the strengths of both, and a sound evolution to an information network. We are already seeing the merging of the SS7 signaling system with data networks. It is possible that circuit-based switches will be retired over time and replaced with packet-based switches.

5. Premium network services will soon become available, offering two classes of service. In addition to the best-effort service that we currently

---

1. Note the next release of Novell's NetWare, version 5.0, is native IP (not IPX encapsulated in IP). Even IPX is fading due to IP's pervasiveness.

have, we will see an additional class of service aimed at priority delivery. This will be the easiest to implement in LANs where one party controls the network. Still though, policy distribution and switch upgrades to those supporting COS will introduce a challenge. In the WAN we will see COS for data that stays within a single carrier's network. Negotiation of COS policy across vendor boundaries will take longer, and the guarantees will probably be less binding.

6. The switch will continue to evolve into the core interconnection device. Burning functionality into hardware for speed will continue to be key to networking. This technique will help satisfy the insatiable appetite of new end-user workstations and PCs that are guaranteed to become increasingly faster in the future. We are seeing more and more intelligence being put into switched devices and many emerging creative solutions. We will see more and more multiservice switches, providing in many ways "a network in a box." As stated early on, *switching solutions help networks scale by addressing performance, robustness, and encapsulating network intelligence.* Switches rule!

7. Switches will evolve to exchange policy information in the same way that routers and routing switches exchange routing information to keep the network topology up-to-date. It is expected that both MPLS and DEN will be instrumental in making this "policy topology" happen. LDAP may become the standard way to access this network data. It is conceivable that we will leverage the updated protocols used by routing to maintain and synchronize policy data. Also, the hierarchical nature established by using BGP between ASs and having OSPF areas may evolve to provide a hierarchical policy solution so that policy may be negotiated across network boundaries, providing true end-to-end. It is expected that hierarchical policy and policy negotiation across networks will take a long time to achieve—in many ways due to the political nature of the problem.

8. Network management will be used to differentiate one vendor from another. Everyone will have fast and fat pipes. Vendors that do the best job of managing their bandwidth and providing fault-tolerant, reliable, value-added, creative network services will be the ones that attract the most customers.

8.13 Conclusions

Clearly, switching solutions are not panaceas to satisfying our demands for networking. They are, however, enabling us to progress fairly quickly and improve our ability to network. Will we ever have network nirvana—network utopia—networks capable of our wildest dreams? Network nirvana is like a pot of gold at the end of a rainbow—we never quite get to the gold, and even if we were to get to the gold, we'd only be searching for a bigger pot tomorrow! Our networks *are* like emerging rainbows: They are becoming brighter and more colorful, largely due to the switching solutions of today and tomorrow.

At this time I give you one final analogy. Hopefully it will leave you thinking about the possibilities of our switched network evolution.

When you go to most restaurants for dinner you are given a menu that allows you to select your food. Restaurants are well aware that different dishes please different people and therefore offer many selections. In addition restaurants must have sufficient food and staff to serve the largely unpredictable number of guests. As you can imagine, this takes a fair amount of management talent, especially as a restaurant grows with distributed chains that span the globe.

Data networks of today serve up bandwidth, without a menu. What will it be, best-effort or best-effort? Tomorrow's switched networks, recognizing that not everyone wants the same entree, will serve up services. Network services will include an entire array of specialties—some part of the normal fare, others as services du jour. Users will be able to select what they want when they arrive at the network, regardless of the network (restaurant) location. Smart network "restaurant chains" (for example, private corporate Intranets, ISPs) will maintain customer profiles and properly "prepare" (send) their data according to their preferences. Tomorrow's networks will have a menu, provide a guarantee of service, and efficiently deliver your order regardless of your current fetish. Networks will evolve to satisfy our demands for networking by offering minimal propagation delay and by being plug-and-play, customizable, and always available—all at a reasonable price.

Bibliography

Bellman, R. *Dynamic Programming.* Princeton, N.J.: Princeton University Press, 1957.

Bellman, R. "IP Switching—Which Flavor Works For You?" *Business Communications Review* (April 1997): 41–46.

Black, D. P. *Managing Switched* Local Area *Networks: A Practical Guide.* Reading, Ma.: Addison Wesley Longman, 1998.

Breyer, R., and S. Riley. *Switched and Fast Ethernet,* 2d ed. Emeryville, Ca.: Ziff-Davis Press, 1996.

Callon, R. "Multilayer Switching Including MPLS and Related Approaches," Tutorial notes, Next Generation Networks 1997, November 1997, Washington, D.C.

Deering, S. "Multicast Routing in Internetworks and Extended LANs." SIGCOMM Summer Proceedings (August 1988).

Dickie, M. *Routing in Today's Internetworks.* New York: Van Nostrand Reinhold, 1994.

Dutton, H., and P. Lenhard. *Asynchronous Transfer Mode (ATM),* 2d ed. Upper Saddle River, N.J.: Prentice Hall PTR, 1995.

Enck, J., and M. Beckman. *LAN to WAN.* New York: McGraw-Hill, 1995.

Ferguson, P., and G. Huston. *Quality of Service: Delivering QoS on the Internet and in Corporate Networks.* New York: John Wiley & Sons, Inc., 1998.

Ferrero, A. *The Evolving Ethernet.* Reading, Ma.: Addison-Wesley, 1996.

Floyd, S., and V. Jacobson. "Random Early Detection Gateways for Congestion Avoidance." *IEEE/ACM Transactions on Networking* (August 1993).

Ginsburg, D. *ATM: Solutions for Enterprise Internetworking.* Reading, Ma.: Addison-Wesley, 1996.

Held, G. *LAN Management with SNMP and RMON.* New York: John Wiley & Sons, Inc., 1996.

Huitema, C. *Routing in the Internet.* Englewood Cliffs, N.J.: Prentice Hall, 1995.

Keshav, S. *An Engineering Approach to Computer Networking: ATM Networks, the Internet, and the Telephone Network.* Reading, Ma.: Addison Wesley Longman, 1997.

Krapf, E. "Serving Up Gigabit Ethernet." *Business Communications Review* (March 1997): 41–45.

Maufer, T. *Deploying IP Multicast in the Enterprise.* Upper Saddle River, N.J.: Prentice Hall, 1998.

McDysan, D., and D. Spohn. *ATM: Theory and Application.* New York: McGraw-Hill, 1995.

Minoli, D., and A. Alles. *LAN, ATM, and LAN Emulation Technologies.* Norwood, Ma.: Artech House Publishers, 1996.

Minoli, D., and E. Minoli. *Delivering Voice over IP Networks.* New York: John Wiley & Sons, Inc., 1998.

Moy, J. T. *OSPF: Anatomy of an Internet Routing Protocol.* Reading, Ma.: Addison Wesley Longman, 1998.

Newton, H. *Newton's Telecom Dictionary.* New York: Telecom Books & Flatiron Publishing, 1998.

Nolle, T. "Switching: Search of the Hassle-Free Network." *Business Communications Review* (March 1997): 35–39.

Partridge, C. *Gigabit Networking.* Reading, Ma.: Addison-Wesley, 1994.

Perkins, C. E. *Mobile IP: Design Principles and Practices.* Reading, Ma.: Addison Wesley Longman, 1998.

Perlman, R. *Interconnections: Bridges and Routers.* Reading, Ma.: Addison-Wesley, 1992.

Roberts, E. "IP on Speed." *Data Communications* (March 1997): 84–96.

———. "Gambling on Switched Networks." *Data Communications* (May 1996): 66–78.

———. "Virtual LANs: How Real? How Soon? Here's How." *Data Communications* (October 1996): 66–75.

Sackett, G., and C. Metz. *ATM and Multiprotocol Networking.* New York: McGraw-Hill, 1997.

Seifert, R. *Gigabit Ethernet: Technology and Applications for High-Speed LANs.* Reading, Ma.: Addison Wesley Longman, 1998.

Smythe, C. *Internetworking: Designing the Right Architectures.* Reading, Ma.: Addison-Wesley, 1995.

Stallings, W. *High-Speed Networks: TCP/IP and ATM Design Principles.* Upper Saddle River, N.J.: Prentice Hall, 1998.

————. *Local and Metropolitan Area Networks,* 4 ed. New York: Macmillan Publishing Company, 1993.

Stein, L. D. *How to Set Up and Maintain a Web Site, Second Edition.* Reading, Ma.: Addison Wesley Longman, 1997.

Stevens, W. R. *TCP/IP Illustrated,* Vol. 3: *TCP for Transactions, HTTP, NNTP, and the UNIX Domain Protocols.* Reading, Ma.: Addison-Wesley, 1996.

————. *TCP/IP Illustrated,* Vol. 1: *The Protocols.* Reading, Ma.: Addison-Wesley, 1994.

Washburn, K., and J. Evans, *TCP/IP: Running a Successful Network.* Essex, England: Addison Wesley Longman Ltd, 1996.

Wright, G., and W. R. Stevens. *TCP/IP Illustrated,* Vol. 2: *The Implementation.* Reading, Ma.: Addison-Wesley, 1995.

Networking Acronyms Used in This Book

ABR	Available Bit Rate
AdSpec	Advertisement Specification
AH	Authentication Header
ANSI	American National Standards Institute
API	Application Programming Interface
ARIS	Aggregate Route-based IP Switching
ARM	Advanced Research Projects NETworks Reference Model
ARP	Address Resolution Protocol
ARPANET	Advanced Research Projects NETworks
AS	Autonomous System
ASCII	American Standard Code for Information Interchange
ASIC	Application Specific Integrated Circuit
ATM	Asynchronous Transfer Mode
BES	Best-Effort Service
BGMP	Border Gateway Multicast Protocol

BGP	Border Gateway Protocol
B-ISDN	Broadband Integrated Services Digital Network
BNC	Bayonet-Neill-Concelman (type of interface connector)
BOOTP	Bootstrap Protocol
BPDU	Bridge Protocol Data Unit
bps	Bits per second
Bps	Bytes per second
BRI	Basic Rate Interface
BSD	Berkeley Software Distribution
BSR	Bootstrap Router
BUS	Broadcast and Unknown Server
CAC	Call Admission Control
CBR	Constant Bit Rate, Committed Burst Rate
CBS	Committed Burst Size
CBT	Core-Based Tree
CCITT	Consultative Committee for International Telegraph and Telephone/Telephony
CDDI	Copper Distributed Data Interface
CDV	Cell Delay Variation
CDVT	Cell Delay Variation Tolerance
CER	Cell Error Rate
CHAP	Challenge Handshake Authentication Protocol

CIDR	Classless Interdomain Routing
CIM	Common Information Model
CIR	Committed Information Rate
CL	Connectionless Service
CLNP	Connectionless Network Protocol
CLP	Cell Loss Priority
CLR	Cell Loss Ratio
CLS	Controlled Load Service
CMIP	Common Management Information Protocol
codec	compression/decompression algorithm
COPS	Common Open Policy Service
COS	Class of Service
CPU	Central Processing Unit
CRC	Cyclic Redundancy Check
CRS	Cell Relay Service
CSMA/CD	Carrier Sense Multiple Access with Collision Detection
CSR	Cell Switched Routers
CSU	Channel Service Unit
CSU/DSU	Channel Service Unit/Data Service Unit
CTD	Cell Transfer Delay
DAP	Directory Access Protocol

DEN	Directory Enabled Networking
DES	Data Encryption Standard
DHCP	Dynamic Host Configuration Protocol
DHL	Distributed Hierarchical Layering
DLCI	Data Link Connection Identifier
DMTF	Desktop Management Task Force
DNS	Domain Name System
DS	Differentiated Service
DS-0	Digital Signal Level 0 (64 Kbps)
DS-1	Digital Signal Level 1 (1.544 Mbps)
DS-2	Digital Signal Level 2 (6.312 Mbps)
DS-3	Digital Signal Level 3 (44.736 Mbps)
DS-4	Digital Signal Level 4 (274.176 Mbps)
DSP	Digital Signal Processor
DSU	Data Service Unit
DVMRP	Distance-Vector Multicast Routing Protocol
E-1	European Signal Level 1 (2.048 Mbps)
E-2	European Signal Level 2 (8.448 Mbps)
E-3	European Signal Level 3 (34.368 Mbps)
E-4	European Signal Level 4 (139.264 Mbps)
EBS	Excess Burst Size

EGP	Exterior Gateway Protocol
EIGRP	Enhanced Interior Gateway Routing Protocol
ELAN	Emulated Local Area Network
ESP	Encapsulated Security Payload
FANP	Flow Attribute Notification Protocol
FCAPS	Fault, Configuration, Accounting, Performance, Security
FDDI	Fiber Distributed Data Interface
FEC	Forwarding Equivalence Class
FIB	Forwarding Information Base
FIFO	First In First Out
FlowSpec	Flow Specification
FOIRL	Fiber Optic Inter Repeater Link
FPS	Frames Per Second
Frac T-1 (FT-1)	Fractional T-1
FRS	Frame Relay Service
FTP	File Transfer Protocol
GARP	Group Address Resolution Protocol
Gbps	Gigabits per second
GS	Guaranteed Service
GSMP	General Switch Management Protocol
GUI	Graphical User Interface

GUM	Global Unified Multicast
HTTP	Hypertext Transport Protocol
IANA	Internet Assigned Numbers Authority
ICMP	Internet Control Message Protocol
IDMR	Interdomain Multicast Routing
IEEE	Institute of Electrical and Electronic Engineers
IETF	Internet Engineering Task Force
IFMP	Ipsilon's Flow Management Protocol
IGMP	Internet Group Management Protocol
IGP	Interior Gateway Protocol
IP	Internet Protocol
IPSec	Secure Internet Protocol
IPv4	IP Version 4 (current version)
IPv6	IP Version 6
IPX	Internet Packet Exchange
IS	Integrated Services
ISA	Integrated Services Architecture
ISAKMP	Internet Security Association Key Management Protocol
ISDN	Integrated Service Digital Network
IS-IS	Intermediate System to Intermediate System
ISO	International Organization for Standardization

ISP	Internet Service Provider
ISR	Integrated Switch Router
ITU-T	International Telecommunications Union–Telecommunication
Kbps	Kilobits per second
L2F	Layer-2 Forwarding
L2TP	Layer-2 Tunneling Protocol
LAN	Local Area Network
LANE	LAN Emulation or LAN Emulation Service
LBS	Label-Based Switching
LCD	Least Common Denominator
LDAP	Lightweight Directory Access Protocol
LDP	Label Distribution Protocol
LEC	LAN Emulation Client
LECS	LAN Emulation Configuration Server
LES	LAN Emulation Server
LIB	Label Information Base
LLC	Logical Link Control
LNNI	LAN Emulation Network to Network Interface
LSA	Link State Advertisement
LSB	Least Significant Byte
LSH	Label Switched Hop

LSP	Label Switched Path
LSR	Link Switch Router
LUNI	LAN Emulation User to Network Interface
MAC	Media Access Control
MAN	Metropolitan Area Network
MARS	Multicast Address Resolution Server
MAU	Multistation Access Unit
M-BGP	Multicast-Border Gateway Protocol
MBone	Multicast Backbone
Mbps	Megabits per second
MBS	Maximum Burst Size
MCR	Maximum Cell Rate
MCTD	Mean Cell Transfer Delay
MD5	Message Digest 5
MFTP	Multicast File Transfer Protocol
MIB	Management Information Base
MIB-2	Management Information Base Version 2
MIC	Media Interface Connector
MOSPF	Multicast Open Shortest Path First
MPLS	Multiprotocol Label Switching
MPOA	Multiprotocol over ATM

MPS	MPOA (route) server
MSB	Most Significant Byte
MTU	Maximum Transmission Unit
NAS	Network Access Server
NCP	Network Control Protocols
NetBEUI	NetBIOS Extended User Interface
NetBIOS	Network Basic Input Output System
NFS	Network File System
NHLFE	Next Hop Label Forwarding Entry
NHRP	Next Hop Resolution Protocol
NHS	Next Hop Server
NIC	Network Interface Card
NIS	Network Information Service
NMS	Network Management System
NNI	Network Node Interface
NNTP	Usenet News
NOS	Network Operating System
nrt-VBR	non-real-time Variable Bit Rate
OC-3	Optical Carrier-3 (155.52 Mbps)
OC-12	Optical Carrier-12 (622.08 Mbps)
OC-24	Optical Carrier-24 (1.244 Gbps)

OC-48	Optical Carrier-48 (2.488 Gbps)
OC-192	Optical Carrier-192 (9.6 Gbps)
O/S	Operating System
OSF	Open Software Foundation
OSI	Open Systems Interconnection
OSPF	Open Shortest Path First
OUI	Organization Unique Identifier
PAP	Password Authentication Protocol
PC	Personal Computer
PCMCIA	Personal Computer Memory Card International Association
PCR	Peak Cell Rate
PIM	Protocol Independent Multicast
PIM-DM	Protocol Independent Multicast Dense Mode
PIM-SM	Protocol Independent Multicast Sparse Mode
PING	Packet Internet Groper
PNNI	Private Network-Network Interface
POP	Point of Presence
POTS	Plain Old Telephone Service
PPP	Point-to-Point Protocol
PPS	Packets Per Second
PPTP	Point-to-Point Tunneling Protocol

PQ	Priority Queuing
PRI	Primary Rate Interface
PVC	Permanent Virtual Circuit
QoS	Quality of Service
QSPF	Quality of Service Path First Routing
RAC	Remote Access Concentrator
RADIUS	Remote Authentication Dial-In User Service
RARP	Reverse Address Resolution Protocol
RAS	Remote Access Server
RED	Random Early Detection
RES-LSA	Link Resource Advertisements
RFC	Request for Comment
RIP	Routing Information Protocol
RM	Resource Management
RMON	Remote Network Monitor
RMON2	Remote Network Monitor Version 2
RMP	Reliable Multicast Protocol
RMTP	Reliable Multicast Transfer Protocol
RPF	Reverse Path Forwarding
RPM	Reverse Path Multicast
Rspec	Resource Specification

RSVP	Resource ReSerVation Protocol
RTCP	Real-Time Transport Control Protocol
RTMP	Routing Table Maintenance Protocol
RTP	Real-Time Transport Protocol
rt-VBR	Real-Time Variable Bit Rate
SCR	Sustained Cell Rate
SLA	Service Level Agreement
SMDS	Switched Multimegabit Data Service
SNMP	Simple Network Management Protocol
SONET	Synchronous Optical Network
SPL	Switched Path Label
SS7	Signaling System 7
STP	Shielded Twisted Pair, Spanning Tree Protocol
SVC	Switched Virtual Circuit
T-1	DS-1 (Digital Signal Level 1) (1.544 Mbps)
T-2	DS-2 (Digital Signal Level 2) (6.312 Mbps)
T-3	DS-3 (Digital Signal Level 3) (44.736 Mbps)
TCI	Tag Control Information
TCP	Transmission Control Protocol
TCP/IP	Transmission Control Protocol/Internet Protocol
TDP	Tag Distribution Protocol

TELNET	Remote Terminal Protocol
TER	Tag Edge Router
TFTP	Trivial File Transfer Protocol
TIA	Telecommunications Industry Association
TIB	Tag Information Base
TM	Traffic Management
TMN	Telecommunications Management Network
TMS	Tunnel Management System
TOS	Type of Service
TPID	Tag Protocol Identifier
TSpec	Traffic Specification
TTL	Time To Live
UBR	Unspecified Bit Rate
UDP	User Datagram Protocol
UNI	User Network Interface
UPS	Uninterrupted Power Supply
URL	Uniform Resource Locator
UTP	Unshielded Twisted Pair
VBR	Variable Bit Rate
VC	Virtual Channel, Circuit, or Connection
VCC	Virtual Channel Connection

VCI	Virtual Channel Identifier
VCID	Virtual Circuit ID
VCL	Virtual Channel Link
VLAN	Virtual Local Area Network
VLSM	Variable Length Subnet Mask
VMRP	VLAN Membership Resolution Protocol
VNN	Virtual Network Navigator
VoIP	Voice over IP
VP	Virtual Path
VPC	Virtual Path Connection
VPI	Virtual Path Identifier
VPL	Virtual Path Link
VPN	Virtual Private Network
WAN	Wide Area Network
WDM	Wavelength Division Multiplexing
WFQ	Weighted Fair Queuing
WRQ	Weighted Round-Robin Queuing
WWW	World Wide Web

Index

Addison-Wesley Computer and Engineering Publishing Group

How to Interact with Us

1. Visit our Web site

http://www.awl.com/cseng

When you think you've read enough, there's always more content for you at Addison-Wesley's web site. Our web site contains a directory of complete product information including:

- Chapters
- Exclusive author interviews
- Links to authors' pages
- Tables of contents
- Source code

You can also discover what tradeshows and conferences Addison-Wesley will be attending, read what others are saying about our titles, and find out where and when you can meet our authors and have them sign your book.

2. Subscribe to Our Email Mailing Lists

Subscribe to our electronic mailing lists and be the first to know when new books are publishing. Here's how it works: Sign up for our electronic mailing at **http://www.awl.com/cseng/mailinglists.html**. Just select the subject areas that interest you and you will receive notification via email when we publish a book in that area.

3. Contact Us via Email

cepubprof@awl.com
Ask general questions about our books.
Sign up for our electronic mailing lists.
Submit corrections for our web site.

bexpress@awl.com
Request an Addison-Wesley catalog.
Get answers to questions regarding
your order or our products.

innovations@awl.com
Request a current Innovations Newsletter.

webmaster@awl.com
Send comments about our web site.

cepubeditors@awl.com
Submit a book proposal.
Send errata for an Addison-Wesley book.

cepubpublicity@awl.com
Request a review copy for a member of the media
interested in reviewing new Addison-Wesley titles.

We encourage you to patronize the many fine retailers who stock Addison-Wesley titles. Visit our online directory to find stores near you or visit our online store: **http://store.awl.com/** or call **800-824-7799**.

Addison Wesley Longman
Computer and Engineering Publishing Group
One Jacob Way, Reading, Massachusetts 01867 USA
TEL 781-944-3700 • FAX 781-942-3076